SPANISH
REPUBLICANS
AND THE SECOND WORLD WAR

Le vent souffle sur les tombes
La liberté reviendra
On nous oubliera
Nous rentrerons dans l'ombre
Emmanuel D'Astier de la Vigerie

SPANISH
REPUBLICANS
AND THE SECOND WORLD WAR

REPUBLIC ACROSS THE MOUNTAINS

JONATHAN WHITEHEAD

PEN & SWORD **HISTORY**

AN IMPRINT OF PEN & SWORD BOOKS LTD.
YORKSHIRE – PHILADELPHIA

First published in Great Britain in 2021 by
PEN AND SWORD HISTORY
An imprint of
Pen & Sword Books Ltd
Yorkshire – Philadelphia

ISBN 978 1 39900 451 0

A CIP catalogue record for this book is available from the British Library.

Typeset in Times New Roman 11.5/14 by
SJmagic DESIGN SERVICES, India.
Printed and bound by CPI Group (UK) Ltd, Croydon CR0 4YY

Pen & Sword Books Limited incorporates the imprints of Atlas, Archaeology,
Aviation, Discovery, Family History, Fiction, History, Maritime, Military, Military
Classics, Politics, Select, Transport, True Crime, Air World, Frontline Publishing,
Leo Cooper, Remember When, Seaforth Publishing, The Praetorian Press,
Wharncliffe Local History, Wharncliffe Transport, Wharncliffe True Crime and
White Owl.

For a complete list of Pen & Sword titles please contact
PEN & SWORD BOOKS LIMITED
47 Church Street, Barnsley, South Yorkshire, S70 2AS, England
E-mail: enquiries@pen-and-sword.co.uk
Website: www.pen-and-sword.co.uk

Or

PEN AND SWORD BOOKS
1950 Lawrence Rd, Havertown, PA 19083, USA
E-mail: Uspen-and-sword@casematepublishers.com
Website: www.penandswordbooks.com

Contents

Acknowledgements

First, a word of thanks to the staff at Pen & Sword who in the difficult circumstances that prevailed in 2020 showed remarkable professionalism and patience. And to Claire Hopkins, Laura Hirst and Chris Cocks in particular for their encouragement and generous support.

I should like to express my appreciation for the work of the Asociación para la Recuperación de la Memoria Histórica in Spain and the unstinting work they have done on behalf of the victims of Franco's regime. Often in the face of obstruction by state and local authorities, they have fought resolutely in pursuit of justice for those who suffered under the dictatorship. At an international level I should like to mention the work of UNCHR in seeking to alleviate the anguish of the victims of the refugee crises that continue to plague the world.

I owe a thank you to Mark Smith for sharing his military and railway expertise and checking the text for anomalies. Any errors that remain are mine.

I am also grateful to James Dorrian of the St. Nazaire Society for his insights into the fate of the survivors of the St. Nazaire raid who escaped capture by the Germans. Similarly, I would like to express my gratitude to Simon Martínez of the Association for the Basque Children of the UK/ BCA'37UK for offering guidance on the contribution to the British war effort made by several of the Basque refugees. The Association works tirelessly to keep alive the stories of the children evacuated to Britain at the height of the Civil War and to record the generosity of those willing to come to the assistance of people suffering oppression wherever they may be.

I should also like to express my appreciation of the work of the Commonwealth War Graves Commission and to thank them for allowing me to use their records. Nor can I forget the International Brigade Memorial Trust and their work to preserve the memory of those who volunteered in the cause of the Spanish Republic.

A special thank-you to Professor Francisco Bolumar of the Universidad de Alcalá for navigating the archives at Alcalá de Henares and uncovering the telegram from the Spanish ambassador in Washington to the Ministry of Foreign Affairs in Madrid (AGA, [10] 26.2, 54/12434).

As always, I must express my gratitude to my son, David, without whom this book would never have been written and to all my friends and family who have directly or indirectly contributed to this work.

Finally, to all those Spanish Republicans who were in the vanguard of the struggle against Fascism, and their children and grandchildren, who have shared their stories with me. History owes them.

Translation and Place Names

All translations that appear in this book from non-English language sources are by the author. Wherever possible, I have cited from English-language editions.

Spanish place names are a minefield because of the multiplicity of official languages. The historical narrative of the book is centred on north-east Spain where there are three official languages. The first is known to non-Spaniards as Spanish, while most Spanish people tend to call it *castellano* (with lower-case 'c'), which translates into English as Castilian. The second is Catalan which is *catalán* in Spanish and *català* in the source language. Finally, there is Aranese (*aranés*) the 'dialect' of Occitan which is spoken by much of the population in the valley that is at the heart of this history.

I use the English names for each of the languages: Spanish, Catalan and Aranese respectively.

As a general rule, for Spanish towns and regions, I have used the names preferred by the majority of the local population. I have therefore chosen to use Catalan rather than Spanish when referring to Catalan towns, e.g. Girona (Gerona) and Figueres (Figueras). Where I think there may be some confusion, I accompany the Catalan name with the Spanish name in brackets, e.g. Lleida (Lérida).

I avoid using English translations of place names, with one exception: Cataluña/Catalunya itself, where the population has become accustomed to using the English name Catalonia.

The Aran Valley, on the border between France and Spain, is called Valle de Arán in Spanish, Vall d'Aran in Catalan and Val d'Aran in Aranese. I prefer Val d'Aran because it is the name used by the people who live there and most historians. It is also the name that is now widely accepted and used by most visitors from the rest of Spain.

ix

Maps

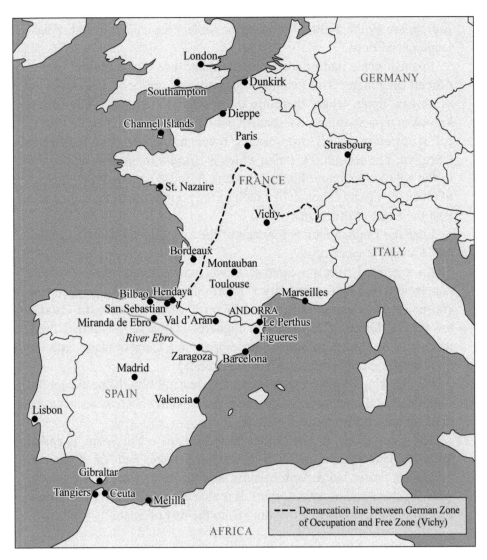

Spain and France (1940) (© Thomas Bohm)

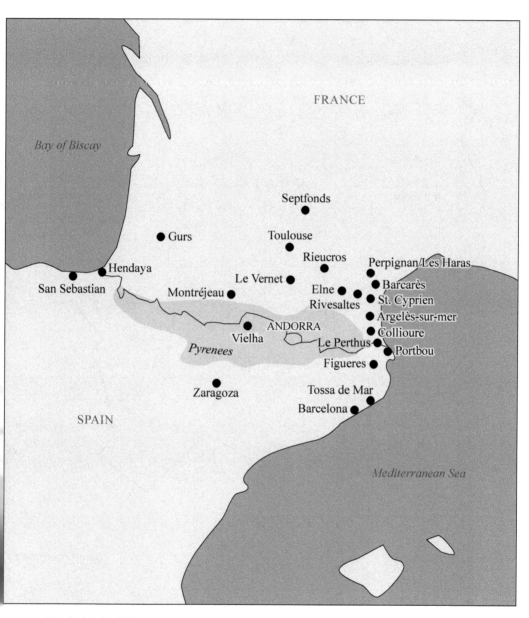

Borderlands (© Thomas Bohm)

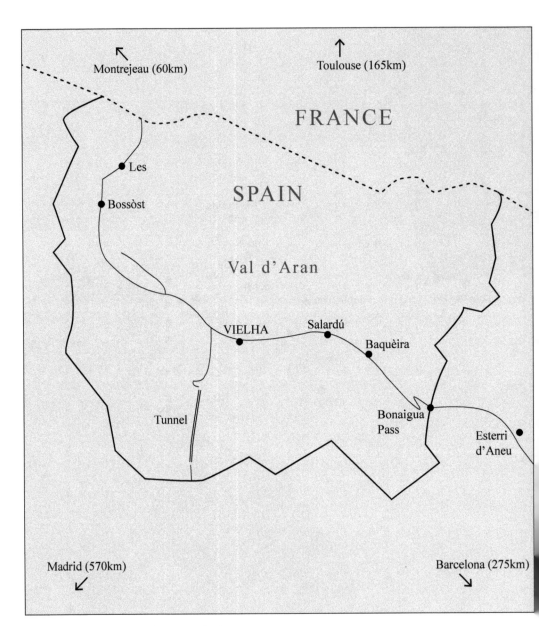

Val d'Aran (© Thomas Bohm)

Timeline

April 1931	Proclamation of the Second Republic
February 1936	Frente Popular wins general election
July 1936	Outbreak of Spanish Civil War
July 1938	Republic launches final offensive across the River Ebro
November 1938	Battle of Ebro ends in defeat for the Republic
January 1939	Fall of Barcelona; mass exodus of Republican refugees into France
March 1939	End of Civil War
August 1939	Molotov–Ribbentrop Pact
September 1939	Germany invades Poland; Britain and France declare war on Germany; USSR invades Poland
April–June 1940	Norwegian campaign
May 1940	German Army launches attack on Western Europe
June 1940	France surrenders; German Army reaches the Pyrenees
July–October 1940	Battle of Britain
October 1940	Franco meets Hitler at Hendaya
June 1941	Operation *Barbarossa*: Germany invades USSR
October 1941	División Azul joins siege of Leningrad
December 1941	Japan attacks US Navy at Pearl Harbor; Germany declares war on the USA
October–November 1942	Second Battle of Alamein, decisive defeat of Rommel's Afrikakorps
November 1942	Operation *Torch*: Anglo-American landings in North Africa

October 1943	Franco orders withdrawal of División Azul
June 1944	D-Day
August 1944	Liberation of Paris; Operation *Dragoon* – Allied landings in South of France
October 1944	Maquis invasion of Val d'Aran
December 1944	German Army launches Ardennes counter-offensive
May 1945	Germany surrenders: end of war in Europe
December 1946	United Nations calls for diplomatic boycott of Spain
August 1953	Spain and Vatican sign Concordat
September 1953	Spain and USA agree Pacts of Madrid
December 1955	Spain joins the United Nations, the end of international isolation
November 1975	Death of Franco
June 1977	First democratic elections in Spain since 1936

Introduction

This history of Spanish Republicans in the Second World War culminates in a description of the Battle of the Val d'Aran, which is no more than a minor skirmish within the context of the Western Front. Indeed, it may be argued that while the offensive was launched from French territory, it was not, strictly speaking, on the Western Front at all. However, it is true that it was also the last victory of the Anti-Comintern Pact powers in the European theatre before the unconditional surrender of Nazi Germany in May 1945. It was also in a sense the last battle of the Spanish Civil War.

Victorious in 1939 in his own war, undisputed Caudillo at the head of a brutal dictatorship that now ruled Spain, friend and ally of Nazi Germany and Fascist Italy, General Francisco Franco knew that the collapse of Mussolini's regime and the impending defeat of Hitler represented a potentially insurmountable challenge to his own position. On the other hand, many Republican veterans, the vanquished of the Civil War, had seen active service in the struggle against Hitler, Mussolini and their allies in France, Norway, Cameroon, Chad, Eritrea, Lebanon, Syria, USSR, Egypt, Libya, Tunis, Italy, Poland, Yugoslavia, Czechoslovakia, Rumania, Hungary, Austria and Germany.

Although in this narrative (as in the entire history of Spain since 1936) the Civil War looms large, so many excellent accounts of the conflict have been written in English by the likes of Hugh Thomas, Paul Preston, Anthony Beevor, Gabriel Jackson and Heather Graham, that it is unnecessary to preface this book with anything but the shortest context.

In July 1936, a clique of disaffected military leaders, supported by the Catholic Church, monarchists, land-owners and industrialists, and the tiny Fascist party (Falange) launched an unsuccessful coup d'état against the Second Republic and the democratically elected Frente

Popular government (Republican parties, supported by the Socialists and Communists) in Madrid. The major cities of Madrid, Barcelona, Valencia and Bilbao all remained loyal to the Republic and Spain became immersed in a savage civil war in which General Franco's insurgent army was supported by Hitler's Germany and Mussolini's Italy. The Republic received weapons from Stalin's USSR, while the British and French imposed a policy of non-intervention (endorsed on paper by all the European powers) and turned a blind eye to the activities of the great dictators.

Chapter 1

Falling of the Dusk

In the autumn of 1938, two years after the military uprising, deserted by the western democracies, and diminished by ideological divisions, the Spanish Republic stood on the verge of defeat. A last desperate counter-offensive across the River Ebro had been driven back by Nationalist forces which enjoyed substantial military superiority. In November, devastated by constant artillery fire and the ever more efficient intervention of air power (generously supplied by Hitler), the last troops of the Popular Army retreated eastward back across the Ebro.

In this final despairing throw of the dice, the Republic had lost its most battle-hardened troops and vast quantities of its artillery, armoured vehicles and aircraft. Approximately 70,000 Republican soldiers were lost: some reports suggest as many as 30,000 Republicans were killed, with some 20,000 taken prisoner. The remaining 20,000 casualties would take no further part in the war. The International Brigades, which had now been ordered to withdraw from combat, also suffered huge losses. The consensus among Hispanists is that at the Battle of the Ebro, the Republic lost its army.[1]

International observers no longer had any confidence in the Republic's capacity to resist and in the face of aggressive Italian and German nationalism, the British and French were committed to a policy of appeasement. Over the three years of the Spanish Civil War they had clung resolutely to their strategy of non-intervention. In spite of the hostile attitude of the political classes in London and Paris, Dr Juan Negrín, prime minister (*Presidente del Gobierno*) since May 1937, still believed they would eventually come to see the Second Spanish Republic as an ally in the global fight against fascism. He and his government rejected the term 'Spanish Civil War' and insisted that the struggle was in fact the 'Spanish War', the opening stage in a European struggle against the forces of Hitler and Mussolini.[2] The key was to resist until the outbreak of a conflict that would engulf the continent and force the western democracies to embrace the Republic as an ally.

Unfortunately, the fate of the Spanish Republic mattered little to the governments in Paris, London or Washington. In September, with Europe ever closer to the war that Dr Negrín had foreseen, British Prime Minister Neville Chamberlain met Hitler, Mussolini and French Prime Minister Daladier in Munich to formalize an agreement on Czechoslovakia and to allow Germany to occupy the Sudetenland. Neither the leaders of Czechoslovakia, nor those of the USSR were invited. When Chamberlain and Daladier returned to their respective countries, they were greeted as heroes who had saved the world from war. Daladier reportedly said of the crowds that met him, 'The fools. If they only knew.' Collective security was dead. Stalin was now aware that an alliance with the West was impossible and he would eventually conclude that the only way to protect the Soviet Union was to follow the path of Britain and France and to seek a deal with Hitler.

Meanwhile, in the USA, President Roosevelt's administration remained true to the spirit of isolationism and had imposed a ban on the sale of weapons to either side in the Civil War (Spanish Embargo Act, 7 January 1937). In his memoirs, the Spanish Foreign Minister Julio Álvarez del Vayo later chastised the US government for its misguided retreat from its international responsibilities and its failure to support friendly nations. He wrote: '[Foreign policy] is not the exclusive property of a country, and one million Spanish lives were lost in a battle that was not only the battle of Spain but the battle of world freedom and peace.'[3] It should not be forgotten that, just as in France and Britain and many other countries, brave men and women ignored the shortcomings of their governments and volunteered to fight for the Republic in the International Brigades, so approximately 2,800 individual American citizens saw active service on various fronts as part of the Abraham Lincoln Brigade (XV Brigade). In the early 1950s, amid the hysteria of the McCarthy era, to have fought fascism before Hitler declared war on the USA in December 1941 was considered un-American, and the volunteers in the brigade were consequently denounced as 'premature anti-fascists'. When President Reagan was asked by the press in 1984 about the role of the American volunteers in Spain, he replied, 'Well, if you get into the moral issue of it, we were certainly tested with regard to the Spanish Civil War I mentioned. I would say that the individuals that went over there were, in the opinions of most Americans, fighting on the wrong side.'[4]

The implication thus being that the right side was represented by the forces of Franco, Hitler and Mussolini.

The perceived absence of a viable alternative policy to appeasement in the context of the Czech crisis may explain the Anglo-French reaction to Hitler's threats. However, the strategy of non-intervention in Spain by which the governments in London and Paris denied weapons supplies to a democratically elected, friendly government in Madrid, while cynically allowing Germany and Italy to provide the insurgents with arms and troops, was morally indefensible and strategically absurd. While it is true that the Republic did receive weapons from the USSR, deliveries were constantly disrupted by the logistical difficulties involved in transporting military equipment either by sea or across Europe. By late 1938, Italian submarines had dislocated pro-Republican shipping in the Mediterranean and the supply route from Murmansk involved transporting weapons the length of France, from Normandy to the Franco-Catalan border, and dealing with unsympathetic French authorities at all stages of the process. To compound difficulties, the government in Paris closed the border at the beginning of 1938 and then again between June 1938 and January 1939 in order to isolate France from the perils of class warfare and to avoid further displeasing Mussolini.

Moreover, the evolution of Stalin's foreign policy and his growing mistrust of western intentions led to a reappraisal of priorities and encouraged a more pragmatic approach to the imminent demise of the Republic. The British historian Gerald Howson's claim that 'the Republicans rarely obtained more than a fraction of what they needed and even then after long delays and a terrible cost, physical and moral'[5] may be exaggerated. The British Hispanist Paul Preston suggested that the equipment supplied by the USSR 'ranged dramatically from obsolete artillery and small arms to state-of-the-art aircraft, tanks and anti-tank guns'.[6] What is certainly true is that the Germans and Italians provided a more reliable, consistent and ultimately decisive service.

The government of the Second Republic did not require the direct intervention of the British or the French; it simply requested that the western democracies uphold its right to buy weapons on the international market in order to defend itself against a military rebellion. Given that German and Italian participation in the conflict was incontrovertible and denounced in sessions of the League of Nations, the policy of 'non-intervention' was in itself 'intervention'. It was not a means to avoid the spread and 'internationalization' of the struggle. At best, in the words of Albert Camus in an editorial of his journal *Combat*, it was an 'abdication of responsibility'.[7] At worst, it was a deliberate manoeuvre to undermine the war effort of the Republic.

Sir Peter Chalmers Mitchell, the former secretary of the London Zoological Society, had retired to Malaga in 1934. On the outbreak of the Civil War, he was detained by militia while on a mission to visit his neighbour, an eminent local monarchist, who was being held in the local prison. The Scotsman later recalled how his guards reassured him that as a national of a 'friendly' democratic country, which 'would be in sympathy with a democracy fighting for its life', he was perfectly safe and that no action would be taken against him. Mitchell, however, was less sure of Britain's response:

> [I] told them that although I personally was entirely with them, they must not deceive themselves. The present Conservative Party would not stir a finger to help the Spanish Government, the Labour leaders would concur, probably with some vague expressions of anger, and the newspaper magnates would flood their papers with the old stories of priests crucified, nuns raped, children blinded [...] But I admit that my pessimism did not reach any conception so degrading to the international reputation and historic fame of England as the Non-Intervention Committee. My new friends refused to believe me.[8]

Indeed, a significant number of people in positions of power in Britain sympathized with Franco's cause, and their horror of social revolution was fuelled by the violence of the anarchists – particularly in Catalonia – and the uncontrolled elements working out of *checas* in the capital. The conservative Catholic lobby was appalled at the attacks on the Church, industrialists feared for their investments and the Conservative Party leadership felt more threatened by communism than by fascism. Antagonism towards the Republic was based on class interest rather than national interest, and by failing to comply with their obligation to support the rights of a democratically elected government, Britain lost an ally of huge geostrategic importance.

From the backbenches, Winston Churchill commended the British government for 'observing a strict and impartial neutrality throughout',[9] but denounced the embargo on the sale of weapons. In February 1939, as he watched the death agonies of appeasement from the backbenches, Churchill denounced non-intervention as 'an elaborate system of official humbug'.[10] Only now as Europe lurched towards war, did the right in Britain begin to recognize their mistake. In an article published in December 1938, Churchill wrote that a victory of the Republic would provide security for British communications through the Mediterranean, whereas if the Nationalists won, 'Nazi Germany would hold, or try to hold, Franco by the scruff of the neck'.[11]

Manuel Azaña, President of the Republic, denounced the British and French and claimed that their refusal to allow a friendly government to buy arms was more damaging to the cause of democracy in Spain than the actual intervention of the Germans and Italians on the side of the insurgent Nationalists. He complained bitterly of the international perception that both sides were equally responsible for the outbreak of war and the ensuing atrocities. It is irrefutable that many barbaric acts occurred behind Republican lines, but they were the work of uncontrolled elements – particularly among the anarchists – and rarely sanctioned by the Republican authorities (and never by the government) who struggled remorselessly to restore order in areas where war had caused a breakdown of police and judicial structures.

On the other hand, for the Nationalists, extreme fear was official policy. In a communiqué of 19 July 1936, the 'Director' of the uprising, General Mola, issued the order that 'We must sow terror'. The Nationalist viceroy in Sevilla, General Queipo de Llano, used his radio broadcasts to harangue his troops and encouraged them to show the wives of Republican soldiers what real men were made of. When the Nationalist Army was halted at the gates of Madrid by the desperate rearguard of a people's army, Franco pioneered the tactic of the aerial bombardment of the civilian population.

Nevertheless, on the international stage, the loyalists became trapped in a vicious circle. The refusal of the French and British governments to support them, or even allow them to purchase weapons, led them to a dependence on the USSR and the Partido Comunista de España (PCE, the Spanish Communist Party), a fact which was subsequently used by the western democracies to demonstrate the original premise: that the Republican government was dangerously subversive.

Furthermore, Soviet intervention came at a cost and Stalin's war aims were dictated not by the needs of the Spanish people, but rather by issues closer to home. While Hitler was anxious to secure mining rights for vital minerals in the Iberian Peninsula, and to provide Göring with a practice ground for methods of carpet-bombing, strafing and dive-bombing both military and civilian targets, he was also genuinely committed to a fascist victory in Spain. Stalin, on the other hand was less interested in securing victory for the Republic than he was in keeping the Germans occupied for as long as possible and as far as possible from the German–Soviet borderlands. In the words of Paul Preston, during Soviet intervention in Spain, 'the agents of the Comintern were not the general staff of world revolution but the frontier guards of the Soviet Union.'[12] Nor was the Soviet government willing to take unnecessary risks. In the first months of the war, they demanded Spanish Prime Minister Largo Caballero and his Finance Minister Juan Negrín, both of the Socialist Party (Partido Socialista Obrero Español, the PSOE), dispatch Republican gold reserves to Moscow to finance the shipments.

Soviet agents in Spain also took advantage of the circumstances to purge the international Communist movement of 'heretics' (i.e. anti-Stalinists). Rogue elements in the International Brigades were relentlessly suppressed under the orders of the French communist hero André Marty, and the Stalinist agent Aleksandr Mikhailovich Orlov of the NKVD (People's Commissariat for Internal Affairs) ruthlessly hunted down 'Trotskyites'. The increasing influence of the PCE and the Catalan section, Partit Socialista Unificat de Catalunya,* and the impunity with which Soviet agents carried out their activities on Spanish soil unsettled many Republican sympathizers, particularly in the armed forces. Worse was the impact abroad. The closer the Republic came to the USSR, the more it alienated conservative lobbies in Paris and London. The fact that it was British and French policy that had left the Republic dependent on Soviet support was ignored.

The Munich Pact proved to be another nail in the coffin of the Republic. Dr Negrín had done what he could. In April, he formed a new government, removing the defeatist Indalecio Prieto from the War

---

* United Socialist Party of Catalonia (PSUC)

Ministry and taking over the portfolio himself. In May he issued a thirteen-point peace plan based on the independence of a democratic Spain free of foreign troops. He promised to protect the rights and delegated authority of the regions (i.e. Catalonia and the Basque Country) within the context of a united Spain, to protect private property and to guarantee freedom of (religious) belief. He proposed agricultural reform in defence of the rights of those victims of the semi-feudalism that still controlled life in many rural areas, and social reform to protect the rights of the working class and to improve their living conditions. He promised an army free of political interference at the service of the nation and renounced war as an instrument of national policy. Finally, he offered an amnesty for all Spanish citizens who were willing to forsake revenge and to work for a better Spain.

Negrín was aware that Franco was confident enough of final victory to ignore the plan. Furthermore, he knew the Caudillo (leader – also translated by Juan J. Linz in a different context as 'chieftain'[13]) had no intention of negotiating terms with the Republic. His war aim was not solely victory, it was victory with an 'ideological holocaust'.[14] However, Negrín's peace plan was designed to appeal not to the Nationalists, but to an international audience and to reassure the world of the democratic credentials of the Republic.

By Christmas 1938, the two sides in the Civil War had been fighting for two and a half years. Given the military superiority of the Nationalists, it is remarkable that Franco's army took so long to achieve final victory. His military procrastination may have been based on incompetence and/or on a determination to extend the war and thus establish his own position and carry out an effective elimination of his enemies. Having made his reputation in the brutal colonial wars of North Africa in the 1920s, Franco gave little value to the life of those serving in the military. He appeared to care little more for the troops under his own command than for those fighting against him. In his counter-offensives, he tended to ignore opportunities to outflank or outmanoeuvre his enemy, and instead insisted upon the destruction of enemy troops and the restoration of his military and political authority throughout the reoccupied territory, irrespective of its strategic importance and the cost in human life. In his description of Franco's tactics during the Battle of the Ebro, Preston wrote, 'With nearly one million men now under arms, he could afford to be careless of their lives. His background in the African wars did not incline him to behave otherwise.'[15] Once the Ebro campaign had been successfully concluded, he was free to turn his attention to Catalonia.

Writing in his diaries in 1937, the Pravda journalist and Stalin's chief agent in Spain, Mikhail Koltsov (aka *Miguel Martínez*), had claimed that Barcelona was the key to the defence of the Republic. Catalonia represented more than a third of the territory of the free Republic. Its manufacturing industry accounted for two-thirds of the total industrial output, and two-thirds of the Republic's proletariat were employed in the Catalan metal, textile, transport, timber, leather and chemical sectors. In agriculture, Catalonia produced high-quality fruit, nuts, olive oil and wine. It had a wide range of mineral resources including potassium, zinc, tin and some coal. It had excellent port facilities and an extensive railway system. In short, 'Cataluña has the capacity to save the Republic and itself from fascism.' However, he concluded enigmatically, 'It also has the capacity to lose the Republic and itself to fascism.'[16]

The final great offensive of the Civil War commenced at Christmas and while survivors of the Republican Army fought brave rearguard actions, the outcome was never in question. The Germans and Italians rewarded Franco with fresh supplies of armaments while the Soviet Union became increasingly unable and unwilling to honour its commitments to a Republican Army that was now facing imminent defeat. At this juncture, in the words of the British historian Anthony Beevor: 'Soviet policy towards the Republic changed from cautious support to active disengagement.'[17]

Martínez Barrio, the President of the Cortes (Speaker), later maintained that the Republic was awaiting delivery of 'thousands of tons of war matériel, tanks, machine guns, rifles, ammunition'[18] that had been delayed en route from Le Havre. In his address to the Standing Committee of the Cortes at the end of March, Negrín later argued that if the weaponry had reached the Republican armies, it would have made a crucial difference both on the Ebro and in Catalonia.[19]

According to Beevor, the Nationalists had 340,00 men, some 300 tanks and 1,400 artillery pieces. The eastern army of the Republic had 220,000 men (many without rifles), 40 tanks (most of which were no longer battleworthy), and 250 field guns.[20] The Nationalist air force had been reinforced with newly trained pilots, Messerschmitt Bf 109Bs and Heinkel He 111s while the Republican air force consisted of a small number of Russian Polikarpovs, strengthened by approximately

45 Polikarpov I-15s (Chatos) assembled in Catalonia. The Republicans had no reserve troops, dwindling reserves of ammunition and little food. In the words of British Hispanist Raymond Carr, once the Nationalists launched their attack, their relentless advance 'was held up only by shortage of petrol'.[21]

In his memoirs, written weeks after the battle for Catalonia, Republican chief of staff, General Vicente Rojo, one of the heroes of the defence of Madrid in 1936, claimed quite simply that by January 1939, the Republic had no army.[22] In his own memoirs, Álvarez del Vayo, the Republican foreign minister, recounts a meeting with the general staff at which the prime minister was told that there were '37,000 rifles for the whole army of Catalonia'.[23] Morale crumbled, new recruits fled in the face of artillery fire, discipline vanished and ever more troops deserted as the 'front' fell back on Barcelona. In the words of General Rojo, 'the spirit of resistance was replaced by the doctrine of escape.'[24]

Two eminent members of the Spanish Communist Party, Manuel Azcárate, son of the ambassador in London during the Civil War, and José Sandoval, war hero both in Spain and later on the Eastern Front against the Wehrmacht, later wrote:

> Republican heroism was confronted with Fascist tanks and aircraft. By the third week [...], the Republican troops had already been decimated. [...] Its initial resistance shattered, the front broken, the Republican Army slowly began a vast withdrawal.[25]

As the enemy advanced throughout Catalonia, the demoralization of the Republican Army was matched by the resignation of the civilian population in Barcelona. Successive military setbacks had undermined any vestige of confidence in the Republic. The disloyalty of the western democracies and the growing indifference of the USSR compounded the sense of isolation. The French border was closed, Nationalist warships patrolled the waters off the Catalan coast and Franco's expanding corridor to the Mediterranean had cut Catalonia off from the rest of Republican territory. In effect, the Catalans were under siege. Power supplies were disrupted by the advancing Nationalist Army, shortages of drugs and food raised the spectre of disease and hunger, each defeat raised the number of refugees and increased the pressure on provisions and services, and constant aerial bombardment sapped the will to resist. The fifth column gained in confidence and many of the population began to believe that even Nationalist conquest was better than the continuing futility of resistance.

On the other hand, morale among the insurgent troops had not been so high since Franco arrived on mainland Spain with this Army of Africa in July 1936. On Christmas Eve 1938, the opening paragraph of the news section of the leading Nationalist newspaper, *ABC* (Sevilla edition) claimed:

> Our troops are used to fighting in all types of weather and in the toughest conditions. They are used to fighting and winning. In the cold, in the heat, on the plains and in the mountains, under the scorching sun or in torrential rain, in the dust-clouds of parched lands or in mud and snow ... Always fighting and always winning. Any weather is good weather for conquest. All roads lead to victory under the providential command of the *Generalísimo*.[*]

By the last week of January 1939, the Nationalists had routed the Republican forces in Catalonia and were poised to take Barcelona. An added dimension to the crisis was that the city was not only the capital of Catalonia, but since October 1937 – when Negrín decided to transfer the government from Valencia – it was also the capital of the Republic. On the 23rd, having received a report from General Rojo on the military situation, the prime minister ordered his secretary of national defence, Julián Zugazagoitia, to make immediate arrangements for the government apparatus to abandon the city. Just as Largo Caballero had ordered his government to Valencia as the Nationalists approached Madrid in 1936, so Negrín now prepared to flee Barcelona. According to Zugazagoitia, he later insisted in a phone call that he personally would only leave when he was told that every other member of his team was gone.[26]

The circumstances in Madrid in 1936 and Barcelona in 1939 were radically different. In November 1936, when the insurgent Nationalists stood at the gates of Madrid, the capital rallied and withstood infantry and tank attacks, relentless artillery bombardment and constant bombing

---

[*] the title of Supreme Military Commander conferred on Franco

raids. The number of those fighting for the Republic was swollen by the troops who had fled the onslaught of Franco's 'Death Column', which had fought its way northward from Sevilla until Madrid stood at its mercy. The survivors of the Nationalist victories at Badajóz and Talavera brought tales of atrocities which increased the resolve of the population to resist, as did the arrival of Russian tanks and aircraft and International Brigade volunteers who rallied to the anti-fascist struggle from across the world. The people of Madrid were also alert to the reality that their backs were to the wall. There was nowhere left to go, retreat was no longer an option, the only feasible military strategy that remained was to make a stand. The spirit of resistance was immortalized in the slogan '*No pasarán*' ('They shall not pass').

However, at the beginning of 1939, the situation in Barcelona was significantly different. The civilian population was faced with extreme hardship, many were close to starvation and they were fully aware that the enemy enjoyed overwhelming military superiority. According to Foreign Minister Álvarez del Vayo, between the 22nd and the 24th, the city was bombed fifteen times by Savoia-Marchettis and Heinkels operating out of the Balearic Islands.[27] The Republicans knew they could expect neither reinforcements nor weapons. Furthermore, the people of Catalonia did have somewhere to flee the advancing Fascist hordes: the border.

Chapter 2

Caminante, no hay camino

On the night of 26 January 1939, as the enemy reached Barcelona, Lluís Companys, the president of the Catalan government (Generalitat), toured the city by car with Josep Andreu, president of the high court in the Catalan capital. Andreu later shared his experience with the historian Ronald Fraser:

> It was a night I'll never forget. The silence was total, a terrible silence, the sort you can only imagine at the height of a tragedy. We drove onto the Plaça de Sant Jaume, said farewell to the Generalitat and to the city. It was 2 a.m. The vanguard of the nationalist army was already on Mount Tibidabo and close to Montjuich. We didn't believe we would return.[1]

In fact, both men did return. After years of exile, Andreu arrived back in Catalonia in 1964. He continued to campaign against Franco and was imprisoned under the dictatorship. With the arrival of democracy in the 1970s, he helped draft the new Catalan Statute of Autonomy and was elected to represent Barcelona in the new Parliament in Madrid. On the other hand, Companys was arrested by the Gestapo in Brittany, in occupied France, in August 1940 and 'extradited' to the military authorities in Spain. Under the terms of articles 237 and 238 of the Military Code of Justice of Franco's new dictatorship and the Law of Political Responsibilities (9 February 1939), a court martial found him guilty of 'military rebellion'. He was sentenced to death and executed by firing squad in the Castillo de Montjuïc on 15 October 1940.

In the words of Republican chief of staff, General Rojo, Barcelona fell '*sin gloria*' (ingloriously).[2] In his seminal work *The Spanish Civil War*, Hugh Thomas claimed the end of the Catalan campaign was less an offensive than a 'victory parade'.[3] Rather than take the city, Franco's vanguard of Spaniards, Italians and North African colonial troops simply occupied it. By then, the political and military leaders were long gone. The fronts had crumbled, and the Republican troops had either retreated or surrendered. The population had neither the means nor the will to mount any resistance. In the aftermath of victory/defeat, some 10,000 Republicans were murdered/executed.[4] There are no official figures. There was of course the customary raping and looting.

On 25 January, the main Barcelona daily paper, *La Vanguardia*, was still calling on the population to resist. An article on the front page echoed the '*no pasarán*' slogan of Madrid's heroic stand against the Nationalists in 1936. Two days later, now in the hands of the invading army, the newspaper appeared on the newsstands with a title that declared itself 'at the Service of Spain and Franco'. On the front page, the new editors gave thanks to the glorious army of Generalísimo Franco and declared: 'Our hearts are filled with the joy of liberation, and the burning desire to serve Spain, immortal Spain, eternal Spain.' The next day the newspaper was rebranded *La Vanguardia Española*.

The Statute of Autonomy (*Estatut de Autonomía de Cataluña*) of 1932 had given the Catalans fairly wide powers of 'self-rule'. When his troops first penetrated Catalonia and occupied Lleida (Lérida) on 5 April 1938, General Franco immediately revoked the statute in line with his declared objective to establish a single language (castellano – Spanish) and a single personality throughout Spain. Now, across Barcelona, the Republican *tricolor* (red, yellow and purple) and the Catalan *Senyera* (five yellow and four red stripes) were pulled down and replaced by the triumphant Monarchist flag (red, yellow, red). Use of the Catalan language was outlawed in state institutions and the media, and would be brutally discouraged by anyone in a position of authority (members of the judiciary, Guardia Civil, employers, teachers etc.) Idealistic *Falangistas** who sought to incorporate Catalonia in their vision of a greater, fairer, more dynamic Spain, were soon bitterly disappointed. Franco was not interested in social reform and integration: he was an authoritarian archconservative who sought to defend and preserve the privileges of the army, Church, industrialists and landowners. The new authorities in Barcelona had no interest in social reconstruction with those who had

---

* members of the Falange – the Fascist Party

resisted the Nationalist movement. Their policy was ideological cleansing: revenge, punishment and the eradication of elements who opposed Franco, might oppose Franco, or had simply failed to support him.

Barcelona's sins were twofold. She had not only defied the sacred Nationalist creed of Spanish unity, but she had also embraced violent social revolution. In the period of nine months after the outbreak of civil war in July 1936, the anarchists and POUM (Partido Obrero de Unificación Marxista, the Workers' Party of Marxist Unification) led not only popular resistance to the military insurgents but also an uprising against the existing social order. Before the street fighting of May 1937, when the less radical members of the Republican front wrested control and reversed the revolutionary process, Barcelona offered Western Europe a vision of the dictatorship of the proletariat. In his passionate account of his own experiences, George Orwell wrote, 'It was the first time that I had ever been in a town where the working class was in the saddle.' He described the revolutionary art that adorned every building, the destruction of the churches, and the collectivization of local businesses and trade. However, he seemed most fascinated by the changes in behaviour and social protocols. Waiters and shop assistants were no longer obsequious, people stopped using the formal *Usted,* tipping was outlawed, and 'Practically everyone wore rough working-class clothes, or blue overalls or some variant of the militia uniform'.[5]

In his own eye-witness account of those early months of the war, Franz Borkenau wrote of his first 'peaceful arrival' in Barcelona in August:

> No taxi-cabs, but instead old horse-cabs to carry us into the town. Few people in the Paseo de Colon. And, then, as we turned round the corner of the Ramblas (the chief artery of Barcelona) came a tremendous surprise: before our eyes, in a flash, unfolded itself the revolution.[6]

The description of the city that follows is not dissimilar to Orwell's, although he puts more emphasis on the fact that so many of the civilian population were armed. When they wrote these words, both men were aware the experiment had been short-lived. Bourgeois elements in Barcelona had not disappeared, they were simply dressed in proletariat clothing, and yet the two writers shared an almost melancholy exhilaration at what they had seen. Orwell concluded, 'I recognized it as a state of affairs worth fighting for.'[7]

Three years later, in January 1939, the leaders of the new military occupation of Catalonia subsequently undertook a campaign to purge the capital of separatists and left-wingers. That the slaughter did not achieve the intensity of Badajoz in 1936 was largely due to the fact that most of the potential victims were gone. Luis Bolín, the man who had been instrumental in arranging the flight that transported Franco from the Canary Islands in July 1936 to take command of the African Army in Morocco, was now head of Franco's State Tourist Board. His take on the need for cleansing was more prosaic. Arriving in Barcelona, behind the first Nationalist troops, he complained of the 'stench' and the garbage in the street, and the inches-thick dust at the Ritz, 'the best hotel in the town':

> I told the manager to summon as many char-women as he could find, for I needed them all. Once they arrived, I reviewed them, complete with brooms, mops and pails. 'Has the day at last arrived for us to resume scrubbing floors?' one of them asked me. 'It certainly has,' I replied. 'Thank God for that!' she answered, throwing up her hands to the skies.[8]

This, according to the American poet Gamel Woolsey, was perhaps the 'real voice of Spain'. Describing her experiences in Andalucía at the outbreak of war in 1936, and the reaction of her servant Maria, she wrote of those made to suffer by the 'folly and presumption of misguided men' which interrupted the 'natural order of birth and burial' and 'sowing and harvest'. She wrote that perhaps, 'when the delirium was over […], we would all sigh with relief and go back to the austere hard-working life of peace'.[9]

Prime Minister Negrín had meanwhile established his seat of government at Figueres, some twenty kilometres from the border with France. On the 28 January, the *Guardian* newspaper described 'the scenes of indescribable confusion' in the town: 'Government officials trying to find their departments, Ministers hunting for their colleagues, crying mothers looking for lost children, small boys and girls begging piteously for bread. The refugees lack shelter from the bitter cold and fires to keep them warm.'

Parliament met on 1 February. Henry Buckley, the correspondent for the *Daily Telegraph*, who had accompanied the government north, described the 'clammy and cold' conditions of the Figueres Castle dungeons where 55[10] of the original 473 deputies now sat in session. Negrín made his final peace proposal: a three-point plan demanding a guarantee of Spanish independence, the right of the Spanish people to choose their own destiny and protection from persecution for those who had fought on the losing side in the civil war. He told the deputies: 'Countries do not live only by victories, but by the examples which their people have known how to give in tragic times.'[11]

Referring to twenty centuries of Christian civilization, and the new barbarism facing Europe, the prime minister also reminded the western democracies of their responsibilities:

> in our own struggle in Spain, we are not only defending the interests of Spain, but also those of other countries which not only have failed to help as they should have, but have proved to be one of the main obstacles in our fight.[12]

When Henry Buckley described the setting as a 'tomb' to his colleague Ilya Ehrenburg, standing next to him in the dungeons, the Russian replied, 'My friend, this is the tomb not only of the Spanish Republic, but also of European democracy.'[13]

Writing at the end of the Civil War, the Republic's foreign minister, Álvarez del Vayo, expressed his admiration for the refugees who now thronged the streets of Figueres. Given the extent of the defeat, the grim reality of what awaited them, and the hardship they now endured on the road to France, del Vayo was overwhelmed by the people's generosity and loyalty to the Republic. Nevertheless, he acknowledged that by now if the government still existed, it was 'more by virtue of their moral superiority and the confidence that they [the ministers] still inspired in the people, than on the grounds of any normal functioning of the administration'.[14] This was the key argument used later by Chamberlain to justify his decision to recognize the Franco régime.

In the meantime, the Nationalists embarked on their final offensive in the north-east to mop up resistance in Catalonia. As the Republican Army fell back, so they sought to slow the advance of the Nationalists by raiding their lines, laying isolated ambushes and launching minor counter-attacks. However, final defeat was simply a matter of time. They lacked the numbers, they were desperately short of weapons and ammunition and the newly conscripted had no will to fight. If, after the fall of Barcelona, it took the Nationalist Army so long to occupy the whole of Catalonia, it was largely because they lacked transport and spent too long celebrating in the capital. By now hundreds of thousands of refugees were on the move, seeking to escape the wrath of the enemy. They fled in cars, trucks, buses, by bicycle, on foot. They were driven not only by their fear of the advancing Nationalists but also the terror of German pilots refining their tactics of low-level dive-bombing and strafing. Most followed the main road through Girona and Figueres towards Le Perthus. Some tramped across the Pyrenees through deep snow. Others followed the coast to the French border at Portbou. Figueres was overwhelmed by the flood of human misery. In his memoirs, published in 1940, Secretary of State for War Julián Zugazagoitia described his sense of shame at having failed in his mission and having brought this suffering upon the people:

> Intimidated by despair, the defenceless mass dared not take any initiative. They waited for someone to lead them somewhere. They wanted someone, anyone, to take charge of leading them to the promised land. [...] They moved aside to avoid being in the way, they made no complaints in order to avoid making things worse, they hid their anguish in order to deal with them on their own. I have never felt so terribly guilty.[15]

On 3 February, when the Nationalists were within fifty kilometres of the border, a further problem arose for the Republican authorities. What to do with the treasures of the Prado Museum which had been shipped to Valencia when the Germans began bombing Madrid and had subsequently been transferred to Barcelona. The foreign minister, Álvarez del Vayo, signed a contract in Figueres with the sub-director of the Louvre, by which the paintings, including classic works by Goya, Velázquez and El Greco, would be transported by road to Geneva, and there delivered into the safekeeping of the League of Nations. The government was faced with the moral dilemma of whether or not to carry out the operation with transport which might otherwise be used to alleviate the suffering of those evacuees fleeing the Nationalists on foot. Once the decision was taken to save the paintings, the Republican authorities were once again humbled by the reaction of those undergoing the tribulations of defeat and deprivation and yet who made no protest when moved aside to facilitate the departure of the trucks bearing the paintings.

On the other hand, Henry Buckley was highly critical of the pressure brought by foreign governments which prioritized art over the lives of the refugees and 'cared nothing about the soul of a people which was being trampled on'. Writing in the immediate aftermath of the defeat he complained:

> the art treasures left for Geneva in 1,842 cases on February 13th; they were well protected from rain and wind. Women and children and sick and wounded men could sleep in the open air, almost uncared for. But the twenty trucks of Prado pictures had great tarpaulin covers and the care of a score of experts.[16]

Less publicly, in order to cover the costs of maintaining the resistance of the central–south zone (based on the Madrid–Valencia axis) and providing for the refugees, Negrín also ordered the transfer of more than 100 crates containing 'treasures' that the Republic had appropriated from both public and private owners.

On 4 February, the constant air raids and advancing Nationalist troops forced the government to abandon Figueres and relocate closer to the French border. The next day, the French government, which had agreed to open the border to civilian refugees at the end of January, also agreed to allow troops to cross. On 6 February, Negrín accompanied President Azaña into France. Once there, Azaña would refuse to return to Spain, either to Madrid or Valencia, on the grounds that such a gesture might be interpreted as a willingness to pursue a war that he considered lost. Together with many generals, he now believed that to fight on involved a futile sacrifice of the lives of young men in a forlorn hope that a sudden change of heart among the western democracies might shift the military balance. Some days later, entrenched in the Spanish embassy in Paris, he told Minister of Foreign Affairs Álvarez del Vayo, 'My duty is to make peace. I refuse to help, by my presence, to prolong a senseless struggle.'[17] Negrín however, was dismayed by Azaña's attitude and relinquishment of his duty.

On his way back into Spain, Negrín met José Antonio Aguirre (first *Lehendakari* – president – of the Basque Country) as he accompanied the president of the Catalan government, Lluís Companys across the border into exile. He told Zugazagoitia that in this case it was a relief to see them go; it meant 'one less thing to worry about'.[18] There remained a lingering frustration with the Catalan leadership and a resentment that they had prioritized the defence of an autonomous Catalonia and withheld support that the Republic desperately needed elsewhere. A British woman, Nancy Johnstone, who ran a hotel in Tossa de Mar – Casa Johnstone – on the Catalan coast, later encapsulated the attitude of the townspeople: 'The Tossencs objected to their young men being sent to defend Madrid. Madrid was not a Catalan town. Catalans had driven fascism out of Catalunya and that should be sufficient.'[19] Paradoxically, while Barcelona had now fallen to Franco's troops, Madrid continued to resist the Nationalist siege which had lasted over two years.

Three days later, the remaining ministers of the Republic, including the prime minister, were also forced to evacuate to Toulouse whence Negrín flew back to Alicante in Spain. Chief of Staff General Rojo ordered his troops to withdraw across the border and was himself one of the last to abandon Spanish territory on 9 February, by which time Franco's army had reached Le Perthus and stood ready to control the border from east to west, from the Mediterranean to the Bay of Biscay. According to the Valière Report, commissioned by the French government and presented to the Chamber of Deputies in Paris on 9 March 1939, a total of 440,000 refugees fled to France between 28 January and 12 February. Of these, 220,000 were men-at-arms, 210,000 civilians (including 170,000 women, children and elderly) and 10,000 wounded. Minister of the Interior Albert Sarraut claimed that by the time the report was published, some 50,000 had already returned to Spain, either to fight or to brave the reprisals of the new regime. Other sources provide different numbers, the modern consensus suggesting that the total number of evacuees was close to half a million.

The German writer Gustav Regler, who had been political commissar of the XV International Brigade, met the eminent *New York Times* correspondent Herbert Matthews in his hotel in Perpignan and decided to accompany him to the border to see if he could assist the International Brigaders still crossing into France. He described the scene he found as 'the abyss between two worlds', like 'a medieval picture of the

Crucifixion'. He saw men who 'still had earth clutched in their hands which they had snatched up as they left their villages'. The French police made one man open his hand and throw the soil on the ground. When a border guard asked one woman what had brought her to this place, another woman replied, 'Anything is better than Fascism.' Regler witnessed women

> with children in their arms, others carrying small dogs, and one was carrying a hen in her apron. The Quakers had sent cars with milk and cocoa up into the hills, and some had picked up women they found on the way. One woman discovered, just as she was passing us, that the child she was carrying was dead. She covered it with her apron and pressed it more tightly against her.[20]

The vast majority crossed the border on foot, short of food and exposed to the harsh conditions of mid-winter. As well as the Quaker Friends Service Council, several international bodies and charitable organizations, including the Red Cross, and the International Commission for the Assistance of Child Refugees in Spain did manage to provide some relief in the form of food and hot drinks, but ultimately, they were as overwhelmed by the crisis as the French state. Many French families responded generously to the plight of the evacuees and provided shelter and food where they could. Unfortunately, the magnanimity shown by the French government in opening the border to the Republican refugees was not matched by the provisions made for their well-being once they were in France. The authorities were unable to cope with the dimensions of the refugee crisis and in all likelihood were not unaware that the worse the conditions in France, the easier it would be to persuade evacuees to return to Spain to rejoin the Republican Army or take their chances with the new regime.

Nevertheless, soldiers were disarmed as they entered French territory and, given the chronic and desperate shortage of weapons on the Republican side, any plans for the generalized repatriation of rifle-less infantrymen to Republican territory seemed futile. The consensus among the general staff was that the war was over and regardless of the vindictive nature of Franco's crusade, the sooner the fighting stopped the better.

On 9 February, the Nationalist government in Burgos approved the new Law of Political Responsibilities (published three days later in the *Boletín Oficial del Estado**) – a legislative aberration of which Hitler and Stalin might have been proud. The law declared that all supporters of the Popular Front including government officers and members of the armed forces who had resisted the coup d'état of July 1936 were guilty of military rebellion. The abject cynicism of accusing of insurrection those who had remained loyal to the Republic and who had resisted the insurgency, confirmed that Franco had no intention of making concessions to the vanquished.

The law was made retroactive (to October 1934) and included provision to punish those who had failed to support the Nationalist cause by act or omission. It thus gave Franco carte blanche in the repression of his enemies: republicans, socialists, communists, anarchists, trade unionists, Basque and Catalan separatists, masons and 'disloyal' members of the military forces. So generic and wide-reaching was the law, that Spanish historian Carlos Hernández de Miguel suggested that under its terms even Franco could have been prosecuted.[21]

According to Sandoval and Azcárate, while Negrín continued to lobby the French and British for support, and those around him sought some semblance of a peaceful solution to the conflict, 'Franco was whetting his knife'.[22]

---

* *BOE*: *Official State Gazette*

21

Chapter 3

Till the Last Gasp

Prime Minister Negrín and Foreign Minister Álvarez del Vayo flew back to Alicante on a mission to organize a final desperate rearguard action against Franco's triumphant army. By now the prime minister's determination to resist at all costs was supported only by the Communists and his own faction within the PSOE. His increasing dependence on the PCE/PSUC further alienated those who sought to bring a rapid end to the conflict. Despite the catastrophe of Catalonia, the Republican government still controlled 30 per cent of Spanish territory including Madrid and Valencia. On the other hand, according to Hugh Thomas, although the Republican Army had half a million men in active service in February 1939, the Army of the Centre (the Madrid zone) had only 95,000 rifles, 1,600 sub-machine guns, 1,400 machine guns, 150 artillery pieces, 50 mortars and 10 tanks. The food supplies for a civilian population on near-starvation rations were almost exhausted and the military leaders had given up. 'All were weary of war.'[1]

In the meantime, the Republican government became painfully aware that the British and French governments were on the verge of recognizing Franco's régime. In London, the only cause for further delay appears to have been the belief that, as a quid pro quo, Franco might yet be forced to issue theoretically binding assurances that there would be no reprisals. On 16 February, Sir Alexander Cadogan, the under-secretary of state, reported that the Republican ambassador in London, Pablo de Azcárate, had visited the Foreign Office and 'practically offer[ed] surrender on terms'. Having dispatched a telegram to Franco in Burgos, Cadogan then wrote in his diary, 'Pray Heaven, with any luck, "Spain" will be over soon.'[2] On 26 February, Azcárate delivered an official note to Foreign Secretary Lord Halifax offering 'an immediate cessation of hostilities', in return for a pledge from Franco that his new regime would desist from any punitive acts of retribution against Republican loyalists, and a commitment to allow the evacuation of leading Republicans by sea. According to Azcárate, he left the meeting convinced that in spite of the secretary of state's customary good manners, the Republic could expect no favours from the British government.[3] Indeed, there is little doubt that Halifax had long since concluded that given the breakdown of Republican institutions, there was no alternative but to declare the unconditional recognition of Franco's government. The decision, taken in tandem with the French government, was announced on 27 February.

The opposition in the British Parliament subsequently tabled a motion of censure claiming that the recognition of insurgent forces which were supported by the intervention of foreign powers hostile to democracy

> was a deliberate affront to the legitimate Government of a friendly Power, [...] a gross breach of international traditions, and [...] a further stage in a policy which [was] steadily destroying, in all democratic countries, confidence in the good faith of Great Britain.[4]

In his reply Neville Chamberlain argued that having taken Barcelona, Franco was now in 'a position which one might call a position of reasonable expectancy of permanence and superiority', while the Republican government of Spain was in a state of disarray from which it would not recover. He further pointed out that the President of the Republic was no longer in Spain, that a number of government ministers were in France, and that many ministers and military advisers were calling for an end to hostilities. In these circumstances the Cortes (Parliament) could not be convened and the diplomatic corps were unable to perform their mission.

He concluded that refusing to recognize Franco 'could not help the Republican Government or the people in Madrid. What it would do would be to embitter our relations with the new Government of Spain and to destroy any influence which we may hope to have with that Government'. When he was attacked from the opposition benches for failing to obtain a guarantee from Franco that there would be no reprisals against the defeated, he read aloud a telegram he had received from the general on the 22nd:

> National Spain has won the war, and it is therefore incumbent on the vanquished to surrender unconditionally. The patriotism, chivalry and generosity of the Caudillo,

of which he has given so many examples in the liberated regions, and likewise the spirit of equity and justice that inspires all the National Government's actions, constitute a firm guarantee for all Spaniards who are not criminals.[5]

Unfortunately, Franco had made it clear in the Law of Political Responsibilities that in the new Spain, all Spaniards who opposed the Nationalist cause, or failed to give active support, were indeed criminals. On the other hand, the decision to recognize Franco's government was no more than the official culmination of the foreign policy of the British government under Stanley Baldwin and Neville Chamberlain. The principles of appeasement and the fear of social revolution had persuaded the government in London that their own interest was best served by the policy of allowing the Germans and Italians to supply the rebels with military supplies, troops and logistic support that would ultimately prove crucial in determining the outcome of the conflict. They cared little for the fate of the millions of Spaniards who had fought on the 'wrong' side. The solution to George Orwell's dilemma over whether the British ruling class was wicked or merely stupid[6] was in fact easy: they were both.

In a personal and confidential letter to Joseph Stalin, written in November 1939 before the Nationalist offensive in Catalonia, Negrín claimed English politics was the key to the behaviour of the French and the other European countries who would officially be allies of the Republic. He continued:

> Unfortunately England is governed by the Cliveden Set, with the Astors, Lord Londonberry, Garvin and other elements hostile to Spain and in thrall to Hitler and Mussolini. Chamberlain is the effective tool of their obstinacy, their folly and their impermeability to public opinion.

He then listed Chamberlain's four key characteristics: 1) empathy with Hitler and Mussolini, 2) a Tory's profound hatred for the Soviet Union, 3) distrust for France, and 4) the repugnance of his class for the working classes and its insular philistinism. While he saw some hope in the opposition faction of the Conservative Party which was gradually forming around Churchill, and the slow awakening of the British people, he described Chamberlain and his clique as 'the worst enemy of Spain'[7].

The eventual shifts within the Conservative Party in response to Hitler's disregard for the spirit of appeasement came too late to save the Republic. According to Azcárate, when he was first introduced to Churchill in August 1936 at a social event which he was attending as the new ambassador of Spain, an enraged Churchill had refused even to shake his hand and had stormed off, muttering, 'blood, blood.'[8] However, by the end of 1937, Azcárate was reporting to his prime minister that Churchill's attitude had undergone a 180-degree change and he now acknowledged that a victory for the Republic was the only outcome 'compatible with the vital and permanent interests of the [British] empire'.[9] The foreign secretary, Sir Anthony Eden, had also resigned (February 1938) over disagreements with Chamberlain's reconciliatory approach to Mussolini's fascist Italy and Il Duce's continued intervention in the Spanish war. Nonetheless, appeasement was only to be reversed when Czechoslovakia had been dismembered and the USSR alienated, and when France's borders were threatened by three adjacent and hostile fascist powers, united in their enmity towards the French state.

In March 1939, the French government dispatched Marshal Pétain to Burgos as ambassador to the new régime. The hero of Verdun, Pétain had fought with Franco in the Rif War (North Africa) in the 1920s. The posting did not last long; the ambassador was soon ordered back to France, eventually to answer a higher calling, which would have a far greater impact on the Spanish refugees now massed in camps on the French side of the Pyrenees.

The decision of the governments in Paris and London to recognize Franco's régime was providential for the President of the Republic, Manuel Azaña, who had been awaiting a pretext to resign for weeks. The president was now living in the Spanish embassy in Paris, and Foreign Minister Álvarez del Vayo had made repeated attempts to coax him into returning to Spain and thus persuade the British and French of the Republic's determination to resist. But Azaña had commissioned a report from members of the general staff and rejected del Vayo's pleas with the words, 'Nobody believes in our powers of resistance, and the most sceptical of all are our own generals.'[10]

On hearing the news from London and Paris, he immediately tendered his resignation and issued a statement in which he claimed he was no longer able to fulfil his functions in the light of these new circumstances and insisted on the need for an immediate end to the fighting in order to avoid further pointless sacrifice.

As the Nationalists stood poised to deal the deathblow, the Republic came under attack from within. Just as at the international level, Negrín had been forced into dependence on the USSR, so at home his only ally in the policy of continued resistance was the Communist Party, which in the absence of Secretary-General José Díaz (receiving treatment for cancer in Moscow) was under the guidance of the Italian Palmiro Togliatti (nom de guerre *Ercoli*),[11] the Comintern delegate in Spain. On 3 March, in order to guarantee his position and the feasibility of his strategy, and to undermine the defeatism of many in the general staff, Negrín made a series of appointments of communists to key posts, including command of the naval base at Cartagena. The port, and the ships of the Spanish Navy that were deployed there, were key to Negrín's plans for the mass evacuation of Republican supporters.

On 5 March, frustrated by Negrín's determination to prolong the war and angered by his affinity to the Spanish Communist Party, Colonel Segismundo Casado López seized power in Madrid. The coup was supported by Anarchists embittered by their treatment at the hands of the PCE and the Comintern, disaffected members of the PSOE who did not trust Negrín, agents of military intelligence (Servicio de Investigación Militar, or SIM), and military officers who were either defeatist or had 'covert sympathy'[12] for the Nationalist cause. Various conspirators, both civilian and military, were dangerously close to the fifth column. Many of the latter were geographical or accidental loyalists: on the outbreak of the Civil War, they had found themselves in areas where the uprising failed to prosper and had trodden the path of caution rather than declare for the insurgency. All the disparate elements behind the coup were linked by their abhorrence of communism and their obsession that Negrín was a puppet of the Comintern.

Fighting broke out in a sub-civil war in Madrid and a three-way battle in Cartagena, where the battle between the followers of Negrín and those of Casado's new Consejo Nacional de Defensa (National Defence Council) sparked an uprising by fifth columnists. Hundreds, perhaps even thousands, of men lost their lives in what proved to be the most significant battle of the final days of the Republic. By this point, Negrín and his entourage had set up a new government headquarters at Elda in the province of Alicante. Aware that Casado would try to capture them and use them as bargaining chips in peace talks with Franco, the prime minister, his cabinet and Communist Party leaders (including Dolores Ibárruri – 'La Pasionaria') flew out of Spain and into exile from the aerodrome of Monóvar.

Having presented his anti-communist credentials, Casado then set out to negotiate with Franco. Assuming that as a professional military officer he would have more success agreeing peace terms with the Generalísimo, he offered to surrender in return for a pledge that there would be no reprisals and a twenty-five-day truce to allow for the evacuation of all those who did not feel able to trust their fate to the new regime. Although talks did indeed take place, Franco was in no mood, and had no need, to settle for anything less than unconditional surrender. He simply waited patiently for the rump of the Republic to implode and by 27 March his troops were in a position to occupy Madrid. The last Republican mayor of Madrid, Melchor Rodríguez (appointed hours before by the Defence Council), and Julián Besteiro, the last remaining member of the council in the capital, subsequently surrendered the city to the *franquista* army. On 1 April, Franco issued his final war communiqué stating that the 'red army' had been made captive and disarmed.

The substantial numbers of Republican and left-wing officials, soldiers, trade unionists, party activists and sympathizers still in Madrid were denied a last opportunity to escape. Nevertheless, thousands of desperate Republican sympathizers did gather in the port at Alicante in anticipation of a rescue operation by the British and French navies. Not only did Casado's coup wreck Negrín's strategy to extricate as many people from Madrid as possible, but with the notable exception of the *Stanbrook* and her captain Archibald Dickson[13], the boats that were expected on the east coast to carry out a mass evacuation failed to materialize. In the words of Henry Buckley:

> The Democracies who had been so anxious that no more blood should be shed in war, showed no perturbation whatever at the fact that thousands of people whose life was in danger […] because they had fought for the progress and independence of their land, were left to face at the worst a firing-squad and at the best a concentration camp.[14]

The men and women trapped in Alicante were eventually detained by the Italian vanguard of Franco's army. The men were disarmed and then held on a hillside (the notorious Campo de los Almendros – The Field of Almond Trees), two kilometres from the port, whence they were transported to prisons and forced labour camps around the new Spain. Those who survived the fascist death squads that constantly searched the camps for personal enemies, the summary justice of military courts, the torture and the inhuman conditions in which they were incarcerated were to remain at Franco's pleasure for as long as twenty years, prisoners of war of a conflict that Franco had triumphantly claimed he had won, but which he was eternally reluctant to admit had ever ended. Writing in the *Evening Standard* in August 1937, Winston Churchill had claimed that regardless of the outcome of the civil war, 'victory will be followed by the merciless extermination of the active elements of the vanquished and by a prolonged period of iron rule'.[15] He was right.

In the prologue to his work, *The Spanish Holocaust*, Paul Preston wrote:

> In all of Spain after the final victory of the rebels at the end of March 1939, approximately 20,000 Republicans were executed. Many more died of disease and malnutrition in overcrowded, unhygienic prisons and concentration camps. Others died in the slave-labour conditions of work-battalions. More than half a million refugees were forced into exile and many were to die of disease in French concentration camps. Several thousand were worked to death in Nazi camps.[16]

Chapter 4

Allez, allez!

Antonio Machado, one of Spain's leading twentieth-century poets and a fervent supporter of the Republic, reached the border ahead of Franco's troops at the end of January 1939 accompanied by his elderly mother. Once in France, they took refuge in the Hotel Bougnol-Quintanain in the small town of Collioure. Machado suffered a chronic pulmonary condition and having undergone the trials of the *retirada* (the retreat across the border), his health quickly deteriorated. He died three weeks later in the same hotel. A letter from the British Hispanist John Brande Trend offering the poet a position at the University of Cambridge arrived too late. In his reply to Trend, Machado's brother, José, expressed his gratitude for the offer and wrote: 'Given his deep and sincere admiration for England, he would have been able to fulfil one of his most fervent wishes: to visit your country […] But dreams do not come true!'[1] Machado's mother, Ana Ruiz, died within three days of his demise. Franco's Spain was not a land for poets. Federico García Lorca had been murdered in Granada at the outset of the Civil War and Miguel Hernández would later die in prison (Alicante, 28 March 1942) of tuberculosis at the age of 31.

In his poem *Españolito*, Machado had described two Spains: one that died and one that yawned. Franco now divided the country into conquerors and vanquished, a country under military occupation by its own armed forces. The Caudillo had no interest in reconciliation. His war aim was the extinction of all Republican ideologies and the restoration of Catholic obscurantism. He converted Spain into a giant concentration camp policed by the army, Guardia Civil, secret police, and the Falange. Inspired by the words and example of Himmler, he offered redemption exclusively through labour. The fate of those that had escaped into France did not appear much better. Pablo Neruda, former consul-general at the Chilean embassy in Madrid during the Republic, described the *retirada* as the 'most painful event in the history of Spain'.[2]

In fact, the mass exodus of January/February 1939 was not the first. According to French historian Geneviève Dreyfus-Armand,[3] 120,000 Republicans had fled on the loss of the Basque Country and the fall of Santander and Asturias in the summer and autumn of 1937. The defeat in the Aragón campaign and the collapse of the Ebro front in 1938 led to the flight of another 25,000 troops and civilians seeking refuge in France. However, as long as Catalonia resisted, many of those forced to retreat across the border were able to reenter Spain and rejoin the Republican Army. Geneviève Dreyfus-Armand suggests that some 40,000 were still in France at the end of 1938.[4] The figures therefore indicate a massive repatriation of Republican troops.[5] In any case, these 'migrations' did not prepare the French authorities for the potentially vast humanitarian disaster that threatened after the defeat of Catalonia. The government in Paris had been generous enough to open the border to all refugees, including members of the Republican Army, but then proved unwilling or unable to provide them with shelter, basic hygiene facilities, medical care or anything more than minimum survival rations.

The abiding memory of many of the refugees was the constant universal command '*Allez, allez!*' of French soldiers, gendarmes, or indeed anyone in a uniform or in authority. Having separated the men from the women, children and elderly, the French commenced the assignment of refugees to internment centres, the most notorious of which was at Argelès-sur-Mer, a small seaside resort between the border and Perpignan.

Some 75,000 to 100,000 men were assembled in a 'virtual' internment camp. French colonial troops from Senegal and Morocco laid a perimeter of barbed wire and the defeated Republicans were then left to fend for themselves. At first there was little food and water and no refuge from the elements; men were forced to dig holes in the sand to protect themselves from the wind and rain, and there were no hygiene or sanitary facilities. In the absence of drugs and medical supplies and facilities, the 'Infirmary' became the place where internees were taken to die. According to Carlos Hernández de Miguel, in the first six months of the camps, there were 14,617 documented deaths. The total number of victims remains unknown as the fate of many of those who died was not recorded.[6]

Eventually more food and water supplies did appear and then timber, with which the internees built latrines and huts for the infirm. Conditions did gradually improve, mostly through the efforts of the 'prisoners' and

Republican exiles and sympathizers, but apart from malnutrition and the cold, the internees suffered lice and scabies and there were widespread cases of typhus, dysentery and malaria. The regional hospital service collapsed under the avalanche of refugees requiring treatment and the pressure on local infrastructures led the authorities to open two spill-over camps at St. Cyprien and Bacarès. Within weeks, there was a network of internment centres across the region of south-west France.

Manuel Azcárate, son of Pablo de Azcárate – who until February had been the Spanish ambassador in London and whom Negrín had now appointed president of the Servicio de Emigración de los Refugiados Españoles* – accompanied his father on one visit to Argelès. An active member of the Communist Party in exile, but at this time installed with his family in the relative luxury of a Paris flat, Azcárate was shocked by the conditions in which his fellow Republicans were forced to live. So humiliated was he to be escorted on their tour of the 'facilities' by camp guards, that he refused to return to the camp:

> I felt terrible shame to imagine what these Spanish men
> thought of us. I did not want to make any more trips, even
> though it would have given me an exceptional opportunity
> to pass on a secret message to the organization of the JSU[†]
> in the camp.[7]

An extraordinary graphic record of life in Argelès was provided by Robert Capa in his article 'The Forgotten Army', published in *Picture Post* in April 1939. Following one visit to the camp, he described Argelès as 'Hell on earth'. After the evacuation of the women and children, he wrote:

> And still today there are 50,000 men who live on the sand
> of Argelès-sur-Mer. Keeping up their morale after two and
> a half years of warfare and the terrible days of the exodus,
> these men manage to stand life in the camp, though in many
> ways it is harder for them to bear than the years of war.
> The elite of a whole people live in these tents and shacks

---

* Spanish Refugee Evacuation Service of the – SERE
† Juventudes Socialistas Unificadas – United Socialist Youth

built on sand. Made almost unrecognizable by the gray sand, they have all begun to look alike. A glacial wind blows almost constantly and envelops the camp in a grey cloud [...] Scientists, musicians, peasants who have left the trenches for the first time in two and a half years mix freely with each other. One question is the same for all of them: what is to become of them?[8]

Many of Capa's most dramatic photographs of the internees and their improvised shelters later reappeared in the *Mexican Suitcase* catalogue.

Nancy Johnstone, the British woman who ran a hotel in Tossa de Mar until she and her partner Archie turned it into a refuge for orphans and children evacuated from war zones, later wrote two accounts of her experiences. As the fascists advanced, she accompanied the children by lorry across the frontier into France and 'safety'. She then spent time as an aid worker in south-west France and experienced the reality of the internees. Writing later after an initial turn at the Les Haras camp (Perpignan), she concluded: 'I thought the men's camp at Les Haras was the worst example of misery and hate I could expect to see. I was wrong. Les Haras was the best concentration camp in the district. The men were under cover; they had water; they had latrines.'[9] Visiting the other camps, she became fully aware of the true extent of the suffering the Spanish Republicans were forced to undergo. Of the French reaction to the crisis, she wrote:

The French were torn between a feeling of hopeless inadequacy and pride in La Belle France. La Belle France would provide for refugees. She provided a sandy waste at Argelès; another at St. Cyprien. She provided several miles of barbed wire; two pounds of bread between twenty-five men *after* they had been behind the barbed wire for three days; a trickle of brackish water; several thousand Senegalese with rubber batons; a number of machine-gun nests directed at the barbed wire; several thousand uncontrollable Spahis, who galloped about in circles with drawn swords, and a number of harassed mobile guards and army officers. [...] La Belle France omitted to provide latrines or the spades to dig them with; she omitted to provide firewood; she ignored such necessities as the most primitive hospital arrangements, leaving the wounded and sick to take their chances with the soldiers and the mules on the bare ground. Admittedly it was a situation without precedent, the exodus of a people, and it was impossible to say whether it was criminal carelessness, deliberate sadism, or just incapacity that was to blame. It seemed a mixture of all three.[10]

Angry at the British failure to support the Republic or to provide sufficient aid to the refugees, she ended her epilogue with a description of a visit by members of a British charitable organization: 'A contingent of plus-four clad gentlemen arrived from England to shoot painlessly the wandering, starving Spanish mules. It seemed a pity that they did not first shoot painlessly the cooped-up, starving Spanish refugees.'[11]

Nevertheless, the SERE was able gradually to mobilize support for the Republicans suffering the tribulations of the concentration camps and eventually provided for the regular delivery of food and clothing. The Emigration Service also set up a centre in Toulouse for the distribution of medical supplies to the camps and negotiated grants to local hospitals in return for the treatment of refugees. Over time, they were also able to provide facilities and equipment for leisure, sports and academic events. In his own memoirs (edited by Angel Viñas), Pablo de Azcárate describes how in little more than two months the desolate stretches of sand were transformed into 'almost towns'. The internees erected makeshift buildings, and there were courses and conferences, football matches, physical education classes, even exhibitions of sketches, paintings and sculptures produced with materials scavenged from within the camps. In the early summer of 1939, an exhibition was held in Paris which proved highly successful in raising both funds and awareness of the plight of the Republicans.[12]

In her autobiography, Federica Montseny describes the remarkable efforts of those in the camps to achieve some form of social cohesion and to defend their cultural identity. Taking full advantage of the Spanish genius for improvisation, the internees were able to arrange a plethora of cultural activities. Montseny concluded: 'Heroic and wretched people, worthy of greater fortune [...] who preserved the admirable integrity of their enthusiasm, their capacity of self-sacrifice, their faith, their generous mysticism, their hope and their dreams.'[13]

To the west, some eighty kilometres from the Atlantic coast, and forty from the Spanish border, the French authorities had opened a camp at Gurs, to deal initially with Spanish combatants that had escaped across the western end of the Pyrenees. The compound was subsequently used to intern veterans of the International Brigades, *gudaris* (literally Basque warriors) and airmen. Pressure was brought to bear on unskilled Spanish refugees who had also been gathered in the compound to accept repatriation. Those that assented were delivered into the hands of Franco's police forces in Irun and dispatched to the infamous labour camp at Miranda de Ebro.

The Gurs camp did have rudimentary huts to provide some shelter from the climate of the Atlantic coast, and crude latrines. Inevitably, rations were poor, but the prisoners were not mistreated by their guards. Republican veteran Antonio Grande Catalán escaped from a forced labour camp in the Pyrenees in January 1940 and crossed into France where he was treated with great kindness by a succession of private French citizens. He was eventually conveyed to Gurs, where he was interned for two weeks. In his memoirs, he described the compound as 'well organized' with 'large billets equipped with beds, blankets, sinks, showers and toilets'. The food, he continued, was 'good and plentiful'.[14] It is possible that this glowing report (written sixty years after the events) was more indicative of the conditions he had experienced in the Spanish labour camp than of those at Gurs. When Frida Stewart, a volunteer worker for the Spanish Relief Committee, visited the camp in 1940, she was allowed to meet two veterans of the International Brigades. One pointed to his uniform and told her, 'This is eighteen months old – I wore it when we crossed the Ebro, and ever since!' The two men told her, 'Our ration is one loaf between four men; in the morning a drink of coffee made from burned barley; midday soup of *garbanzos* (chickpeas) or lentils; in the evening a drink of watery cocoa.'[15] The Vichy regime and the Nazi occupiers would later use the centre as a holding compound for 'rebel' Germans detained in their occupied territories, Jews, French hostiles, and even some common criminals.

After Argelès-sur-Mer, the most infamous camp north of the Pyrenees was Le Vernet d'Ariège. In addition to more than 10,000 Spanish refugees, the complex also held veterans of the International Brigades who were unwelcome both in France and in their own countries and who were incarcerated in barracks that became known as the 'leper colony'.

Vernet combined the functions of holding centre, prison, punishment facility and forced labour camp. One of its more famous inmates was Hungarian writer Arthur Koestler (granted British nationality in 1949) who had been detained and sentenced to death by Francoist authorities in Sevilla while covering the Civil War as a correspondent for the *News Chronicle*. His wife in London successfully lobbied for his release and he made his way to Britain and then to France. Although he had first entered Spain as an agent of the Comintern, he became disenchanted with Stalinism, particularly following the Ribbentrop–Molotov Pact and abandoned the Communist Party. Nevertheless, this failed to protect him from arrest on the outbreak of the *drôle de guerre* – the phoney war – as an 'undesirable alien'. He was first held at the improvised base at Roland Garros stadium before his transfer south to Vernet. His first impression of the camp was a 'mess of barbed wire and more barbed wire'.

In his book *Scum of the Earth*, he offered the following description of conditions:

> There were no windows, only rectangular slabs cut out of the wall planks, which served as shutters. There was no stove during the winter of 1939, no lighting, and there were no blankets. The camp had no refectory for meals, not a single table or stool in the hutments; it didn't provide dishes, spoons, or forks to eat with, nor soap to wash with. A fraction of its population could afford to buy these things; the others were reduced to a Stone Age level.[16]

The men slept five to a 105-inch-wide compartment, each on his side (in his own '*Lebensraum* of 21 inches'), all of them forced to face in the same direction. They ate their meals 'standing or sitting on the frozen earth'. The lack of proper latrines was exacerbated by 'epidemics' of diarrhoea and dysentery. Koestler was told by German prisoners who had undergone imprisonment in such camps as Dachau, that 'as regards food, accommodation and hygiene, Vernet was even below the level of Nazi concentration camps'.[17] During the day, internees worked mainly on road construction or camp maintenance. Discipline was brutal.

Another inmate during the early months of the Second World War was the German writer Gustav Regler, a friend of Koestler and Hemingway, and veteran of the XII International Brigade. He described the compound as an 'eerie cemetery' and wrote that, 'The huts stood like great coffins on the plain'.[18] After the occupation of Vichy France by the Wehrmacht in 1942, the Germans used the camp as a collection point for Jews en route to the extermination camps.

Many other camps were opened or converted to cope with the refugee crisis throughout southern France, including Rieucros, Bram, Agde, Rivesaltes, Septfonds, Prats-de-Molló, Le Boulu, Arles-sur-Tech and Barcarès. Some were specifically for women and children or the elderly and some, particularly the smaller ones, with substantially better conditions than Argelès or Le Vernet. As many as 13,000 Spanish Republicans were also held in camps in Algeria, Tunisia and Morocco. Those who had fled to North Africa were joined by men considered too dangerous or politically unreliable to be kept in mainland France. Many of the veterans were set to work on the infamous Trans-Saharan railway that was designed to link French territories in North Africa and sub-Saharan Africa. At a meeting in London in April 1943, between de Azcárate and Donald Downes of the OSS, the American claimed that in the aftermath of Operation *Torch*, there were still 4,000–5,000 Republicans in camps in Algeria and another 8,000–10,000 in Morocco.[19] The conditions in such labour camps as Rlizane, Bou-Arfa and Camp Morand were worse than the camps in France. The brutality of such punishment camps as Hadjerat M'Guil, Ain-el-Ourak, Meridja, Berrouaghia or Djelfa was unspeakable. The commandant of Djelfa reportedly welcomed new arrivals with the words, 'Spaniards, you are now at Camp Djelfa. You are in the middle of the desert. The only escape possible is death.'[20]

The French state was simply overwhelmed by the dimensions of the crisis and successive governments were unsure of how to deal with the tide of human tragedy. The brutality with which the authorities dealt with many of the Civil War veterans was indefensible, but it was also true that they were ill-prepared for such a disaster and if they lacked the will to provide the refugees with proper food, accommodation and healthcare, it is also true that they lacked the necessary resources and logistical infrastructures. There were indeed cases where groups of refugees (essentially the women, their children and the aged) were interned in far more reasonable conditions. The writer Luisa Carnés tells of her own experiences in the premises of a school summer camp in St. Nazaire in the north-west, where some one hundred Republicans were given sufficient food and adequate sanitary and sleeping facilities.[21]

Some help for those trapped in the more primitive camps was also forthcoming from other sources. The Red Cross provided what meagre supplies and funds it had available and many of the population in the areas surrounding the camps responded generously to appeals for support. The world-renowned cellist Pablo Casals was a member of that privileged sector of the evacuees that could count on personal funds or a support network in France that allowed them to avoid the camps and to enjoy greater hospitality from the French state. He had taken up residence in the Grand Hotel at Prades and subsequently made a series of visits to the camps at Rivesaltes, Le Vernet, Le Boulou, Septfonds and Argelès. He later wrote, 'The scenes I witnessed might have been from Dante's Inferno,' and reported that 'Scores [of refugees] had perished from exposure, hunger and disease. At the time of my arrival the hospitals at Perpignan still overflowed with the sick and dying'.[22] From his hotel room, he launched a campaign to raise funds for refugee relief. As a result of appeals to individuals and organizations in France, Britain and the USA, 'Gifts of food, clothing, medical supplies and money poured into Prades'.[23] He also embarked on a series of benefit concerts in Paris and other major cities in France.

Help of another kind came from a Swiss nurse, Elizabeth Eidenbenz, who had volunteered for relief work in Madrid in 1937, had then been transferred to Barcelona, and on the fall of Catalonia had escaped to Switzerland. She now made her way to the South of France to work with the refugees. She toured the concentration camps at Argelès, St. Cyprien, Barcarès and Rivesaltes and was sickened at the conditions and by the lack of healthcare facilities. Unofficial sources claimed that the infant mortality rate among the internees was between 90 and 95 per cent.[24] Eidenbenz subsequently took over a small semi-abandoned château at Elne and with the aid of funds donated by the Cartel Suisse de Secours aux Enfants charity, she was able to refurbish the mansion and set up a maternity unit where pregnant refugees from the camps could give birth. She also commandeered a van (known to the staff at Elne as *Rocinante*) from the Republican military authorities to use as transport for those under her protection.

In 1942, she widened her net to include Jewish women fleeing the Nazis. However, the outbreak of war had cut off funds from private donors and she had become dependent on the Red Cross. She was thus required to comply with the neutrality protocol that proscribed political involvement and obliged Eidenbenz to respect the laws of the territory in which she was operating. Once the Nazis had occupied Vichy, she simply disguised the names of the newborn infants on the birth records in order to protect both the Jewish women who sought refuge at Elne and their infants.

Nevertheless, she was not always able to save those in her care from the Nazi authorities. In one account given to the Catalan historian Assumpta Montellà she described an incident with a Gestapo agent:

> The German officer ordered Lucie [one of the mothers] to pack her things and she took advantage of the opportunity to escape. Thinking that it had been my idea, he warned me that if Lucie did not come back, I would take her place. I packed in less than 5 minutes and having given instructions to my staff to carry on as normal, I handed myself over to the officer. My responsibility was to preserve the work of the unit as a whole, I could not put the maternity clinic at risk. [...] At the very last moment Lucie reappeared. She left with the Gestapo and gave her life in order to save mine.[25]

Eidenbenz was eventually ordered by the occupying Wehrmacht forces to close the hospital in April 1944. The last of the babies delivered in the clinic was a girl (Danielle Louise C.), born on 30 April. By this time, the unit had provided safe and comfortable conditions for 597 women to give birth (including approximately 400 Spanish Republican exiles).

Eidenbenz also received assistance from Mary Elmes, the Irish aid-worker, who collaborated closely with the Quakers. During the Civil War, she had worked with young children in clinics in Almeria and Alicante (the capital and Polop, a small town in the province) before crossing the border into France in May 1939. After a short trip to Ireland, she returned to France in July to work with the refugees. Much of her time in the camps was spent organizing classrooms and lessons for the children and providing cultural facilities for adults – including a remarkably well-stocked library. She also took responsibility for rescuing pregnant women from the camps and delivering them to the Elne maternity hospital. She continued her work after the defeat of France, saving the lives of many Jewish children by hiding them with families in remote villages or smuggling them out of the country. She was eventually arrested by the Gestapo and detained first in the Saint-Michel prison in Toulouse and then in the Fresnes prison, outside Paris. When asked about her experience as a prisoner of the SS and the Gestapo, she gave the now famous response, 'we all suffered inconveniences at that time.' On her release, she returned to the south and continued her work. In 2013, she was recognized by the Israeli state as 'Righteous Among Nations'.[26]

Before the Nationalist Army occupied Madrid, and General Franco proclaimed his victory in the Civil War at the end of March 1939, Hitler had torn up the Munich Accords and had ordered the invasion and eventual dismantlement of the rump state of Czechoslovakia. On 31 March, aware that their trust in the Führer may have been misplaced and that the policy of appeasement was flawed, the British and the French offered Poland a guarantee under which they would protect the Poles if their independence was threatened by Germany (but not the USSR). As Europe tottered on the verge of war, close to half a million Spanish Republican refugees found themselves north of the Pyrenees in territory that, if not hostile, was certainly inhospitable. In human terms, their plight meant little to those in power in Paris and London; indeed, the Daladier government had already introduced the decree law of November 1938 which made provision for the detention of *étrangers indésirables* (foreign undesirables). Nevertheless, the presence in France of 'hordes' of Spanish Republican veterans was a major embarrassment and for many on the right it represented an unacceptable drain on national resources. It was clear to the authorities in Paris that long-term internment was not a viable option, but before a definitive solution could be found, France was consumed by a far greater crisis.

Chapter 5

Diaspora

Before the defeat of June 1940, the preferred short-term policy of the authorities in Paris was immediate repatriation for all those refugees that could be persuaded or bullied into throwing themselves on the mercy – malevolence – of Franco. At a meeting with a representative of the French Ministry of the Interior in August 1939, Pablo de Azcárate, president of the SERE, was told that some 150,000 of those in exile in south-west France had elected to return to Spain.[1] The fortunate ones (mostly among the women, children and elderly) found family or friends willing to support them. According to Álvarez del Vayo, writing from exile in Mexico in 1940, many of those civilians who consented to voluntary deportation quickly decided even the internment camps in France had been preferable to 'the vast prison that is Spain today'.[2] Worse was the fate of ex-combatants and members of left-wing political parties and trade unions. The lucky ones were transferred to work camps to seek redemption through labour, the less privileged were executed. Del Vayo claimed that, 'the grave-digger at the Irún cemetery, horrified at the mass executions of returning Spaniards, himself escaped to France'.[3]

Of the perhaps 300,000 refugees who chose exile, the vast majority remained in southern France, either because they wished to stay close to Spain or because they were given no other option. However, in the period between the end of the Spanish Civil War (March 1939) and the outbreak of the Second World War (September 1939), various 'pockets' of Republicans (including the majority of the political leaders) did escape to more comfortable, though not necessarily much safer territories.

Manuel Azaña, President of the Republic (1936–9), abandoned Paris at the end of February and settled temporarily in Collonges-sous-Salève on the Swiss border where he devoted his time to his memoirs. In Madrid, the dictatorship decided to take legal action against him under the Law of Political Responsibilities, and the former president was vilified as an enemy of the army, the Church and the *Patria* (fatherland); a sexual pervert, a mason and a Marxist. In his absence, his assets were bestowed on the Falange and he was ordered to pay a fine of 100 million pesetas.

Francisco Largo Caballero (President of the Government 1936–7), the self-anointed 'Spanish Lenin', had crossed the border into France at the end of January 1939 and moved into a small flat in Paris with his family, although two of his sons remained imprisoned in Nationalist Spain. Escaping from the last outpost of the Republican government in Elda (Alicante) via the tiny aerodrome at Monóvar, Largo Caballero's successor, Juan Negrín, fled first to Toulouse and then Paris. Following his dismissal as minister of war in April 1938, Indalecio Prieto had been appointed ambassador plenipotentiary for the Republic in Latin America and was in Mexico when the Civil War ended.

Colonel Segismundo Casado, the man who masterminded the anti-communist coup against Negrín at the beginning of March 1939, fled Madrid at the end of the month. The Council for Defence advised Republican supporters who wished to be evacuated to make for Alicante on the east coast. While thousands of Republicans waited in vain at the port for the ships they had been promised, Casado and some 150 of his staff were driven to Gandia, 110 kilometres to the north, to await their rescue by the Royal Navy. On 30 March they were taken on board HMS *Galatea* and carried to safety. The intervention of a British ship and the carefully coordinated operation inevitably led Negrín's supporters to suspect the involvement of the British secret services in the coup that had destroyed any possibility of further resistance to the Nationalist advance. Casado immediately took up residence in the United Kingdom.

The two men who had remained in Madrid to facilitate the surrender to Franco's occupying army, Julian Besteiro and the mayor, Melchor Rodriguez, were both detained and incarcerated by the new authorities.

The cupola of the Communist Party, some of whom had moved to Elda with Negrín, escaped to North Africa and France from the same Monóvar aerodrome as Negrín, hours after the premier had departed. In her memoirs, La Pasionaria described her last moments in Republican Spain:

> The flight mechanic closed the doors of the airplane. The propellers turned ... The machine moved forward, along the last strip of Spanish land that remained free. The soldiers

stood in formation … A moment later they broke ranks. They were the last image I kept of Spain. With their rifles held high as a salute, as a promise, as a hope.[4]

Under the supervision of La Pasionaria, the party held a series of low-profile meetings on French soil, but with a European war looming, by spring the bulk of the politburo had embarked on ships for the USSR. The secretary-general, José Díaz, had been diagnosed with cancer months before and had already left Spain in December 1938 for treatment in Moscow. The last of the ships, the *Cooperazya*, left Le Havre on 11 May.[5] According to the Spanish historian of the PCE, Gregorio Morán, Spanish migration to the Soviet Union consisted of 2,895 children who had emigrated over the course of the Civil War and a total of 1,248 adults (900 party members and their families, the 122 teachers who had accompanied the children, 157 pilots who were undergoing instruction in Soviet academies, and 69 sailors whose ships had docked in Russian ports at the end of the war).[6] While the most important leaders settled in Moscow, various others were dispatched to the Americas where they dispersed between the USA, Cuba and Mexico.

Meanwhile, huge numbers of rank-and-file members, some detained initially by Casado's Defence Committee and then transferred to the custody of the Nationalist authorities, were executed, incarcerated or condemned to the labour camps. Extraordinarily, and crucially for this narrative, those who had escaped across the border were left essentially without leaders and without a leadership structure.

Following the Non-Aggression Pact, Franciso Antón, last of the upper echelons of the PCE on French soil and partner of La Pasionaria, was detained by the French authorities and interned in Le Vernet. He appointed Togliatti's former personal assistant and typist, Carmen de Pedro, as representative of the party in France and entrusted her with the task of coordinating party members on the ground and liaising with party structures elsewhere. In his 900-page memoirs, Santiago Carrillo, perhaps the most influential figure of the PCE of the twentieth century, makes a solitary passing mention of de Pedro, without a single reference to her role either before or during the Second World War.[7] His indifference might reflect the shadow that later purges cast over the Stalinist era of the PCE, but that such a 'lowly' official should be left in charge of party affairs is indicative of the attitude of the Comintern towards the tens of thousands of rank-and-file communists left behind in France.

And thus, vast numbers of men and women who were relatively detached from the dramas of power struggles, purges and realpolitik that characterized the history of the PCE, but had resisted the fascist insurgency in Spain with courage and discipline, now found themselves bereft of party hierarchy and, therefore, free to act with a remarkable level of local autonomy. Few foresaw the deal that Stalin was about to make with Hitler.

Meanwhile, the leaders of the PSOE were in control of the public funds of the now extinct Republic and were thus in a better position to provide aid to the refugees in south-west France. Indeed, since the outset of the Civil War, the Republican government had been moving assets outside Spain, primarily for the purchase of weapons and supplies. Amaro del Rosal, one of the Socialist leaders responsible for arranging the transfer of Republican gold reserves to Moscow, recounts an episode in November 1936, when the then minister of finance, Dr Negrín, and a delegation of bankers accompanied another cargo of gold from the Bank of Spain vaults in Madrid on a flight to Paris, where it was to be used as collateral for future transactions. Bad weather made it impossible to land the Douglas DC-2 in the French capital, and when the fuel supply was exhausted, the pilot, Pedro Tonda, was forced to make a crash-landing in countryside outside Orleans. Both passengers and cargo were unharmed.

As defeat threatened, and it became almost impossible for the Republic to buy arms, so the priority switched to the welfare of the vast number of Republican loyalists expected to flee into exile. Unfortunately for the Socialist Party, their efforts to assist those interned in the camps exposed and exacerbated the rift in the party between the prime minister (now in exile), Dr Negrín, and his former minister of war, Indalecio Prieto, whom he had sacked in May 1938.

In February 1939, the government set up the Servicio de Evacuación de Refugiados Españoles* (SERE) in the French capital. Negrín persuaded Pablo de Azcárate, previously ambassador in London, to take on the presidency while real executive power lay in the hands of Francisco Méndez Aspe – the last minister of finance of the Republic.

---

* Spanish Refugee Evacuation Service

The Comité Técnico de Ayuda a los Refugiados Españoles* (CTARE) was set up in Mexico under Dr José Puche to coordinate the activities of the SERE in Latin America.

However, on 26 July 1939, the rump, or Standing Committee (*Diputación Permanente*) of the last Parliament (Cortes) voted by fifteen votes to five effectively to dissolve the government by declaring it *'inexistente en realidad'* ('non-existent in reality')[8] and grant itself powers to control the financial resources of the defunct Republic. The Junta de Auxilo a los Republicanos Españoles (JARE),[†] under the de facto control of Indalecio Prieto, was established five days later to wrest responsibility from the SERE.

The scandals and intrigues surrounding the activities of the two associations remain unresolved. At the very least it is fair to say their accounting systems were opaque; it may also be true that funds that might have been invested in the welfare of the refugees were used for other purposes; for example, to cover the expenses of leading members of the Republican political class, or held in funds in provision for an eventual campaign to overthrow Franco's dictatorship. In a sense, the opposing views of Negrín and Prieto in 1938 and 1939 on whether to resist or acknowledge inevitable defeat were reflected in their priorities in the post-(Civil) war era. In his biography of Negrín, the American Hispanist Gabriel Jackson wrote that:

> [he] and those who accepted his leadership between 1939 and 1945, believed in the continuing legitimacy of the Negrín government and that within a few years (presumably after the Allied victory) the Republic would be restored. It was therefore Negrín's view that only about a quarter of the resources should be spent on refugee needs, and the rest retained to finance the Republican re-establishment in Spain.[9]

Consequently, in spite of pressure from the British authorities, Negrín insisted on spending most of the war years (after the fall of France) in Britain. He viewed London as the headquarters of democracy in Europe and was determined to keep a presence alongside other exiled leaders,

---

* Spanish Refugee Aid Technical Committee
† Spanish Republican Assistance Board

delegations and governments-in-exile. The British ambassador in Madrid, Sir Samuel Hoare (June 1940–December 1944), on a 'special mission' to ensure Spain's neutrality, was particularly anxious to avoid causing General Franco any offence. He advocated the removal of Negrín to the Americas in order to avoid any suggestion of complicity between the British government and the premier-in-exile. When a 'fractious' Foreign Secretary Lord Halifax subsequently complained to his Foreign Office staff about the decision to grant Negrín asylum, Sir Alexander Cadogan (under-secretary of state and the person responsible for negotiating Negrín's admittance to the UK) responded with a curt 'all right: turn him out'.[10] Cadogan, however, estimated that Halifax was as frightened of his War Cabinet colleague Clement Attlee as he was of Negrín, and that the Labour leader would know how best to protect the interests of his fellow socialist. Indeed, in his notes on the cabinet meeting of 1 November 1940, at which the Negrín question was discussed, Cadogan reported that, 'Any Spanish topic makes the politicians go all hay-wire and Attlee, otherwise a dormouse, becomes like a rabid rabbit'.[11]

Nevertheless, Attlee was persuaded in cabinet to approach Negrín with a politely worded request that he absent himself from London, as his presence was not conducive to good relations with the new regime in Madrid. In fact, Attlee seemed to show little interest in the man who stood as the symbol of the Second Republic. In his memoirs, he mentions Negrín only once, in an account of his visit to Spain during the Civil War in 1937, and describes him as 'a distinguished scientist and Socialist'.[12] In the index to the memoirs, the Spanish prime minister is listed as 'Negrin, Ivan'.

Hoare reported in his memoirs that two years later, in the run-up to Operation *Torch* (the invasion of North Africa, 1942), the German propaganda machine in Spain was encouraging rumours that the Allies were intending to set up a 'communist government under Dr Negrín' who they claimed 'had lunched with Mr. Churchill in Downing Street, and been received by the King at Buckingham Palace'.[13] In fact during the time Negrín spent in London, the British government chose simply to ignore the Spanish leader and deny him the status offered to other figures such as de Gaulle, Queen Wilhelmina, Edvard Beneš or Sikorski. In a memorandum to Churchill at the end of November 1942, Hoare described Negrín as 'riff-raff'. He also forwarded a comment from Spanish Foreign Minister Francisco Jordana who expressed his delight at a conversation between Churchill and Spanish ambassador, the Duque de Alba, in which the British prime minister had expressed his dislike of the Republican leader.[14]

The most dramatic incident in the rivalry between the Negrín and Prieto was the case of the treasure of the *Vita*, a small ship commissioned by the former to transport the goods he had 'smuggled' out of Figueres into France in order both to finance further resistance and to cover the basic welfare needs of the refugees. Legend has it that the *Vita* had originally been the Royal Yacht *Giralda* belonging to Alfonso XIII. It was slightly more than sixty metres in length and had a maximum speed of 18 knots per hour. Its captain for the mission was José de Ordorica, apparently affiliated to the Basque Nationalist movement. The ship was manned by elite members of the Cuerpo de Carabineros (a combination of armed coastguard, border patrol, and customs and excise officers) under the command of Enrique Puente.

The *Vita* docked in Le Havre at the end of February and took on board 110 cases that Negrín had dispatched from Figueres. The ship set sail on 28 February for Mexico. Unfortunately for Negrín, a breakdown in communications meant his agent, José Puche, did not appear when the *Vita* docked in the port of Veracruz a month later. Puente subsequently contacted the Republic's ambassador in Mexico, Indalecio Prieto, who, after consulting with the Mexican president, Lázaro Cárdenas, instructed him to unload his cargo at Tampico. The 'bounty' was then transported overland to Mexico City under Prieto's protection.

Amongst the treasure were vast quantities of valuables appropriated by the Caja General de Reparaciones (General Reparations Board) set up under the auspices of the Ministry of Finance in September 1936 to appropriate the assets of civilians who had supported the military insurgency. There was also a number of religious artefacts 'liberated' from various cathedrals. The contents of the 110 crates contained priceless coin collections, jewels, historical objects and even perhaps one of the oldest editions of *Don Quixote*.[15] What happened to these goods remains a mystery. It is widely believed that most of the more valuable gold and silver items were melted down. Whatever the truth, the treasure disappeared, and it is impossible to know how much of the funds were spent on protecting those refugees who re-immigrated to Latin America. In later years, certain items were found in tin boxes at the bottom of a lake close to the Nevado de Toluca volcano in the state of Mexico. The finds encouraged rumours that at least part of the cargo had been stolen.[16] Amaro del Rosal, director-general of the Caja General de Reparaciones, described Prieto's coup as 'the act of political and economic piracy of the century'.[17]

When Negrín visited Mexico at the beginning of June 1939, he sought a meeting with Prieto on several occasions. Prieto refused. In his letter of 16 June to his former colleague and friend, Negrín wrote that they should overcome any differences and arguments concerning the past (specifically Prieto's dismissal as minister of war in 1938). He continued:

> What concerns me is to mend a friendship that you alone
> are determined to break once and for all; and I know that it
> is my duty to leave aside all personal feelings in the interests
> of union and solidarity among those in exile which are vital
> for our compatriots and for Spain.[18]

A week later, Negrín asked in vain for clarification of the whereabouts of the cargo of the *Vita*. By then, it was clear no reconciliation was possible.

Despite the conflict between the two refugee services, and Prieto's animosity towards Negrín, the SERE did manage to implement some rescue plans. Through their efforts and those of other international associations and individuals, a happy, albeit relatively small group of refugees, was able to start a new life far from the troubled continent of Europe, primarily in Mexico, the country which had proved to be the most loyal ally of the Republic. Between June and July 1939 three ships commissioned by the SERE reached Veracruz: the *Sinaia* (with 1,599 evacuees), the *Ipanema* (998), and the *Mexique* (1,200).

Seventy-five years after the crossing, Julián Atilano a refugee on board the *Sinaia*, recalled the voyage in an interview with the newspaper *El País*:

> There was an unforgettable moment when we passed the
> Peñón de Gibraltar and we were about to leave Spain behind
> forever. Some members of the Madrid Symphony Orchestra
> who were passengers on the ship began to play *Suspiros de
> España*. That is when we knew we would not come back.[19]

Also aboard the *Sinaia* was Nan Green, who had seen service in Spain during the Civil War. In December 1936, in response to calls from the Republican government for international support and following a fact-finding mission by an all-party team of British MPs to Madrid, representatives from various aid associations met in London to set up an umbrella organization to be known as the National Joint Committee for Spanish Relief (NJCSR). Its aims were 'the care of refugees', 'the removal of civilians from battle areas', and 'medical aid'. In a booklet published in February 1937, the committee explained:

> Our appeal is to relieve the suffering of children, of civilians, helpless in face of the terrors of modern war, of the sick and wounded. We believe that whatever divergent political views may be held on the conflict itself, the urgency of the need is so great that no one can question the necessity for action.[20]

Nan Green's husband, George Green, had volunteered to drive an ambulance to Spain for the Spanish Medical Aid Committee (represented on the NJCSR) in February 1937 and she was later recruited to the administrative personnel to coordinate efforts on the ground. Her husband had meanwhile joined the British Battalion (XV) of the International Brigades and was killed in action on 23 September 1938 in the final skirmishes of the Battle of the Ebro, when the Brigades had officially been withdrawn from the front. Back in Britain, the war now lost, Nan Green was invited to join the crew of the *Sinaia* as an observer.

The proposal that she accompany the refugees had been made by Leah Manning, Labour Party activist and secretary of the Spanish Medical Aid Committee. She too had worked with the relief services in Spain and had been instrumental in organizing the evacuation of 4,000 Basque children to England in 1937 before Franco's Army of the North occupied Bilbao. She had also accompanied the children on their voyage to Southampton on board the SS *Habana*.[21]

Nan Green described her experiences of the expedition in her memoirs, and contrary to the claims made by Prieto and his faction that Negrín was using SERE funds to help only his own supporters, Green reports that the lists of those to be rescued from the camps were drawn up 'with great care – to make sure that whole families were enrolled and to try to ensure that the list reflected the *political* composition of the

Republican side, without bias towards any particular group'.[22] Once at sea, she was made responsible for providing meals for the very young and spent so much of the voyage in the galley that she claims she was rarely able to get up on deck. The ship made a first stop at Madeira and then docked in Puerto Rico. Green recounts how the US authorities refused the passengers permission to disembark in order to enjoy a banquet that the local population had prepared in their honour. The Puerto Ricans subsequently transported all the food to the quayside and used ropes to haul it onto the ship.

The *Sinaia* finally docked in Veracruz after twenty-three days at sea. They were welcomed by local dignitaries and Dr Negrín who was visiting Mexico. Green spent some time touring the area around Mexico City and was impressed both by the efforts to integrate the new arrivals and to find them suitable employment, and the enthusiasm of the refugees. She quoted the example of surgeons 'who cheerfully packed up the sets of instruments with which they had been provided by the National Joint Committee for Spanish Relief and set off for remote areas with unselfish resolve' and some agricultural workers who 'to the joy and admiration of the villagers' were able to repair in a day a tractor that had stood idle for some time.[23] Indeed, Spain's loss was Mexico's gain. Franco's refusal even to contemplate a degree of reconciliation caused a drain on Spain's human resources and a deficit of professionals and skilled workers as well as the enforced and often self-imposed exile of many figures from academia and the arts.

Nan Green finally returned to London but before she could embark on a speaking and fund-raising tour, the outbreak of world war introduced a new dimension to the refugee crisis.

The most famous of the voyages of the ships that ferried evacuees across the Atlantic to safety was that of SS *Winnipeg*. Chile's greatest poet, Pablo Neruda, had been posted to the Republic as consul during the war. Inspired by the bravery of those who fought in defence of the Republic, and the population of Madrid that suffered the aerial bombardment of Franco's air force, he wrote one of his most popular works, *España en el corazón* (*Spain in My Heart*). He was later transferred to Paris as Consul in Charge of Spanish Immigration and given special responsibility for the Republican refugees seeking to re-immigrate to Chile. In his memoirs, he describes how the traditionalist diplomatic staff sought to sabotage his mission even to the extent of refusing to supply him with writing paper. Neruda was allocated an office on the fourth floor of the embassy and was outraged to discover that the use of the lifts was denied to the 'wave of undesirables: wounded soldiers, lawyers and writers, professionals who had lost their clinics, skilled workers from every sector'. Many of those who struggled up the stairs to plead their case for inclusion in the scheme were 'war-wounded and survivors of North African concentration camps'.[24] Nevertheless, with the collaboration of the SERE, and the intervention of Negrín and the Quakers, and having overcome last-minute political wrangling in Santiago, Neruda was able to charter an old French cargo ship, SS *Winnipeg*, and equip her to carry a large number of evacuees across the Atlantic.

The ship left the port of Pauillac on the western coast of France on 4 August 1939 with 2,200 Spanish Republicans on board. She docked first in Arica on 26 August to allow some passengers to disembark and reached her final destination, Valparaiso, at the beginning of September. The bulk of the refugees came ashore on 3 September, the very day that on the other side of the world, Britain and France declared war on Germany. Among those Chilean authorities waiting the next day on the dockside to welcome them, was the newly appointed minister of health, Salvador Allende. The majority of the Republicans then travelled to Santiago by train, while others remained on the coast. A small number travelled on to Argentina. Neruda claimed the voyage of the *Winnipeg* was his greatest work, a poem that no critic could ever destroy.

There can be no doubt that Negrín himself genuinely feared for the well-being of his troops and the civilian population in the loyalist zone, and the refugees in France. Once an eventual victory became impossible and intervention by the western democracies equally unlikely, his policy of resistance was designed to allow more time for those in danger to be evacuated and to provide a final bargaining asset with which to wring concessions from the victors in the treatment of the vanquished. The Law of Political Responsibilities had made Franco's intentions explicit and the number of deaths that followed the 'liberation' of every loyalist town and city provided the world with ample evidence of his methods. Apart from 'extra-judicial' assassinations by semi-autonomous Falange death squads, the numbers of officially sanctioned executions of Republican soldiers, freemasons, 'leftists', liberals and other social undesirables in the immediate aftermath of each Nationalist victory were staggering: Cádiz – over 600, Zaragoza – 2,578, the province of Valladolid – over

3,000, Badajoz – approximately 3,800, Toledo – more than 800, Málaga – 1,574 and so on throughout the war, the length and breadth of Spain.[25] Casado's coup wrecked Negrín's strategy, undermined efforts to rescue Republican supporters in substantial numbers, and facilitated the ideological cleansing of the immediate post-war.

Nor did Negrín hold grudges against his rivals and those who had undermined his position in government. He made repeated efforts at reconciliation with Indalecio Prieto – each one rejected – and when he finally fled the Nazis in 1940 aboard a Greek freighter out of Bordeaux, he invited Largo Caballero and Manuel Azaña to accompany him. However, both men had their own reasons for staying in Spain.[26]

According to Zugazagoitia, secretary of national defence in the last Republican government, in the final weeks of the Civil War Negrín had told the French ambassador, Jules Henry, and the British chargé d'affaires, Ralph Stevenson, that he would surrender himself to the Nationalists and sacrifice his life as a 'symbolic punishment' in return for a commitment from the Nationalists not to carry out reprisals against the population.[27] The suggestion was ingenuous; Franco had long made it clear that those who had supported the Republic would only find redemption through hard labour or death. His plans for the new Spain included neither compassion nor compromise.

On the outbreak of world war, Negrín attempted another approach. In his own memoirs, Manuel Azcárate, son of Pablo de Azcárate (the last Republican ambassador in London and president of the SERE), refers to an entry in his father's diary describing a meeting with Negrín and del Vayo in Paris on 26 September 1939. Negrín informed his colleagues that he had advised Franco's ambassador in Paris, José Félix de Lequerica, that he was willing to negotiate the transfer of funds and materials that remained in the hands of the Republican authorities in Mexico and London to the new régime in return for an amnesty for those refugees still trapped in France and incarcerated Republicans in Spain. On 18 November, in the absence of any response, Azcárate approached the British government and outlined Negrín's offer to Sir Alexander Cadogan, the permanent under-secretary at the Foreign Office.[28] The British response to requests for support was that Franco was unlikely to welcome any interference from London on 'internal affairs'. Indeed, Franco ignored the initiative. Manuel Azcárate wrote: 'The most significant conclusion from these events is the implacable inhumanity of Franco.'[29]

Chapter 6

Fraternité

The movement of refugees out of France continued over the following months and years. According to the French historian Bartolomé Bennassar, more than 7,000 Spanish refugees escaped to Mexico in the years between 1940 and 1943. He also describes how in the period from November 1939 to May 1940, a further 3,000 Republican re-emigrants made their way across the Atlantic to the Dominican Republic aboard the steamships *Flandres*, *Saint-Domingue*, *De La Salle* (three voyages) and *Cuba* (two).[1] Dreyfus-Armand calculates that Mexico received closer to 14,500 refugees between 1939 and December 1942, when the French state and Mexico broke off diplomatic relations.[2]

Nevertheless, discounting the many who chose to chance their luck by returning to Spain and the fortunate now settled in Latin America, in the summer of 1939 more than 200,000 Spanish Republican refugees remained in France. Some, who were fortunate enough to have family or friends to vouch for them in France, were released into their 'custody' on the understanding they would not participate in subversive activity. The majority still wallowed in the misery of the concentration camps.

The issue facing the French state was to find a solution to the refugee crisis beyond internment in concentration camps, which was both an embarrassment in a republic based on the principles of '*liberté, egalité et fraternité*' and a drain on its social welfare resources. In general terms, there were two broad options, one civilian and the other military. On the one hand, impending war and conscription meant a potential labour shortage and the Spanish Republican population offered a convenient, even fortuitous, supply of skilled and unskilled labour. On the other, it had not escaped the attention of military chiefs that among the ranks of the Spanish internees there was a substantial number of battle-hardened troops that would be an asset to any land army.

Nevertheless, many in positions of authority in France approached the dilemma with less enthusiasm and questioned the expediency of the military or economic integration of the refugees. Endemic xenophobia was compounded by ideological mistrust of politically undesirable social elements (i.e. communists and anarchists) and there were many, in both the public and private sectors, who sympathized with the authoritarian and obscurantist conservatism of General Franco, and would later support much of Pétain's quasi-fascist 'National Revolution'. Feelings against the Spanish exiles were widespread among those social sectors that feared the Popular Front experiment both at home and abroad.

Luisa Carnés was part of a group of Spanish women transferred to Brittany by train as a first step in relieving the pressure in the south. She later described the reaction of a party of local well-to-do citizens waiting on the platform when the gendarmes ordered a hundred refugees to disembark at Le Boule:

> They kept a prudent distance – they could not ignore the fact that the refugees, in addition to being reds (in other words lower class, without culture, probably illiterate and in many cases murderers and thieves), were in all likelihood carriers of innumerable contagious diseases. [They] examined this cargo of suffering human flesh, which had endured the most terrible of trials, now in the epilogue of their misfortunes, as though they were plague-infested outcasts. The French people made comments and offered opinions, without disguising their repugnance.[3]

Nevertheless, the unfolding international crisis and subsequent economic pressures in the South of France, at least for the time being, overcame the concerns and reservations of the French right.

Men of fighting age – given the flexibility imposed by circumstances, this appears to have been from 18 to 44 years of age – were offered the opportunity to volunteer for service in the French Foreign Legion. The exact number of men who were recruited remains unknown – it was probably a little over three thousand. The men were released from their camps in France and North Africa and dispatched to Sidi Bel Abbés (Algeria). Integrated in the13e Demi-Brigade Légion Étrangère, their most significant involvement in the Second World War was their role in operations in Norway which were truncated by the German attack on the Low Countries and France.

Following the invasion of Poland, the French Ministry of War made provision for foreign citizens to join the French Army as infantrymen in the Régiments de Marche de Volontaires Étrangers (RMVE), military units of recruits who enlisted for the duration of the conflict and were to be deployed as support personnel or reinforcements on the front line. In his work on the French response to the refugees, the historian Scott Soo calculates a total of 6,000 Spanish Republicans were under French military discipline in the Legion and the RMVEs by the time of the German offensive in the spring of 1940.[4]

A far greater number of men were recruited to the Compagnies de travailleurs étrangers (CTE), unarmed paramilitary work battalions established under the terms of a Decree-Law passed by the Daladier government in April 1939. Each company was made up of 250 men and formed an integral part of the French military apparatus under the orders of the Ministry of Defence. Recruits were subject to military discipline and were deployed to assist with logistics, maintenance and construction. According to Soo, some 55,000 Spanish Republican refugees enlisted in the companies[5] and were dispatched primarily to the Maginot Line, the system of fortifications that the French had built along their border with Germany in the misguided belief that this would prevent invasion by the Wehrmacht. The men were employed in various projects which included the upkeep of the existing installations and the digging of anti-tank trenches. Other recruits were posted to the Swiss border, to the south coast area adjacent to the Italian frontier and to the north coast area near Dunkirk. They received a small daily allowance and their conditions depended largely on the attitudes of the French officers that commanded each company.

In response to demands from both the agricultural and industrial sectors in the south-west, another 40,000 refugees were given work on the land and in factories.[6] Although not subject to military discipline, their rights, particularly of movement, were heavily restricted. Their conditions of employment depended on local circumstances. Nevertheless, the use of Spanish refugees to cover the labour shortages in south-west France was a major step towards the long-term settlement of the waves of homeless, destitute migrants that had at first overwhelmed the authorities. According to Dreyfus-Armand, as many as 40,000 exiles were soon usefully employed in industry and agriculture. Over the following months, efforts were made both to ensure fair wages and, wherever possible, to reunite families that had been separated at the border. In a relatively short time, those that had sought asylum across the Pyrenees were in a position to make a significant contribution to the area. The policy of repatriation was reversed, pressure on the French social welfare budget was eased and the bases were laid for eventual integration.

Unfortunately for the refugees, history had not finished with them. On 23 August, Molotov and Ribbentrop, respective foreign ministers of Stalin and Hitler, met in Moscow and signed the Treaty of Non-Aggression between Germany and the Union of Soviet Socialist Republics. According to Article 1 of the treaty: 'The two Contracting Parties undertake to refrain from any act of violence, any aggressive action, or any attack on each other, either individually or jointly with other powers.' The Nazi–Soviet Pact included a secret protocol that would not be revealed until the defeat of Germany and which recognized spheres of influence in Europe for the two powers. Germany thus consented to the Soviet occupation of eastern Poland, the three Baltic states, Finnish territory adjacent to Leningrad (St. Petersburg) and Bessarabia and Northern Bukovina in Rumania.

Despite universal condemnation of the secret protocol in the post-war world, the pact itself was as much a product of Anglo-French diplomatic incompetence as it was of Soviet perfidy. Those that had supported appeasement could hardly complain when Moscow negotiated with Berlin. In the words of British historian A.J.P. Taylor:

> The Russians in fact did only what the Western statemen had hoped to do; and Western bitterness was the bitterness of disappointment, mixed with anger that professions of Communism were no more sincere than their own professions of democracy. The pact contained none of the fulsome expressions of friendship which Chamberlain had put into the Anglo-German declaration on the day after the Munich conference.[7]

The Anglo-Russian historian Alexander Werth concurred and reported that the Soviet press subsequently 'maintained a marked aloofness vis-à-vis Nazi Germany' and avoided any favourable references to Hitler. He did claim, however, that during Ribbentrop's visit to Moscow, Stalin privately offered a toast to his counterpart in Berlin: 'Since the German people love their Führer so much, let us drink the Führer's health.'[8]

The Non-Aggression Pact turned the diplomatic world on its head. The Anglo-French refusal to enter serious negotiations for a military alliance with the USSR was the final failure of the 'appeasers'. Frustrated by British prevarication, Stalin simply put his own interests and those of his homeland above any ideological imperative. Within days, Georgi Dimitrov, the Bulgarian secretary-general of the Comintern, had officially congratulated Stalin on his contribution to world peace in the face of the warmongers of the west. For Hitler, the pact was a masterstroke. Having secured his border with the USSR, he felt confident enough to attack Poland a little over a week later and then to launch the devastating invasion of Western Europe the following spring. How far the pact served Stalin's interests is a more complex question. The original 'popular front' strategy had failed, and the western democracies had refused to include the USSR in a realistic system of collective security. Although this was the bitterest of pills for many loyal Stalinists, most party members (unaware of the secret protocol) did come to accept the pact as a last resort. In any case, at this stage, the Communist movement retained a largely blind faith in the leadership and wisdom of Comrade Stalin. In the short term, the pact allowed him to annex adjacent territory and gave the Red Army another twenty-one months to recover from the purges of the high command and to prepare for war. He did not use the time well. When Hitler ordered Operation *Barbarossa* in June 1941, and in spite of the warnings he had received from military intelligence, Stalin was still taken unawares, and his army was ill-prepared for the Wehrmacht's blitzkrieg.

Those of the leadership of the Spanish Communist Party that had by now sought refuge in Moscow were unlikely to question the hand that fed them. Many years later, in his memoirs, Santiago Carrillo wrote: 'We thought that the USSR was trying to gain time in order to improve conditions in preparation for the inevitable war with the Nazis, and had undone the plan of the English and French to launch Germany against it (the Soviet Union).'[9] He also expressed his bitterness at the cowardice of the British and French in their policies in Abyssinia, Spain and Czechoslovakia, and suggested they had now reaped their fair reward. Nevertheless, questioning whether the struggle that broke out against Hitler in the first week of September was an imperialist conflict or an anti-Fascist war, Carrillo suggested that the one Communist leader who had been right from the outset was Harry Pollitt, secretary-general of the Communist Party of Great Britain (CPGB).[10] In the pamphlet *How to Win the War*, issued on 14 September, Pollitt wrote:

> The Communist Party supports the war, believing it to be a just war. [...] The common people of Britain who have entered into the war, calm, deadly serious and prepared to make whatever sacrifices are necessary, do not in the slightest degree share any ulterior or imperialist motives which this Government may hold. [...] Now that the nightmare of war is upon us, we Communists cannot stand aside.

Forced to resign for opposing the 'Moscow line', Pollitt returned to his roots as a boiler-worker. He was later reinstated after Operation *Barbarossa* in June 1941.

Meanwhile in France, the government of Édouard Daladier reacted with dismay and anger at news of the Nazi–Soviet deal; within days, the prime minister ordered the closure of *L'Humanité*, the Communist newspaper, and on 27 September, he outlawed the party. The French Communist Party (PCF) was split on whether to follow the official Comintern line or to support the French war effort. According to British historian Roger Moorhouse, twenty-one PCF deputies resigned from the party. The largest trade union, the Confédération General du Travail (CGT), denounced the pact. Nevertheless, 3,000 party members were arrested and another 2,500 lost their jobs in public administration.[11] The PCF leader, Maurice Thorez, having been conscripted, promptly deserted and fled to Moscow, apparently on the orders of the Comintern,

The Nazi–Soviet Pact was a double blow for the Republican refugees, and in particular those who belonged to the PCE/PSUC. It was the Germans who had rescued the floundering military uprising of July 1936 by airlifting Franco's African Army across the Straits to Sevilla. It was the German Condor Legion that had ruthlessly bombed Durango and Guernica (March/April 1937) and it was the German navy that had used its artillery against the civilian population of Almeria (May 1937). The Nazis had provided the Nationalist insurgents with vital logistic support and cutting-edge weaponry. The Soviets on the other hand had supported the Republic when it could find no allies in the West. The Comintern had organized the International Brigades. Soviet pilots flew the legendary Polikarpovs (I-15 Chatos and I-16 Moscas) which for so long had challenged the Messerschmitts for control of the skies above northern and central Spain, and 'Russian' tank crews had operated the T-26s in decisive moments of the land battles.

And yet now, Stalin, without warning or notice, had signed a deal with the enemy. The oft-repeated adage among Spanish communist refugees in France, '*Si Stalin lo hace, por algo será*' ('Stalin must have his reasons'), sounded hollow when Hitler ignored the Anglo-French ultimatum and invaded Poland. If the psychological and strategic setbacks were not enough, once the British and French declared war on 3 September, Spanish communists in France were seen as agents of a hostile country. They owed ideological, if not political, allegiance to a foreign power that was now an ally of the enemy. In the case of a German invasion, the communists represented a potential fifth column. Nevertheless, on the ground, it soon became evident that while substantial numbers of communists across the continent performed Orwell-inspiring feats of intellectual gymnastics to justify the new policy, the Spanish refugees, who had already fought the Nazis once, were less inclined to trust the new realignment. In fact, over the next four years, and before the French population commenced its own mobilization, the Spanish Republicans (primarily members of the PCE and PSUC) were committed to the unconditional fight against Nazism with whatever weapons were to hand, at all times, and wherever its exponents appeared.

Chapter 7

Fall Rot

Throughout the 'twilight war' as Churchill called it, or the 'phoney war' or *dròle de guerre* as it became known (September 1939–April 1940), most of the French population remained confident that their army and the Maginot Line would prove effective in preventing a German invasion. Having made a promise to defend Poland, and then declaring war on Germany on 3 September 1939, the British and French failed to take anything but token measures to counter Nazi aggression until the following spring. They declared a blockade on Germany and there were skirmishes at sea, including the Battle of River Plate in December. On 12 February 1940, the Royal Navy minesweeper HMS *Gleaner* was able to destroy the German submarine *U-33* in the Firth of Clyde. The crew recovered two Enigma rotor wheels which were delivered to Bletchley Park. On land, the French Army did launch the Saar Offensive on 7 September 1939, in order to relieve pressure on the Polish Army, and advanced a few kilometres into German territory. However, given the rapid victory of the Germans in their war against the Poles, and the fear that Hitler would order the deployment of reinforcements from the Polish front, within ten days the French troops were ordered to withdraw to the Maginot Line. In fact, Hitler had committed so many of his military resources (particularly the Luftwaffe) to the Polish campaign, that had they not opted for a purely defensive strategy, the French might have caused considerable disruption to the Wehrmacht's plans for the Western Front.

After the defeat of Poland, the Red Army became embroiled in the 'Winter War' with Finland. The western allies (Britain and France) made tentative preparations to reinforce the Finnish Army but were pre-empted by a peace settlement, and they subsequently turned their attention instead to Norway. Hitler was equally aware of the strategic importance of Scandinavia and the demands of German industry for the vital iron ore imports from Sweden. He thus launched his second main offensive of the war (against Norway and Denmark) as the French and British were mounting their own operation to occupy key areas of the Norwegian seaboard. In his history of the secret services, Nicholas Rankin described the battle for Norway as the 'first major grapple of Allied and Axis forces'.[1] He wrote: 'Open warfare in 1940 began almost accidentally, as if two bands of robbers, intent on burgling the same house, bumped into each other in the dark, triggering a chaotic sixty-two-day struggle over the rugged kingdom.'[2]

Meanwhile, at the beginning of February, the French military authorities had founded the 13e Demi-Brigade de Légion Etrangère from volunteers in the two North African bases of Sidi Bel Abbés and Saïda as part of the expeditionary force preparing to deploy to Finland to intervene in the Winter War against the Soviet invasion launched in November 1939. Of the 2,000 men that formed the new unit, a little under half were Spanish Republican evacuees. Dreyfus-Armand calculates that a total of 6,000 Spanish refugees were 'recruited' by the Foreign Legion for a period of five years or the RMVEs for the duration of the war.[3] Most saw enlistment as the only escape route from the tedium and hardships of life in the internment camps and the threat of repatriation.

On 10 February, the Demi-Brigade embarked on an odyssey that would take them from Algeria to the Arctic Circle. They left the port of Oran and disembarked in Marseille two days later. After one night in the Fort Saint-Jean, they were transferred by road to the Camp du Larzac in the Masif Central, where they were provided with equipment and weapons for the campaign in Finland. Finally, they were transported by rail and road, via Lyon, to Belley close to the Italian and Swiss borders, where they linked up with the Brigade de Haute Montagne (BHM) under the command of Colonel Antoine Béthouart. In the French Alps, they underwent special training for the conditions that awaited them in the North. However, before their mission could begin, the conflict between Finland and the USSR was brought to an end by the Moscow peace settlement of 12 March 1940. The first unit of the BHM which was already en route to Cherbourg was ordered back to barracks. The combined forces of the BHM and Foreign Legion Demi-Brigade spent another three weeks on their base, before the authorities in London and Paris agreed on a new plan for the invasion of Norway.

On 5 April, they were ordered to Brest on the north coast, for their transfer to Britain. While the BMH sailed to the west coast of Scotland, the Demi-Brigade came ashore at Southampton and were taken to an encampment outside Brighton. They were subsequently transported by rail to Glasgow, where the dockers were still unwilling to work at weekends and the French force was consequently instructed to board the luxury passenger ship, the *Monarch of Bermuda*, which had been reserved for British troops. They then joined the FP3 convoy at Scapa Flow and headed for the ports of Harstad and Narvik in the north of Norway. By the time they arrived, and despite the ebb and flow in the fighting, the Anglo-French command were coming to terms with the reality that any positive outcome was increasingly unlikely. They had failed to recapture Trondheim and faced a frustrating stalemate at Narvik which had been held by a vastly inferior German force. Events in France now persuaded the government in London that they could no longer sustain a front in Norway. Churchill later wrote:

> it was decided with almost universal agreement that we must concentrate all we had in France and at home. The capture of Narvik had however to be achieved both to ensure the destruction of the port and to cover our withdrawal. The main attack across Römbaks fiord was begun on May 27 by two battalions of the Foreign Legion and one Norwegian battalion under the able leadership of General Béthouart. It was entirely successful. The landing was effected with practically no loss and the counter-attack beaten off. Narvik was taken on May 28. The Germans who had so long resisted forces four times their strength retreated into the mountains, leaving four hundred prisoners in our hands.[4]

The British commander at Harstad, Major-General Mackesy, had firmly resisted the plan for an amphibious attack on Narvik. The British Second World War historian Martin Gilbert suggests this was due to a reluctance to involve the local civilian population in the hostilities. He quotes a telegraph message to London in which the general claimed: 'There is not one officer or man under my command who will not feel shame for himself and his country if thousands of Norwegian men, women and children in Narvik are subject to the bombardment proposed.'[5] General Béthouart – he had been promoted as his troops embarked on the campaign – believed Mackesy's resistance was due to fear of an 'arctic

Galipolli'.[6] The British commander was also concerned at the shortage of both basic equipment – goggles and proper boots – and consequent incidences of snow blindness and frostbite among the troops. Nor did his troops enjoy adequate air cover against the Stuka dive-bombers deployed by the enemy, which had first been tested against the civilian population during the Spanish Civil War.[7] Nevertheless, Mackesy later reported that:

> The arrival of a Demi-Brigade of the Foreign Legion and of a Polish Brigade, coupled with gradually improving weather conditions and an accession of much needed equipment (notably anti-aircraft artillery, a very limited number of landing craft and a French company of light tanks) facilitated the undertaking of more active operations on the Narvik front.[8]

At last, on 13 May, following naval bombardment from the ships under the command of Lord Cork, General Béthouart was able to land the Demi-Brigade at Bjerkvik. Mackesy, whose reluctance to engage the enemy had secured him adversaries both in London and in the field, was relieved of his command and replaced by Lieutenant-General Auchinleck who later reported, 'I am constrained to express my admiration for the way in which the whole operation was conceived and effected by all concerned. I was particularly struck by the business like efficiency of the French Foreign Legion which carried out the landing.'[9] Mackesy concluded his own report with the statement, 'That I once commanded an Allied Force containing such fine troops, British, French and Polish alike, will for ever remain a source of great pride to me.'[10] The fact that the Spanish troops in the Demi-Brigade were classified as French is understandable, given the nature of the Foreign Legion – but the absence of any reference to their nationality was an omen of the invisibility to which they would be submitted in Second World War historiography.

After fierce fighting between the Wehrmacht and Norwegian, Polish, British, French and French Foreign Legion units, Narvik fell to the Allies on 27 May – a result celebrated as the first Allied land victory of the war. In assessing the role of the Franco-Spanish force, Auchinleck reported, 'Thus ended an operation which, in my opinion, reflects great credit on the judgment and pertinacity of General Béthouart and on the fighting qualities of his troops.'[11]

The triumph was short-lived. The situation in France was critical and although Winston Churchill, who had become prime minister on 10 May, was loath to give ground in Scandinavia, he was primarily concerned with preparing Britain for an impending invasion. The decision to withdraw was taken on 24 May, although the Norwegian authorities were not informed until 1 June. A week later, King Haakon VII and the Norwegian cabinet were evacuated by HMS *Devonshire* and joined other foreign governments in exile in Britain. The last Allied troops were withdrawn on 8 June after destroying what they could of the railway system and port facilities. According to Pons Prades, the Allies – British, Norwegians, French, Polish and Spanish – lost approximately 4,000 men in the campaign, of whom some 500 were Spanish Republicans.[12] The Norwegian Army surrendered to the Germans on 10 June 1940. With the obvious exception of the USSR, Norway resisted a ground attack by the Nazi aggressors longer than any other country in the Second World War.

The troops of the Foreign Legion were returned safely to Greenock in Scotland, but were immediately transferred to Brest in northern France to participate in the struggle to establish the Breton Redoubt, a last foothold of a free French government in Brittany. At the same time, in a final desperate attempt to avoid the capitulation of the French Army and to persuade the government that further resistance was possible, Churchill made an extraordinary proposal to create a single Franco-British state based on the 'indissoluble union of the two countries', 'common citizenship' and 'a formal association of the two Parliaments'. The plan involved 'a surrender of national sovereignty [...] that went further than anything before in the history of war-time alliances'.[13] In his memoirs, Jean Monnet, the most eminent of the fathers of European unity, who had collaborated with Churchill in drafting the proposal, wrote that in the circumstances, the Allies had no choice but to 'join their destiny in war and beyond'. Monnet also claimed that, somewhat surprisingly, Charles de Gaulle, soon to put himself forward as the leader of the *France libre* (Free France – more commonly referred to as the 'Free French') movement, also supported the initiative.[14]

However, by this stage the French authorities, civilian and military, had lost the will to resist; they saw Churchill's offer as an empty gesture made even more futile by the impending invasion of Britain by the Germans.

Béthouart was ordered to withdraw his men and return to Britain. On 16 March, French Prime Minister Reynaud was replaced by Maréchal Philippe Pétain. His government asked the Spanish ambassador in Paris, José Félix de Lequerica, to convey to the Germans a request that they set out their conditions for a ceasefire. The next day Brigadier-General Charles de Gaulle escaped to London and on 18 June, he delivered a first appeal to the French people from the BBC:

> I, General de Gaulle, now in London, invite the French officers and soldiers who are on British soil or who might find their way here, with their weapons or without their weapons, I invite the engineers and the specialized workers of the armament industries who are on British soil or who find their way here, to report to me. Whatever may happen, the flame of French resistance must not, and will not be extinguished.[15]

On 19 June, the first boats out of Brittany docked in Plymouth; the 'Norwegians', the troops who had fought in Norway, were transferred to Trentham Park in Staffordshire with other non-British evacuated infantry forces. Ten days later they received a visit from de Gaulle. The self-proclaimed leader of the National Committee of the Free French was unable to dissuade General Béthouart from his plan to return to French territory. Nevertheless, the commander of the forces that had fought with such bravery in Norway departed for North Africa, 'with the firm intention of getting back into the line one day – which indeed he was destined to do, effectively and with glory, later'.[16] Nevertheless, de Gaulle did recruit Lieutenant-Colonel Magrin-Verneret, leader of the 11ème Demi-Brigade. In his memoirs, consistent with the post-war Gaullist narrative that sought to ignore (or delete) the role of Spanish Republicans in the Free French movement, de Gaulle makes no reference to the Spanish survivors of the Norway campaign. However, Serapio Iniesta, a Spanish Republican who fought in Norway, recalled in his own memoirs the fact that de Gaulle addressed the Spanish contingent separately and requested that they join forces with the Free French and continue to defend 'the France of human rights'.[17] He also reports that few Republicans responded to the general's rhetoric and that 'more than a thousand' ignored the call to take one step forward.

Both de Gaulle and Iniesta report that two British colonels (Chair and Williams) then addressed the assembled infantrymen on behalf of the War Office, and declared, 'You are perfectly free to serve under General de Gaulle. But it is our duty to point out to you […] that if you do so decide you will be rebels against your Government.'[18] If the two officers were aware of the presence of a Spanish contingent, they might have chosen their words more carefully.

On 1 July, those Spanish *legionnaires* who had elected to return to French territory were preparing to embark on their transport ship at the small port of Newton, when they discovered their destination was Morocco and not Sidi Bel Abbés, the Legion's main base in Algeria. Fearing that once in Morocco, they might be 'repatriated' to the Spanish protectorate, 300 Spanish Republicans subsequently 'mutinied', laid down their weapons, and were taken into custody by the British authorities and escorted back to Trentham Park. Thus, almost by default, they joined the forces of the Free French. Given that British military regulations precluded the recruitment of foreign nationals to serve in a combat role, those Spanish troops who insisted in their refusal to serve under de Gaulle were recruited into the No. 1 (Spanish) Company of the Royal Pioneer Corps (the Sappers).

Meanwhile, the Republican exiles that remained in France discovered that their nightmare was not to finish with defeat in the Civil War or the misery of the camps. Having fought the Germans in Spain, they were now faced with a second defeat and a new tyranny. As Negrín and his government had sought to warn the world, the war against fascism would never be confined exclusively within an area south of the Pyrenees.

Chapter 8

Sauve qui peut

Hitler ordered the main thrust of his western offensive against the Low Countries and through the Ardennes for the second week of May 1940. Neither the British nor the French, and much less the Dutch and the Belgians, were able to deal with the speed and efficiency of the Wehrmacht. The defence systems were brushed aside and the impregnable Maginot Line was neutralized by the main attack through the forest of the Ardennes. The Germans then advanced on Allied positions in the north and by reaching the coast they cut off the British Expeditionary Force (BEF) and an important section of the French Army.

German blitzkrieg overwhelmed the British and French forces and the demoralized Allies retreated in disarray. An unknown number of recruits in CTE 118 which had been assigned to the British Expeditionary Force (BEF) fought in the rearguard as hundreds of thousands of Allied troops massed on the beaches of Dunkirk. Approximately thirty Spaniards[1] were later rescued alongside French troops in the final hours of Operation *Dynamo*. Others escaped westward. Many were captured by the Nazis and would be repatriated to face the 'justice' of the new Spain.

The Spanish who had signed up for service in the Régiments de Marche des Volontaires Étrangers for the duration of the war were assigned to the 21st, 22nd and 23rd regiments, which were formed and trained at Le Barcarès. Prejudice against the Republicans and the credence given to unfounded Francoist claims which dismissed the Popular Army as an undisciplined rabble was enough to persuade the French military authorities to deny the Spanish the privilege of forming their own units with their own officers. The regiments were ordered north in April and deployed defensively in the southern sector of the Ardennes offensive and against the June attack south from the Somme. Alongside other Italian, Polish and central European Jewish volunteers, they resisted the combined pressure of German artillery, panzers and Stuka dive-bombers until the armistice of 22 June.

The 500 Spanish Republicans serving in the 11ème Régiment Etranger d'Infanterie were stationed on the Maginot Line when the Germans launched the first stage of the western offensive (*Fall Gelb* – Case Yellow). On 20 May, they advanced to the front and came under heavy artillery fire and aerial attack from Stuka squadrons. They were ordered to join up with troops withdrawing from positions in the west under the onslaught of the panzer divisions. They dug in east of the River Meuse, and resisted the German advance at what became known as the Battle of the Bois d'Inor. They defended their position, at times in desperate hand-to-hand fighting, until ordered to withdraw on 9 June. In the face of the inexorable advance of the Wehrmacht and overwhelming odds, they made a last stand at Saint-Germain-sur-Meuse, before crossing the river and destroying the two bridges in the town. When they finally laid down their arms, after the signing of the armistice, more than three-quarters of the 3,000 men of the 11th Regiment who had started the war on the Maginot Line were dead.

Meanwhile, on the other side of France, survivors of the 185th CTE were stranded near St. Nazaire (Loire-Atlantique) on the west coast. Internees at the Gurs camp, they had been recruited by officers of the BEF to assist in the construction of storage facilities for the supplies and equipment shipped into France from the UK via the port at the mouth of the Loire. The new French premier, Reynaud (who had replaced Daladier in March 1940), had considered prolonging the struggle by withdrawing to the Breton Redoubt but despite encouragement from Churchill and de Gaulle, it soon became clear that he lacked political support from within his own government. Moreover, Commander-in-Chief General Weygand, whom he had himself appointed, dismissed the idea as militarily unfeasible. According to Major-General Edward Spears, Churchill's personal liaison officer to the French leadership, Weygand claimed that 'the *réduit* had never existed save in the *Président du Conseil*'s imagination.'[2]

By mid-June the military débâcle was complete, and all thoughts of resistance had dissipated. Churchill ordered the implementation of Operation *Cycle* to extract British and Polish troops from the Normandy ports and Operation *Ariel* to rescue all remaining British military personnel and civilians from the north-west. As part of the withdrawal plan, HMT *Lancastria* was ordered to St. Nazaire to pick up evacuees from the Loire estuary. By early afternoon of 17 June, the ship had taken on board as many as 9,000 evacuees. The exact number is unlikely ever to be known. In their haste to remove as many British nationals as possible before the German Army reached the coast, and following orders from naval authorities in London, Captain Rudolph Sharp suspended normal protocols and allowed as many 'passengers' to embark as space permitted.

In spite of German aerial bombardment of the coast, the captain of the *Lancastria*, was more concerned by U-boat activity in the area, and elected to wait for destroyer escort before putting out to sea. The ship then received four direct hits from a Junkers Ju 88 bomber and quickly capsized. Many of those who were able to abandon ship found themselves trapped in the oil leaking from the sinking vessel which was then ignited as German aircraft strafed survivors. While as many as 2,500 people were rescued from the water by smaller boats involved in the operation, the number of dead remains unknown. Churchill was concerned that coming in the aftermath of the military fiasco of the Battle of France, the sinking of the *Lancastria* would have a devastating impact on national morale. He subsequently issued a D-notice imposing a 'voluntary' ban on public disclosure of the event. In his memoirs, he recorded his reaction:

> When this news came to me in the quiet Cabinet Room during the afternoon I forbade its publication, saying: 'The newspapers have got quite enough disaster for to-day at least.' I had intended to release the news a few days later, but events crowded upon us so black and so quickly that I forgot to lift the ban, and it was some years before this horror became public.[3]

In fact, on 26 July 1940, the *Scotsman* and the *Daily Herald* did report the sinking, but the nation was by then involved in a life and death battle with the German Luftwaffe. Britian's worst-ever maritime disaster remained, and remains, shrouded in mystery. Reports suggest that some classified documents will not be made available until 2040. Estimates suggest that more than 4,000 perished in the attack.[4] According to figures available at the National Archives, the total BEF casualties reported by the War Office included 4,206 dead and 47,959 missing.[5] Researchers have compiled lists of those known to have died on the *Lancastria* and of others presumed to be have been aboard.[6] The lists do not include the names of any Spanish Republicans working alongside the BEF in St. Nazaire, though it seems reasonable to suppose that some must have found their way on board the ship. If they had, they almost certainly would have used false identities in order to gain access to the ship.

One Spanish Republican, Antonio Grande Catalán, and a group of approximately fifteen comrades who had been recruited from the Gurs camp by British colonels of the Manchester Regiment were more fortunate. According to Grande's own account,[7] the 250 men selected in early 1940 were transported to a village between Nantes and St. Nazaire, where they were issued new clothes and an armband that read 'Allies of the British Expeditionary Force'. They were well treated, well fed and well paid and accommodated in an old Benedictine monastery (Blance Couronne). They were initially employed building warehouses and then in unloading the trains and trucks that arrived from the port.

However, by 18 June, the Germans had advanced to within forty kilometres of their base and the Republicans were informed by their commanding officer that only British troops were to be evacuated. Assuming, that if they were captured by the Germans, they would be repatriated, Grande and fifteen more of the men decided to take their chances with the British Army after all. They salvaged British uniforms from the warehouses that had been set on fire to prevent supplies falling into the hands of the Germans, commandeered a truck and its driver, and made their way to the port of St. Nazaire, where they mingled with British troops and embarked on the last ship to leave the docks. Unable to speak English, they were quickly discovered once at sea but managed to persuade the authorities that given their service in France, they deserved to be evacuated with the Manchester Regiment.

They arrived in Plymouth on 20 June and Grande later recalled that while they waited to disembark at the port, he was overwhelmed by the sound of thousands of voices singing 'historical English songs' and immediately concluded that if they displayed such spirit in defeat, the 'English' could not lose the war.[8] His faith in the morale of the British people was shared by Basque leader José Antonio Aguirre who listened to British troops singing as they retreated towards Dunkirk. With the benefit of hindsight, he later wrote, 'People who can sing in the middle of such gunfire cannot be vanquished.'[9] Grande and his companions were eventually recruited into the No. 1 (Spanish) Company of the Royal Pioneer Corps.

The French Prime Minister Paul Reynaud meanwhile resigned on 17 June and was replaced by Marshal Philippe Pétain, the hero of Verdun. Following the approach by the Spanish ambassador to France, José Félix de Lequerica, to the German military authorities, on behalf of the French government, an armistice was signed on 22 June at Compiègne. France was divided into the *zone occupée* (occupied zone – including Paris and the Atlantic coast) under the control of the Germans, and the *zone libre* (unoccupied zone) under Pétain in the south, with its capital in Vichy. As head of state, Pétain swiftly dismantled the democratic institutions of the Third Republic and established a dictatorship based not on '*Liberté, égalité, fraternité*' but on the new motto of '*Travail, famille, patrie*' ('Work, family, fatherland'). More resolutely opposed to the principles of the Third French Republic, which had sowed the seeds of defeat, than to those of the enemy that had invaded France and crushed its army, the new regime embraced the principles of ultra-conservative authoritarianism based on the traditions of a rural, paternalist and Catholic society.

As the Germans turned their attention to Britain, mainland Western Europe was forced to adjust to a new peace. For three years, between 1936 and 1939, those who had supported the Second Republic had warned the governments of Western Europe that if they failed to resist fascism in Spain, they would soon become the next victims. Prime Minister Negrín had insisted that the conflict in Spain was not a civil war, but rather the War of Spain, the first battlefield in the struggle against fascism in Europe.[10] The Republican Ministry of Propaganda had published a poster showing a young girl killed in an air raid, with the slogan, 'If you tolerate this your children will be next'. However, for the Spanish exiles who had escaped Franco in 1939 and found refuge north of the Pyrenees, the fact that history had proved them right was hardly consolation. They were now confronted by the realities of a new order, trapped within the borders of the unholy alliance of Hitler, Mussolini, Pétain and Franco.

Chapter 9

The Wall

In the summer of 1940, for the second time in little more than a year, many exiled Spanish Republicans found themselves on the losing side to fascism. Those stranded in northern France were at the mercy of the Germans. They faced either repatriation to a hostile homeland, or incarceration or execution by the Nazis. On the other hand, those who had remained in the south or managed to evade capture by the Wehrmacht long enough to cross into the unoccupied zone found themselves the unwelcome guests of a regime of the same ilk as Franco's.

Having drawn the dividing line between occupied and unoccupied zones, the Germans proceeded to impose from Paris a ruthless suppression of the rights and freedoms of the French people. Although lacking the extreme savagery that followed the invasion of the USSR, the occupation nevertheless exposed the population to the barbaric methods of the SS (Schutzstaffel – Protection Squadron) and the Gestapo (Geheime Staatspolizei – Secret State Police). The Spanish Republican exiles of the CTE and RMVE who were captured in battle and in the immediate aftermath were treated with particular brutality.

Franco's regime failed to respond to German requests for guidance on how to treat these prisoners and by refusing to acknowledge them as the responsibility of the Spanish state, denied them any rights or protection they might have enjoyed as Spanish nationals. The administrative decision was then taken by the German authorities to transfer 10,000 'Rotspanier' (Red Spaniards) to labour camps in 'Greater Germany'. The vast majority (approximately 7,500) were sent to Mauthausen (Austria). Once issued with camp uniforms, they were identified by an inverted triangle with a white S (for *staatlosen* – stateless) superimposed on a blue background. Another 750 were interned in Dachau (near Munich), 600 in Buchenwald (near Weimar) and approximately 175 women were imprisoned in Ravensbrück (north of Berlin). Others were dispatched to such camps as Bergen Belsen and Auschwitz (Poland), Sachsenhausen (north of Berlin) and the Channel Islands.

The most infamous episode in the Nazi deportation of undesirable Spanish refugees was the case of the Convoy de los 927. In August 1940, in the first mass transfer of civilians to German camps, entire families interned in the Les Alliers camp in Angoulême were forced to board a train on the understanding that they were to be transported either to the unoccupied zone or to the Spanish border.[1] Their destination was in fact Mauthausen, where they arrived four days later. Without preamble, the camp guards ordered the adult and adolescent males from the train. The women and children, on the other hand, remained in the cattle trucks and were returned to France and then to Irun where they were 'released' into the custody of the Spanish police authorities. The most plausible explanation for this extraordinary decision to transport the women and their children half way across Europe and back was that the authorities in Angoulême did not wish the local French population to witness the harrowing scenes of the separation of husbands and wives and parents and children.

In Mauthausen, SS-Hauptsturmführer (Captain) Georg Bachmayer, the second in command, greeted the men with the pledge that if they ever left the camp, it would be through the crematorium. With customary Nazi pragmatism, zeal and efficiency, the camp officials immediately set the inmates to work finishing the construction of their own prison and constructing a network of smaller sub-camps in the area, the most important of which was Gusen, the final destination for most of the Spanish prisoners. Of the 470 males who arrived at Mauthausen on 24 August 1940, only sixty-one would survive the war before their liberation by American troops on 5 May 1945.

The Spanish inmates became famous for their bravery and refusal to submit to the tyranny of the SS and the *kapos*. According to a manuscript published by his family, Ukranian prisoner Vasily Bunelik was assigned to a construction team (Brigade 2), where he experienced the Spanish gifts of courage, ingenuity and contempt for authority:

> The senior worker, a Spanish tradesman, Pedro Garcia, was pretending to work diligently, banging about with his trowel and at the same time keeping watch for the approach of the SS guards whilst we rested in the shed. Garcia was working on the second floor and had a good view from there to shout the signal: 'MATERIAL' when the SS were approaching.

With this pre-arranged signal we had time to grab our buckets and spades and get to our work places. Seeing how 'busy' Garcia was and having checked on the amount of raw materials down below, the SS guards continued on their rounds and we dodged back into the shed until the next warning signal from Garcia.[2]

In historiographical terms, the most significant achievement of the Spanish inmates was inspired by three men, Francisco Boix, Antonio García Alonso and José Cereceda,[3] who were assigned to the *Erkennungsdienst* (camp records department) with access to the pictorial files of the camp. With the help of comrades working both inside and outside the camp, they were able to make copies and to smuggle out and conceal huge numbers of both prints and negatives before the advance of the US Third Army through Austria forced the camp authorities to order their destruction. Boix later appeared as a witness at the International Military Tribunal in Nuremberg and provided photographic evidence to refute SS-Obergruppenführer (General) Ernst Kaltenbrunner's claims that he knew nothing about the extermination camps. The court was shown photographs and negatives of Kaltenbrunner touring the camp in the presence of Reichsführer Heinrich Himmler. Boix was also able to identify Albert Speer (minister of armaments) from his own visit, and to deliver proof of the atrocities denied by the SS officers serving in the camp.[4]

Answering questions in French, Boix described his own experience in the French services prior to deportation:

Either in infantry battalions or in the Foreign Legion, or in the pioneer regiments attached to the Army to which I belonged. I was in the Vosges with the 5th Army. We were taken prisoners. We retreated as far as Belfort where I was taken prisoner in the night of 20–21 June 1940. I was put with some fellow Spaniards and transferred to Mulhouse. Knowing us to be former Spanish Republicans and anti-fascists, they put us in among the Jews as members of a lower order of humanity (Untermensch). We were prisoners of war for 6 months and then we learned that the Minister for Foreign Affairs had had an interview with Hitler to

discuss the question of foreigners and other matters. We
knew that our status had been among the questions raised.
We heard that the Germans had asked what was to be done
with Spanish prisoners of war who had served in the French
Army, those of them who were Republicans and ex-members
of the Republican Army. The answer ...

At this point the French prosecuting counsel, Charles Dubost, interrupted
his own witness with the words, 'Never mind that',[5] and Boix was
denied the right to denounce the collusion of the Spanish government
with the Nazi authorities and Franco's part in the transfer of thousands
of Republican exiles to German death camps.

In fact, on at least four occasions, the Nazi authorities in Paris had
requested instructions on how to deal with the Spanish Republicans in
France from Ramón Serrano Suñer, minister of the interior, minister of
foreign affairs, chief of the Falange and Franco's brother-in-law (he was
married to the sister of Franco's wife). As far as Serrano was concerned,
the *Rojos* that had fled to France had lost all rights to their nationality
and diplomatic assistance, and he subsequently declined to reply. He
would later deny knowledge first of the camps and then of the existence
of any Spanish inmates.

However, given that he visited Berlin in September 1940 to hold
talks with leaders of the Nazi Party, that he personally accompanied
Heinrich Himmler when the Reichsführer made an official visit to Spain
as a prelude to the Franco–Hitler summit of Hendaya (October 1940),
that the Germans were conscientious in reporting their activities via
the Spanish and German embassies in France and Spain respectively,
and that his ministry negotiated the release and repatriation of two
prisoners (Fernando Pindado and Joan Bautista Nos Fibla) who had been
incarcerated in Mauthausen, Serrano's claims appear implausible.[6]

His predecessor as foreign minister, Juan Luis Beigbeder, had indeed
asked for information on the fate of those men interned in Mauthausen.[7]
When the German government responded with a detailed report on the
measures taken, an official at the ministry wrote in the margin, 'as it
does not appear opportune to do anything to help the internees, this
document should be filed.'[8]

In May 1945, it was the remaining Spanish inmates of Mauthausen
that produced a banner to welcome the US troops of the Third Army

with the slogan: '*Los españoles antiFascistas saludan a las fuerzas libertadoras*' ('The Spanish Anti-Fascists Salute the Liberating Forces'). In the rush and excitement of the moment, the inmates misspelt the last word, which read '*liberadoras*'. According to Hernández de Miguel, a total of 7,532 Spanish exiles had been interned in the Mauthausen complex between the summer of 1940 and the liberation of the camps in 1945.[9] In August 2019, the Ministry of Justice published a list in the *Boletín Oficial del Estado* (*BOE – Official State Bulletin*)[10] of 4,427 Spaniards who had died in Mauthausen-Gusen. The ministry also published the names of 695 other Spanish victims who did not appear in the original records but whom researchers discovered through other sources. They included Republicans who had been interned across the board of Nazi death-camps: Mauthausen-Gusen, Auschwitz, Bergen-Belsen, Dachau, Ravensbrück, Buchenwald etc. The information had been transmitted by the French authorities to Franco's government in Madrid, but the dictatorship elected to hide the documents. Publication in the *BOE* finally allowed for the official registration of the deaths.

The last known Spanish Republican survivor of Mauthausen died in October 2020 at the age of 101. Juan Romero was born in Córdoba in 1919, and was still a teenager when he enlisted in the Republican Army in 1936. He fought at Guadarrama, Brunete, Guadalajara, Teruel and was wounded at the Battle of the Ebro. Having crossed the Pyrenees in 1939, he was interned in the Vernet d'Ariège camp and subsequently enlisted in the French Foreign Legion. After an initial posting to North Africa, Romero returned to France with his regiment and was captured by the Germans in May 1940. Together with other Spanish Republicans he was taken first to Stalag III-A (Luckenwalde) near Berlin and then transferred to Mauthausen (prisoner 3,799). After the liberation, Romero settled in Aÿ in northern France and was awarded the Légion d'honneur in 2016. In 2020, the Spanish government issued a document acknowledging his contribution to the struggle for freedom and democracy. At the presentation, Deputy Prime Minister Carmen Calvo insisted that 'we will always owe a debt of gratitude to the Spanish antifascists'.[11]

Compared to their compatriots on German territory, the refugees in the *zone libre* appeared to have escaped the worst consequences of Hitler's victory. Although his regime owed its existence to the Germans, Pétain chose not to see Vichy as a puppet state and although the constraints imposed by the Nazis were tangible, his *Révolution nationale* was as much a 'French' strategy to undo the social change of the Third Republic as it was to gratify the new authorities in Paris.

Nevertheless, the Maréchal's ideological proximity to the Franco regime in Spain was an obvious concern for the Spanish Republicans. Indeed, Pétain was no stranger to Spain or Spanish dictators. In the second half of the 1920s, he had played a central role in the joint Franco-Spanish campaign against Abd al-Krim[12] in North Africa. At the beginning of the decade, Spanish efforts to expand their influence into the central Rif had led to an uprising among the Berber tribesmen. In the summer of 1921, the Spanish African Army suffered a crushing defeat at the Battle of Anwal (casualties included 8,688 dead, 4,500 wounded and 570 taken prisoner). The rebel leader subsequently proclaimed an independent Rif Republic, and was able to extend his authority over much of Spanish Morocco. However, when he sought to expand his power base into the French protectorate, the two colonial powers in Morocco agreed to launch a combined attack to overthrow him.

In July 1925, Pétain travelled to Morocco as envoy of the French government to discuss strategy with the Spanish authorities. He held talks with the new dictator, Captain-General Primo de Rivera, whom the king had appointed head of government and chief of the Military Council after the coup d'état of September 1923. He also met the young General Francisco Franco.[13] The French general was suitably impressed by the Spanish forces which had been overhauled since the Anwal débâcle. On his return to Paris the next month, he put forward a plan for a major offensive against Abd el-Krim in a joint operation with the Spanish Army. At a dinner in Algericas on 21 August 1925, both flattered by the attention of the Spanish authorities and impressed by the achievements of the new dictatorship, Pétain allegedly declared, 'I toast Primo de Rivera who through his intelligence and patriotism was able to re-establish discipline and order in Spain. Perhaps circumstances may make it necessary to do in France as was done in Spain.'[14]

Under the command of Primo, and with substantial naval and aerial support, a combined force of some 13,000 troops effected an ambitious landing in the Bay of Alhucemas in September 1925. The first such 'amphibious' operation in military history allowed the Spanish to establish a secure bridgehead in the north while their French allies, under the command of Pétain, attacked from the south. The following spring, overwhelming military superiority facilitated a complete victory for the colonial powers and Abd el-Krim was forced into exile.

In the meantime, Pétain had made an official visit to Madrid (February 1926), where he was welcomed with great ceremony by dictator and king alike. In the presence of military and civilian authorities who had gathered in the Alcazar de Toledo (Toledo Citadel), Alfonso XIII bestowed on Maréchal Pétain the most prestigious Medalla Militar in honour of his services in North Africa.

Once France had recognized the Franco regime in March 1939, Daladier appointed Pétain the new ambassador in the temporary capital of Burgos. A distinguished soldier, an intensely reactionary conservative, a devotee of the Catholic Church, an enemy of the freemasons, and a proven friend of a previous Spanish autocrat, it seemed likely that he would sympathize with the new tyrant. Ambassador Pétain used his time in Franco's Spain to travel, to explore the political situation in post-Civil War Spain, and in all likelihood to ponder on the format for a new French state, in case he be called upon to rescue France.[15] He also caused some concern in Paris by maintaining cordial relations with Eberhard von Stohrer, the German ambassador in Madrid, even after war had been declared.[16] The French embassy staff were bewildered when in October 1939, he shook hands with his German counterpart at an official ceremony in front of the entire diplomatic corps.[17] Nevertheless, it is also true that Pétain made genuine efforts to improve French–Spanish relations, damaged in the eyes of the new regime in Burgos by the perceived support of the French for the Republic. Primarily he lobbied for the return of Spanish gold deposited in French banks by the Republic (5,500,000,000 francs)[18] to the new regime in Madrid. The decision of the Daladier government to authorize the transfer in July was a major step forward in the normalization of relations.

At a meeting at the French embassy in Madrid in the autumn of 1939, David Eccles (economic advisor to the British government) felt that the Maréchal showed 'no sign of being anxious to get his hand on the (sic) power'. However, the ambassador did say that, 'he had restored French morale at Verdun, and was probably the only man who could do the same in this war'.[19] Franco later claimed that when Pétain was invited by Reynaud to return to Paris as deputy prime minister in the new government in May 1940, he urged the ambassador to remain in Madrid on the grounds that he had nothing to gain by joining forces with those people who would lead France to defeat. Pétain apparently replied, 'I know, but my country calls and I must do my duty.'[20] His return to Paris now was the prelude to a compromise with Hitler that would allow the 84-year-old general to implement his design.

Franco and Pétain met once more, after the Caudillo's visit to Mussolini in Bordighera in February 1941. On Franco's return trip to Spain, he broke the journey at Montpellier to hold talks with the man who was now chief of the French state. It was the confirmation of a new spirit of cordiality and fraternity between the two governments of Madrid and Vichy. Apart from their obvious abhorrence of socialists and communists, the two autocrats shared a hatred of the Masonic movement, an aversion to all things modern (even in the military), a tendency towards anti-Semitism (though not comparable with that of the Nazis), a determination to defend the Catholic Church, and contempt for democratic institutions, political parties and politicians. It was also true that Adolf Hitler had played a key role in both men's ascension. The substantial difference between the two regimes was that Franco had claimed power through military victory and his regime was based on the legitimacy of conquest; Pétain on the other hand had come to power as a result of military defeat.

Pétain's attitude to the Spanish refugees reflected both his deep distrust of the communists and his growing awareness of the vital role the exiled population had to play as a cheap labour force. By the law of 27 September 1940, the Vichy government launched the Groupes de travailleurs étrangers (GTE), to replace the CTE of the Third Republic and to provide labour to both the industrial and agricultural sectors. The law was officially designed to protect the status and conditions of French workers by regulating foreign labour, limiting its use, and as far as possible compelling the accommodation of foreign labourers in base camps. Dreyfus-Armand estimated that in August 1943, of the 37,000 workers in the GTE, 31,000 were Spanish.[21]

Under the terms of the 'peace' settlement with the Germans, French prisoners of war were to remain in German camps for the duration of the war. The continued resistance of the British thus exposed the dependence of the Vichy economy on the immigrant workforce and the authorities were forced to review their policy. Those who had already found work independently were allowed to remain in their jobs, families were granted permission to reunite, salary demarcations were eliminated, and in many cases foreign workers became entitled to paid holidays. By late 1942, Spanish Republican refugees were a vital workforce on the land, in factories, in the construction of military facilities, and in forestry, the timber industry and even in the production of charcoal. Some were given living quarters in camps, dormitories or agricultural outbuildings, but others were authorized to find lodgings for themselves and enjoyed a considerable level of individual freedom within the constraints imposed by an authoritarian regime approved by the Nazis.

As the war progressed, Germany made demands on both zones in France to supply labour to German industry on German soil. The infamous *relève* of June 1942, whereby Prime Minister Pierre Laval negotiated the export of French workers in return for the repatriation of French prisoners of war failed to satisfy Nazi needs and demands. Laval's declaration in defence of the policy, '*Je souhaite la victoire de l'Allemagne*' ('I hope for a German victory') and promises of excellent conditions were not sufficient to persuade the mass enrolment of volunteers. In February 1943, facing increased German pressure, the Vichy government subsequently introduced the *Service du travail obligatoire* (STO – compulsory work service) whereby all men of working age were liable for transfer to the Reich. By D-Day, more than half a million French workers had been dispatched. Whether they used Spanish immigrants either to satisfy the Reich's demands for workers or to fill the shortages of labour at home, the authorities were forced to acknowledge the crucial role of the refugees in the Vichy economy. To compound the insatiable labour demands of German industry and civil and military engineering projects, the abduction of immigrants (especially the Spanish) and their deportation to Germany or transfer to labour units working on the Atlantic defences encouraged many refugees to join the ranks of the incipient Resistance movement.

It is not clear to what extent Franco actually wished for the mass return of the Spanish refugees from southern France where they could do far less damage to his new dictatorship than they might do on Spanish territory. Spanish prisons were overcrowded, and food supplies were short. A repatriation of elements he continued to think of as the enemy might even prove to be a destabilizing factor. Nevertheless, he was determined to vent his thirst for revenge on Republican leaders who had defied his military rebellion. In fact, the three most wanted: former President Manuel Azaña, Prime Minister Dr Juan Negrín and Indalecio

Prieto (leader of the anti-Negrín faction in the PSOE) proved to be beyond his reach. Prieto had been in Latin America since losing his cabinet position in April 1938 and Juan Negrín left France in mid-June 1940 to take up residence in London as the unrecognized leader of a Republican government-in-exile. Manuel Azaña, President of the Republic until the recognition of Franco by the French and British governments, his health now failing, escaped from his chosen place of exile (Collonges-sous-Salève – 300 metres from the French border with Switzerland) as the armistice was signed at Compiègne. He then settled in Pyla-sur-Mer on the Atlantic coast near Bordeaux, where Negrín paid him a visit on 20 June and offered him a place on the boat that was standing by to take the prime minister to Britain. Given the political animosity between the two men, Azaña acknowledged Negrín's generosity but claimed he was too ill to undertake the voyage. Nevertheless, his family and colleagues decided to transfer him to the relative safety of Montauban in the unoccupied zone.

On 23 June, the Mexican ambassador in France, Luis Ignacio Rodríguez Taboada, had received a telegram from President Cárdenas requesting he inform the German and Italian governments that Mexico would accept responsibility for all Republican refugees in France and Belgium. In light of rumours of a *falangista* squad sent to France to abduct him and the demands from the Spanish Foreign Ministry and the ambassador in France for the return of some 636 '*Jefes Rojos*' (Red leaders),[22] Azaña was now moved into a hotel under the protection of the Mexican ambassador. However, his health had been seriously undermined by defeat and exile, and he underwent a series of cardiac and pulmonary episodes. He finally died on 3 November 1940. In his last public address, in the Barcelona City Hall, in July 1938, Azaña had told the audience:

> When the torch is passed on to other hands, to other men, to other generations, let them remember, if ever they feel their blood boil and once more the Spanish temper flares with intolerance and hate, and a passion for destruction, let them think of the dead and heed their lesson: the lesson of all men who have fallen bravely in battle, fighting nobly for a splendid ideal and who now rest in the soil of their motherland, who no longer feel hate, nor thirst for

revenge and they send us, with a glittering light, as calm and remote as the light of a star, the message of an eternal homeland which says to its children: 'Peace, Compassion and Forgiveness'.

Compassion did not feature in the dogma of the new Francoist regime and their friends, any more than peace and forgiveness. Under the direct orders of the Vichy authorities, the prefect of Montauban refused to authorize any funeral honours due to a head of state. When he further denied Azaña's family the right to cover his coffin with the 'illegal' flag of the Republic, Rodríguez once more intervened and provided a flag of the Mexican Republic in place of Franco's new *rojigualda* (one yellow and two red stripes and a superimposed black eagle – introduced in February 1938). In July 1941, Azaña's widow, Dolores Rivas Cherif, was allowed to cross the Atlantic and to seek refuge in Mexico. Cárdenas refused to recognize Franco's new regime and closed the embassy in Madrid on 1 January 1940. The Mexican Republic subsequently rejected any attempt to restore diplomatic relations with Spain throughout the dictatorship.

The fact that Azaña, Negrín and Prieto were now beyond their reach did not discourage the authorities in Madrid in their pursuit of other leading Republican figures. However, the Vichy authorities refused to bow to pressure and insisted individual extraditions should be processed through established judicial channels. When Federica Montseny, minister of health in the Largo Caballero government (November 1936– May 1937) and the first female minister in Spain, was detained by the Vichy authorities, the judges refused to sanction her extradition on the grounds that she was pregnant. Although she spent some time in prison, she was at least spared Franco's reign of terror, and survived the war.

Francisco Largo Caballero, Prime Minister of the Republic (4 September 1936–17 May 1937), appeared before the court at the same extradition hearings. He too was saved by the determination of the Vichy authorities to uphold the tradition of asylum. Although the court rejected the demands of the Spanish government, Largo Caballero was nevertheless still considered a danger to national security, and was detained in makeshift prisons. In the aftermath of the occupation of the *zone libre*, he was arrested by the Germans and transferred first to Gestapo headquarters in Lyons under the control of the notorious Klaus

Barbie, and then to Paris. In July 1943, he was moved to Berlín for further interrogation, and then finally he was interned in the Sachsenhausen (Oranienburg) concentration camp for the duration of the war.

The Germans did indeed prove to be far more cooperative with the Spanish government. In July 1940, acting on information and instructions from Ambassador José Félix de Lequerica, the Gestapo arrested Julián Zugazagoitia (minister of the interior and then secretary-general of National Defence under Negrín) in Paris, and Francisco Cruz Salido (a journalist who had acted as Zugazagoiotia's assistant) in Bordeaux. The Germans felt no compulsion to comply with French judicial mechanisms and, with other detainees on Spain's list of fugitives, the two men were delivered into the custody of Franco's police. They were accused of rebellion, tried before a summary court martial, sentenced to death and then executed by firing squad on 9 November at the wall of the Almudena Cemetery in Madrid alongside another fourteen Republican prisoners. According to testimonies given by witnesses at the trial, Zugazagoitia had worked to improve the conditions of Nationalist prisoners of war in Republican hands and had protected those most in danger of reprisals, particularly men and women of the Church.[23]

Lluis Companys, president of the Catalan Generalitat, made no attempt to abandon the occupied zone, although he did leave Paris as the city fell to the Wehrmacht and withdrew to a small village in Brittany. His son Luïset, who had been diagnosed with schizophrenia and was under treatment in a clinic near the French capital, became lost amid the hordes of refugees fleeing south. Urged to escape to Mexico by family and friends, and warned that the Gestapo were closing in, Companys refused to leave until he had traced his son. He was subsequently hunted down and detained by the Germans in mid-August 1940. A fortnight later, Madrid's most sinister agent in France, Pedro Urraca, delivered him into the custody of the Spanish police at the border crossing at Hendaya. After severe beatings and torture in the Dirección General de Seguridad (Police Headquarters) in Madrid, he was transferred to Barcelona to face a court martial. The court ignored witness statements that during the war he had provided Nationalist sympathizers with passports to enable their escape, and that he had repeatedly demanded anarchist 'leaders' halt 'revolutionary violence'. He was found guilty of 'military rebellion' and sentenced to death. He was executed by firing squad outside the

Montjuic Castle prison on 15 October. Legend tells that he removed his shoes so that he could feel the soil of Catalonia beneath his feet.[24]

Urraca, later described by his granddaughter as 'Franco's eyes in Spain',[25] had set up a network of Francoist informers north of the Pyrenees to monitor the activities of Republican exiles and was also involved in the detention of Julián Zugazagoitia. Recent research[26] suggests he played an active part in the search for the Jewish artist Antoinette Sachs and the subsequent detention of her friend, the inspirational Resistance leader Jean Moulin, in June 1943. During the Spanish Civil War, although working in the French Air Ministry, Moulin had ignored the non-intervention policy of his own government and assisted in a plan to smuggle arms across the border to the Republican Army.[27]

Urraca worked closely with the Comisión Central Administradora de Bienes Incautados (Central Administrative Board for Confiscated Property) set up in January 1937 to appropriate the assets of those organizations and individual citizens who had failed (actively or passively) to support the insurgency. He was also recruited into the service of the Gestapo (as Agent E-8001, alias *Unamuno*) and acted as consultant in the creation of intelligence networks in Holland and Belgium designed to uncover elements hostile to the Reich.

The most extraordinary story of the exiled Republican leaders was the case of Lehendakari (First Minister of the Basque government) Aguirre, who had moved his government to Catalonia following the defeat of the Republic in the north, and who accompanied Companys as he abandoned Catalonia and crossed the border into France in February 1939.[28] He settled with his family in Paris and took the misguided decision to visit relatives in Belgium just as the Germans launched their attack against the Low Countries in May 1940. He crossed back into France and witnessed the retreat to Dunkirk before travelling to Brussels and then on to Antwerp. He grew a moustache, bought some glasses, and leaving his family in the relative safety of Belgium, he travelled to Hamburg and Berlin under a false name (Dr Alvarez) and with a Panamanian passport.

While in the Nazi capital, he attended the memorial service for Alfonso XIII, whose exile had heralded the Second Republic and who had recently died in Rome. Aguirre sat in the St. Hedwig's Catholic Cathedral on Unter den Linden in the company of Franco's diplomatic corps (including Ambassador General Espinosa de los Monteros). On another occasion, he waited outside the Chancellery, amid enthusiastic crowds, to catch a glimpse of Adolf Hitler, as he emerged onto the balcony with Japanese Ambassador Baron Ōshima Hiroshi, the man that William L. Shirer described as 'more Nazi than the Nazis'.[29]

Aguirre was eventually joined in Berlin by his wife and family (travelling under Venezuelan passports), and with the assistance of friends (especially Germán Guardia, a Panamanian diplomat), Basque sympathizers and unwitting German administrators, they were able to obtain visas and travel passes to enter neutral Sweden. Once there, they took a boat to Brazil and then spent time in Uruguay before moving on to New York where Aguirre took up a post at Columbia University.

The experiences of many of the Republican leaders trapped in France is simply a tiny reflection of the fate of Republican supporters and sympathizers who had remained in Spain. In the absence of official records and figures, it is impossible to provide anything but estimates of the numbers of victims who paid the price of the Nationalists' wrath. Apart from the 500,000 who were originally forced into exile, at least 20,000 Republicans were executed in the immediate aftermath of the Civil War. Herbert Matthews, the *New York Times* correspondent, reported that in the months following the war, there were between 200 and 250 executions a day in Madrid alone.[30] Tens of thousands more died in prisons, concentration camps and seeking 'redemption' through forced labour. In 1941, there were still 233,373 prisoners (of war).[31] Amnesty International reports that 114,000 people who disappeared at the hands of the Franco dictatorship are still missing, buried in unmarked pits and mass graves.[32]

Chapter 10

Forests of the Night

By the beginning of 1941, the French population was slowly adapting to the new reality of crushing military defeat. The Germans had suffered a setback in the Battle of Britain, but mainland Europe remained at peace. The north of France and the Atlantic coast as far as the border with Spain was occupied by the Germans. The *zone libre* with its capital in Vichy maintained a façade of independence and the regime was embarking on a *Révolution nationale* to dismantle the reforms of the Third Republic and to restore the conservative, 'rural' values of the past. Vast numbers of French troops remained in Germany as prisoners of war, and the German authorities in Paris were making increasing demands on the available workforce in France. The still relatively unknown Charles de Gaulle ('Washed up from a vast shipwreck on the shores of England'[1]) made regular attempts from London to inspire his people to resist the invader, but his Free French Army, supported by British troops and ships, had been defeated by Vichy troops when they attempted to seize the port of Dakar (23–25 September). Worse, the Royal Navy had attacked the French fleet at Mers-el-Kébir (Algeria) before it could be appropriated by the Nazis, and in so doing had killed more than 1,000 French sailors.

Such complex circumstances led to an equally complex response from the French people: from overt collaboration with the Germans and enthusiasm for Pétain's regime, to resignation and fear, to resolve to fight back once conditions became more favourable, to the lingering doubts of the communists (whose spiritual homeland was still an ally of the Nazis), to the extreme courage of those who risked detention, torture and death in their determination to support the British war effort and to protect those most in danger. The reaction of the Spanish Republicans, on the other hand, was less ambiguous. Despite the primary instinct to seek survival and the reflex of some who chose to ingratiate themselves with those who held authority over them, few Republicans wavered in their ultimate goal to defeat the enemy, be they the forces of Hitler, Mussolini, Pétain or Franco.

The first resistance came in the form of the rescue lines that were set up to help smuggle Allied troops (escapers and evaders), RAF aircrew, anti-Nazi refugees and Jews across occupied Europe and the Pyrenees, and then to the safe havens of Portugal and Gibraltar. Perhaps the most famous were the Ligne Comète and the Pat O'Leary Line, although the Shelburn Line (Brittany), the Marie-Claire Line (from Paris and the occupied zone to Marseille) and the Mission Martin/Possum Line (Belgian Ardennes and Reims) all made significant contributions to the war effort.

The operational complexity of an escape line was huge. The first stage involved the fielding of escaping or evading enemies of the Third Reich either through a direct approach or through a network of contacts whereby brave Belgian, Dutch or French families offered refuge to fugitives and then sought agents of a coordinated strategy to deliver them to safety. The lines then needed a network of safe houses the length and breadth of occupied Western Europe either as relay stations or hideouts. They also required the assistance of printers able to produce fake identity cards and travel permits. Many of those rescued could not speak French and were unable to travel on the railways or indeed engage in any type of interaction with the local population and authorities without the help of escorts. They often required medical assistance. People from all walks of live provided support: local policemen who could monitor Gestapo activities, railway workers who would signal to indicate when it was safe to abandon a train, hotel, restaurant and bar owners who allowed their premises to be used as a meeting point. Finally, there were the *passeurs/pasadores* who would guide the fugitives across the Pyrenees and wherever possible into the safekeeping of the British consulates in Bilbao and Barcelona. In London, MI9 was set up to assist and fund attempts by British troops to evade capture or to escape from POW camps.[2] They initially agreed to pay a fee of £40 for each officer and £20 for 'other ranks'.[3] The escape line leaders were able to maintain contacts with London either through the consulate staff or by radios provided by MI9. Those behind the Ligne Comète in fact rejected offers of a radio or radio transmitter on the grounds that they wished to maintain their independence from MI9.

It was precisely the size of the operation that made each member so vulnerable. However compartmentalized the activities, the brutal efficiency of German interrogations meant each man and woman who worked with the networks did so at great and terrifying risk to their own safety. The Ligne Comète evolved primarily from the bravery of three Belgian citizens – the '3 Ds' – Henri de Bliqui, Arnold Deppe and Andrée 'Dédée' de Jongh – who resolved to coordinate local assistance to escaping and evading Allied soldiers and RAF crews. Thousands of men had been left behind in northern France in the summer of 1940. Some had fought in the rearguard actions during Operation *Dynamo*, others from the garrison in Calais had been ordered to defend the town until the last round in order to delay the German assault on Dunkirk, and others were victims of the debacle of Saint-Valéry-en-Caux – where a breakdown in communications and bad weather prevented the Royal Navy from evacuating the British troops (mainly 51st Highland Division) waiting on the coast. Of these men, some avoided capture, others escaped while en route eastward to prisoner-of-war camps in Greater Germany. Many private French and Belgian citizens eschewed caution and offered them food, clothing and shelter, but by the spring of 1941 it became crucial to move them away from the occupied areas of Europe, and if possible, to the relative safety of neutral (later 'non-belligerent') Spain.

As Bomber Command became Britain's only offensive resource against the Germans, MI9 made it their priority to rescue RAF aircrew who baled out or crash-landed on the European mainland, or escaped from a *Stalag*. In 1942, Churchill also authorized two cross-Channel raids against the German occupiers in northern France. In March, a combined British Navy–commando force steered a specially prepared HMS *Campbeltown* into the port at St. Nazaire and rammed the dry dock. The explosives that had been fitted in the bows of the ship were detonated by timer and destroyed the installations, which were crucial to the German Atlantic fleet. In the meantime, commandos disembarked and wreaked havoc in the defensive and port facilities. Despite the success of the mission, fewer than a third of the 622 men involved in the operation were able to make their way safely back across the Channel. The rest were killed in action (168) or taken prisoner. Five men were rescued, at huge personal risk, by the local French population and smuggled south to the Vichy zone, and then across the Pyrenees, and eventually back to England: Corporal Wheeler, Lance-Corporal Douglas, Lance-Corporal Howarth, Lance-Corporal Sims, and Private Harding.[4] Lance-Corporal Arnold Howarth (3448514) of No. 2 Commando had been caught in an explosion on the dock and received shrapnel in his back and face. Having changed into civilian clothes that he found in a cellar where he had taken refuge, but in great pain, he managed to walk past German sentries and to escape from the town. He was taken into hiding by members of the local community (the Barette family) and then escorted by train to Bordeaux. He crossed the demarcation line but was detained by the Vichy authorities and interned in Fort de la Revère near Nice. In September 1942, he took part in a mass breakout of some fifty prisoners, and escaped to Gibraltar. It seems probable that he was a member of the party organized by the O'Leary group that was taken off the beach at Canet-Plage and transferred to HMS *Tarana* (see below). After recovering from his injuries, he returned to active service in Italy and died in November 1944 at the age of 23 from wounds he received at the fighting in Salerno. He was awarded the BEM and Croix de Guerre.

In August, the Allies launched the ill-fated Dieppe Raid designed as a rehearsal for an eventual invasion of France, to gather intelligence and to destroy German installations. The vast majority of the original force of 6,000 troops were Canadian and they saw the brunt of the desperate fighting against impossible odds. More than half of those who took part in the raid were killed, wounded or captured. The Canadians suffered 916 fatal casualties. When it became clear that no more troops could be rescued from the beaches, a small number of Canadian troops were similarly saved by French citizens and directed to the escape routes. Some joined local Resistance groups, others found their way to Spain.

In April 1941, de Bliqui had been betrayed by a contact, detained and subsequently executed. Four months later, Deppe was arrested while accompanying Belgian anti-Nazis through France. De Jongh and her father, Fédéric, continued the work and were able to establish a series of safe houses as far as the Spanish border. Dédée made contact with the British consulate in Bilbao and Michael Creswell, the second secretary of the embassy in Madrid and MI9 agent (codename *Monday*), was dispatched to liaise with her. She demanded that her network should remain independent of MI9, but requested funds to facilitate her operations: 6,000 Belgian francs for the journey to St. Jean-de-Luz and 1,400 pesetas for the mountain guides.[5] In total she made more than thirty crossings into Spain at the western end of the Pyrenees across the River Bidasoa. Following an infiltration of the line by Gestapo agents, she was captured in early 1943. Her place was taken by Jean François Nothomb (aka *Franco*). In the months leading up to D-Day, and on the instructions of MI9, the Ligne Comète was responsible for the creation of holding camps in northern France to offer evaders and escapers refuge until the liberation of France. According to the Escape Lines Memorial Society, the Comète network was responsible for the safe passage to Britain of over 800 men. On the other hand, more than 60 per cent of those Comète agents detained by the Gestapo were executed, tortured, or starved or worked to death in concentration camps.[6]

The activities of the line became heavily reliant on Florentino Goikoetxea Beobide, a Basque anti-*franquista* and part-time smuggler. He was recruited as a *passeur/pasador* in the spring of 1942 and, until the liberation, was responsible for leading 227 Allied airmen[7] and numerous anti-Nazi fugitives across the border. According to Airey Neave (codename *Saturday*), who interviewed the military personnel fortunate enough to make it to Britain, those who were rescued by Florentino 'spoke of him in awe'. 'He was,' they said, 'indifferent to fatigue or danger.' Neave concluded that, 'Without him, Dédée and the Comet escape line which followed her could never have rescued so many airmen'.[8] Florentino was captured by the Germans in July 1944, following an ambush in which he received four gunshot wounds. Fortunately, he was not identified by his captors and the three members of the Resistance disguised as Gestapo agents rescued him from hospital[9] and kept him hidden until the liberation of south-western France. Goikoetxea was later awarded the George Medal for gallantry. Popular legend has it that at the medal ceremony at Buckingham Palace, when King George VI asked him what he did for a living, he replied 'import–export'. There is now a memorial in Hernani, Goikoetxea's birthplace, honouring his bravery and that of three other Basque guides: Tomas Anabitarte Zapirain, Juan Manuel Larburu Odriozola and Martín Errazkin Iraola. American historian Mark Kurlansky has described the last operation of the *ligne,* which involved the delivery to the British authorities of a list of Gestapo agents in France and Belgium who had fled to Spain.[10] According to Kurlansky, the Basques assumed there would be a hunt for war criminals after the Allies liberated Spain.

The Pat O'Leary Line was born of the efforts of Ian Garrow, a Scots officer who evaded capture after the surrender of his 51st Highland Division at Saint-Valéry-en-Caux and made his way the length of France to the Mediterranean port of Marseille where he was interned in the Fort St. Jean. He escaped and joined forces with the Reverend Dr Donald

Caskie, former head of the Scottish Kirk of Paris who abandoned the city hours before the arrival of the Wehrmacht. Caskie took over the Seamen's Mission in Marseille and made it a safe house for civilians and escaping soldiers alike. A second safe house was run by Dr Georges Rodocanachi, his wife (Fanny) and his maid (Seraphine) from the doctor's surgery.[11]

Meanwhile Albert-Marie Guérisse, an officer in the Belgian Army, had been evacuated from Dunkirk but had then chosen to return to mainland Europe as an agent of the Special Operations Executive (SOE). Sailing out of Liverpool, he assumed the identity of a French Canadian acquaintance, Pat O'Leary, in case of capture and in order to shield his family in Belgium from reprisals. He served on the Q-ship HMS *Fidelity* out of Gibraltar, and was involved in a joint insertion/ exfiltration operation at the beaches near Perpignan. HMS *Tarana*, a requisitioned trawler fitted with concealed guns and based in the British colony, also played a key role in both infiltrating agents and rescuing fugitives. In order to avoid unwelcome attention, each time the *Tarana* left Gibraltar her crew removed their naval uniforms, painted over the battleship grey' of the upper hull, and 'adorned' the decks with fishing gear. Before her return to base, and in order to maintain the deception, the process was reversed and she re-entered the harbour under the White Ensign and restored to her more traditional grey. HMS *Fidelity* followed a similar procedure on the two operations she carried out in the Mediterranean. The crew painted her from waterline to mast in yellow and then a reluctant few dressed in civilian clothes and posed on the deck as passengers.

In April 1941, Pat O'Leary was stranded off the coast of France when the launch he was using to extract agents ran out of fuel. Unable to make his way back to the *Fidelity,* he swam ashore and was arrested by the French authorities. He was subsequently held at the St. Hippolyte du Fort, but managed to escape and make contact with Garrow at the Rodocanachi safe house.[12]

As with the other lines, Garrow's network fell prey to constant betrayals and infiltrations. Garrow himself was arrested in the autumn of 1941 by the Vichy police but was later rescued and finally smuggled back to Britain. In his absence, Pat O'Leary took over command of the network that would later bear his name (also known as the 'Pat Line'). The network was hit by a series of setbacks which included the treachery of the

British agent Harold Cole (aka *Paul Cole*), who revealed the structure of the line to the Germans, and the infiltration of the organization by turned Gestapo agent Roger le Neveu (aka *le Légionnaire*), which led to the virtual dismantlement of the system. O'Leary/Guérisse was arrested in March 1943. According to his biographer, Vincent Brome, O'Leary was then tortured brutally by the Gestapo (long periods of time locked naked in a refrigerator interspersed with vicious beatings) but did not reveal any details of his network. He was eventually transferred to Dachau.[13] In the meantime, Marie Louise Dissard (codename *Françoise*), a member of the French Resistance, took charge of what remained of the group and successfully kept the line open until the liberation of France.

Just as at the western end of the Pyrenees, so the Pat O'Leary Line required the support of Spanish *passeurs/pasadores* to guide escapers and evaders into Spain. The most significant was Francisco Ponzán Vidal, a teacher and anarchist from Oviedo who had made contact with the British intelligence services during the Civil War. Detained for a second time by the French authorities in 1939, he was held in the Vernet camp until a M. Jean Bénazet from the village of Varilhes offered him a contract as a mechanic in his workshop and thus obtained his release.[14] He subsequently set up a team of men and women (including his own sister Pilar) to guide fugitives from the Nazi and Vichy authorities across the Pyrenees. He also made daring raids across the border to rescue comrades from Franco's concentration camps.

Ponzán soon made contact with Garrow and O'Leary and although his priority was to prepare for a guerrilla war against Franco, his group made a huge contribution to British operations. In return, he received a substantial amount of money to finance his activities in Spain and two radio transmitters. Following the 'Cockleshell' raid on German shipping in Bordeaux, the two surviving commandos, Major 'Blondie' Hasler and Marine Bill Sparks, were able to contact the Marie-Claire network in Toulouse which transferred them into the safekeeping of the Pat O'Leary Line. Ponzán's group guided them across the mountains and delivered them to the British consulate in Barcelona. According to BBC journalist Edward Stourton, there is also compelling evidence to suggest that the group escorted Airey Neave across the Pyrenees following his escape from Colditz.[15] In his own memoirs, Neave refers to the assistance he received from the Pat O'Leary Line but does not refer by name to the *passeurs* who accompanied him over the border to the consulate in Barcelona.[16] Vincent Brome, Guérisse/O'Leary's biographer, gives a detailed account of Neave's journey to Barcelona with eleven other fugitives, but only refers to the *passeur* as 'José'. In the end, Neave had a relatively uneventful journey to Gibraltar and then back to Britain where, under the codename *Saturday*, he went on to play a key role in the operations of MI9 in Room 900 at the War Office in London. According to Ponzán's sister, in the two years between April 1941 and March 1943, the Pat O'Leary Line was responsible for the safe delivery in Spain of some 700 fugitives, of which 200 were RAF pilots.[17]

Ponzán was detained by the Germans in April 1943 in Toulouse and held in the Saint-Michel Prison. Days before the town was liberated in mid-August 1944, he was one of fifty-one anti-Nazis executed by the Gestapo in the village of Buzet-sur-Tarn in the French Pyrenees. The Germans burnt the bodies of their victims before abandoning the area.[18]

Not all *passeurs* were members of a network; many worked freelance, some worked for more than one escape line. Their motives varied: some sought an active role in the struggle against fascism, some saw an opportunity to demand weapons from the British, and many were smugglers who simply needed to make a living. Many of those who worked throughout the escape network played other roles in Resistance operations or as couriers. Most who acted as *passeurs* faced a double risk, moving between hostile territory in Vichy France, and enemy territory in Franco's Spain, where capture would lead to imprisonment, hard labour or execution. Not only did they save many lives and assist in the passage of trained and expert pilots and crew back to Britain where they were able to resume their own combat roles, but they also forced the Gestapo and Abwehr (German military intelligence) to expend valuable time, manpower and resources in their attempts to neutralize their operations.

According to Airey Neave, in joint operations between the escape lines, MI9 and the American counterpart MIS-X, a total of 4,000 evaders/escapers were brought back to Britain before D-Day. He also estimated that 500 Dutch, Belgian and French underground escape workers lost their lives.[19] Neave's colleague at MI9 was J.M. (Jimmy) Langley, who had lost an arm in the fighting of 1940 at Dunkirk and yet still managed to escape from the military 'collecting centre' in Lille and make his way to Marseille. He was subsequently repatriated via Madrid and Gibraltar.

Langley calculated that the ratio between the servicemen who escaped back to Britain and the resisters in Holland, Belgium and France who lost their lives helping them was in fact one to one:

> The number of people who were shot, died under torture or in concentration camps to achieve these successes will never be known, but I believe it to be far in excess of 500 recorded names. In all three countries hundreds of men and women were arrested and condemned to death under the charge of having helped the Allied cause, with no specific details given. That for every successful evader, a Belgian, Dutch or French helper gave his or her life would, I think, be a fairer estimate of the price paid.[20]

The expedition across the Pyrenees took long hours, even days and often involved great hardship. In winter there were freezing temperatures and blizzards. The terrain was difficult and the unmarked paths over challenging mountain slopes tested even hardened servicemen. To the west, escapers were frequently required to ford the Bidasoa River that was at best cold and at worst treacherous. The escapers and evaders also lived with the constant fear of capture or death at the hand of border guards, especially after Operation *Torch*, when the Germans took over control of the entire frontier and imposed a 'no-go' order on a fifteen-kilometre-wide zone on the French side. Once they were successfully across the Pyrenees, the Allied aircrews, refugees and escaped POWs faced the final stage of their ordeal: passage through a neutral but intimidating Spain to Portugal or Gibraltar.

Although it was widely assumed that once across the Pyrenees those that had eluded the Nazi tyranny would find security and refuge, Spain was still an unwelcoming and intimidating territory for those who challenged German hegemony in Europe. General Franco made no secret of his ideological solidarity with Hitler and Mussolini. Indeed, it was their support that had been crucial in his victory in the Civil War. Nor could he ignore Hitler's warnings that his own regime was unlikely to survive a German defeat. In April 1939, he had officially joined the Anti-Comintern Pact, thus aligning himself with Germany, Italy and Japan. He later ordered Spanish clocks to be moved forward one hour (GMT +1) in order to bring Spanish time in line with Berlin and the occupied zones, and adjusted Spain's status in the world conflict to 'non-belligerent' rather than 'neutral'.

In June 1940, as Paris fell to the Germans, the Caudillo ordered Spanish troops in North Africa to occupy the Tangier International Zone, which by the convention signed in Paris 1923, was under the joint control of France, Britain and Spain. The US later complained that the presence of 100,000 potentially hostile Spanish troops under the command of General Orgaz (high commissioner) in the protectorate of Spanish Morocco was an unwelcome distraction for the US occupying forces in North Africa after Operation *Torch*.[21]

In July 1941, in an address to the National Council of the Falange, Franco claimed that the Allies had miscalculated in their approach to the war and had been defeated. He denounced the 'plutocratic democracies' that had allied themselves to the Soviets, attacked the British blockade of continental Europe, and warned the USA against the folly of intervention. He then declared his admiration for the military leadership of the Wehrmacht in a war that Europe and Christianity had long awaited. He repeatedly assured Hitler and Mussolini at the summits in Hendaya (October 1939) and Bordighera (February 1941), through Serrano Suñer (minister of foreign affairs) and in private correspondence that Spain was committed to joining the war once conditions permitted. In other words, when the country had recovered from the devastation of the Civil War and when the Germans could guarantee alternative supplies of cereals and fuel which until then depended on the 'goodwill' of the British and the system of *navicerts* (certificates dispensed by British officials exempting cargo from seizure by British navy patrols as part of the blockade of mainland Europe).

Despite the best efforts of the British diplomatic corps and the Ministry of Economic Warfare, Franco continued to supply Germany with the wolfram (tungsten) that was so vital to their steel and weapons industry (in the production of reinforced armour). Bizarrely, much of the wolfram was transported through the international railway station at Canfranc, a vast and hugely impressive construction five kilometres inside the border with France in Huesca (Aragon), which serviced the single-track line between Pau and Zaragoza. Opened in 1928 in the presence of King Alfonso XIII and the President of the Third Republic, Gaston Doumergue, the station was designed to deal with freight and passengers whose journey was disrupted by the different gauges used on French and Spanish railways.

Closed in the Civil War to prevent the Republic smuggling arms through the Somport tunnel that linked Spain and France, service had been renewed following the Nationalist victory. To expedite connections, one platform was officially recognized as French territory, with its own border post. The import–export activities of the Spanish and Germans thus came under the partial supervision of the French chief of customs, Albert Le Lay, who besides his official responsibilities, ran (or at least facilitated) two other operations. The first was a spy ring by which Spanish agents carried intelligence gathered by the Resistance into Spain for delivery to the British consulate in San Sebastian via Zaragoza. It is also believed that Le Lay was responsible for arranging the delivery of the first radio transmitters to the French Resistance to enable them to communicate with London. The second was the smuggling of Jewish refugees and other fugitives (possibly Allied military personnel) into neutral Spain. In 1943, Le Lay was able to escape with his family to Zaragoza after he had been warned that the Gestapo had orders to detain him. Franco had given free rein to German military intelligence and the Gestapo on Spanish territory and the Abwehr personnel in Madrid were the most numerous outside Germany. While the Gestapo operated in the borderlands with France, they were more than willing to share information on infiltration by Republicans and to train the Spanish police forces in investigation and interrogation techniques. After the war, Le Lay was awarded the French Légion d'Honneur and the Resistance Medal. However, he declined all offers to publish his memoirs.[22]

The Caudillo also ordered his civil governors to prepare a Jewish archive which contained the names of 6,000 Spanish Jews (almost entirely Sephardic) living in Spain. It seems improbable that the reference to 6,000 Spaniards at the Wannsee Conference, convened by Heydrich to draft plans for the Final Solution, was simply a coincidence.

Finally, Spain provided the Kriegsmarine and the Regia Marina with facilities for refuelling, repairs and maintenance. And yet, crucially, Franco neither declared war on Great Britain, nor allowed the Wehrmacht to cross Spanish territory and take the British colony of Gibraltar. As a result, so long as Spain remained hostile, but not a belligerent, fugitives from the Third Reich were safer south of the Pyrenees than they were north of the Pyrenees. They were also one step closer to passage to Britain or the New World. Nevertheless, for many, this last test proved to be the most unpleasant.

In their work on MI9, M.R.D. Foot and J.M. Langley point out that under international law (Geneva Convention – 1929), evaders that reached neutral territory were to be interned for the duration of the war, while escapers were free to return to their own country. As a result, those aircrew who had been rescued by the Resistance and who wished to fight on were required to argue that they had in fact escaped detention. Escapers in the hands of a neutral police force were in theory allowed to contact their country's military attaché. In the words of Foot and Langley this was a process 'that took minutes in Switzerland, hours in Sweden, weeks or even months in Spain'.[23]

It is also true that for long periods of the war, Spain claimed to be non-belligerent rather than neutral. Those combatants detained by the Spanish authorities were transferred to the concentration camp at Miranda de Ebro. Built in 1937 by the Nationalists for their Republican POWs, it was later used to intern Republicans who chose to return from exile in France and veterans of the International Brigades. The first foreign inmates, excluding Civil War volunteers, were the 105 crew of Belgian patrol boats that had navigated their way to Spain when the Germans invaded the Low Countries and that had arrived at the camp at the end of June 1940.[24] Situated in the north of Spain (province of Burgos) and with good communications with both Barcelona and Madrid, it was ideally suited as a holding compound for unwanted exiles fleeing the Nazis.

Cedric Brudenell-Bruce, Earl of Cardigan, had been captured at Calais, but escaped as he was transported to Germany. He found his own way through France and across the border but was then detained by the Spanish police. After spending time in the prison and then the fortress of Figueres, he was transferred to Cervera and finally to Miranda de Ebro. In his memoirs, he describes his first impression of the compound as 'modern and civilised' and later added, 'It looks to me as if those who designed it had honestly intended to create a "model" prison camp, for the barrack rooms are reasonably large and airy, there is plenty of space for exercise and there are special buildings set aside for medical and recreational purposes.'[25] Nevertheless, in his time in the camp, he observed frequent beatings, witnessed the torture and execution of some prisoners who had sought to escape, and was forced to work in a chain gang.

Neave also recalled that the hardships of the camp were mitigated by the visit of the British assistant military attaché (Brigadier Bill Torr) from Madrid, who brought food, tobacco, money, news of the battle raging over Britain and also secured the release of those British internees who had been longest in the camp. In his own memoirs, E. Martínez Alonso, one of a group of pro-Franco but also pro-British members of the higher echelons of Spanish society, reports that in fact he and the assistant military attaché made weekly visits to the camp. He also recalls providing the prisoners with irons with which to kill the lice and other miscellaneous vermin that infested their clothes. These visits and his assistance to other British nationals who evaded detention in Spain brought him to the attention of the authorities and the Gestapo, and he was eventually forced to flee to London via Portugal.

Prisoners of other nationalities were less fortunate, as the governments of their own countries were often unwilling or simply unable to provide them with any assistance. The British authorities did make efforts to help but their priority remained to secure the release of those agents most useful to their war effort. As the war progressed, the conditions in the camp deteriorated, particularly under the supervision of Paul Winzer, intelligence expert and Gestapo officer who was instrumental in training Franco's new secret police services. Both Queen Wilhelmina, the Dutch queen in exile in London, and the Free French registered formal complaints against the deplorable conditions in which internees were kept.[26]

British and Commonwealth prisoners released from Miranda de Ebro and those who eluded the Spanish authorities were taken into the custody of the British embassy in Madrid. The new ambassador, Sir Samuel Hoare, the arch-appeaser, defined his 'special mission' to Spain as an assignment to ensure that Franco was not tempted to abandon neutrality (or non-belligerence). While the intervention of the Spanish armed forces may not have substantially altered the balance of power in the rest of Europe, a land offensive against Gibraltar, by German troops, Spanish troops, or both, would have had a profound impact. Not only was the British colony now an effective gateway in and out of continental Europe, but it was also a hugely significant naval base without which Britain's access to the Mediterranean would be compromised.

Hoare was consequently reluctant to jeopardize his diplomatic 'overtures' to General Franco by encouraging the opposition or by making any gestures that might be interpreted as hostile to the new regime. Neither was he unaware that unwelcome British activity on the

Iberian Peninsula might be used by Hitler to justify a 'friendly' invasion of Spain to protect Spanish interests against further British infiltration and subversion. He insisted to his staff and the authorities in London that he would not tolerate any activities on Spanish territory by the Special Operations Executive (SOE) unless/until war was declared.

Nonetheless, despite Hoare's own aversion to undercover operations that risked jeopardizing the compromise he believed he had established in Hispano-British relations, the ambassador in Madrid did agree to support Creswell (aka *Monday*) in Madrid and Donald Darling (*Sunday*), the MI9 man posted from Lisbon to Gibraltar, in their efforts to ensure the safe return to Britain of as many fugitives and military personnel as possible. In his memoirs, he reported: 'Escaped prisoners of war, refugees of many countries, crashed airmen and stranded submarine sailors are not normally the concern of a diplomatic mission. In Madrid, their affairs occupied more of our time and thought than any other single question.'[27] In his own account of his escape from occupied France, J.M. Langley, the MI9 officer, recalls an incident in the Spanish capital when the ambassador chastised his group of BEF escapers for their behaviour at the French–Spanish border, when an inebriated private (who had fought for the International Brigades) loudly insulted the figure of the Spanish head of state.[28]

Most of the responsibility for the welfare of the fugitives fell to Brigadier Bill Torr, the military attaché, who, apart from constant visits to Miranda de Ebro with essential supplies obtained from Gibraltar, was involved in endless negotiations with Spanish military authorities in order to secure the release of escapers and refugees. On the other hand, it was Creswell (*Monday*), assisted by his colleague Henry Hankey, who organized transport, often in their own vehicles, and were responsible for 'ferrying British escapers and evaders round Spain'.[29]

Those fortunate enough to evade capture and who made their way to the British consulates in Bilbao or Barcelona were discreetly transferred by road or train to the embassy in Madrid. The less fortunate who were detained in such prisons as Figueres and Girona and then Miranda de Ebro – when the British diplomatic corps were made aware of their presence – were eventually released into British custody. An annex was built in the embassy grounds at Calle Fernando el Santo, 16 – perpendicular to the Avenida del Generalísimo (today Paseo de la Castellana) to cope with the overflow.

Although many non-British refugees preferred to exit the continent through Lisbon, for British agents and aircrew, the next stop after the Spanish capital was Gibraltar. Some crossed the border into the colony with the blessing of the Spanish border authorities, others were smuggled across by Creswell and Hankey in their car boots. According to the reports of Donald Darling, two men who had made their own way south even tried to reach safety by swimming across the Bay of Algericas. They were both fortunate enough to be rescued by naval patrol boats.[30]

Not all escape stories ended well. The New Zealand Brigadier Reginald Miles became one of the highest-ranking officers to escape an Axis prisoner-of-war camp when he and his partner Brigadier James Hargest tunnelled their way out of the Vincigliata PG 12 mountain fortress near Florence and with the help of the Resistance managed to make their way first to Switzerland and then to Spain. Miles had seen action in Greece and North Africa and was indignant at the needless sacrifice of young men by incompetent military planners. He had lost his only son during the Norwegian campaign. By the time he reached Figueres in October 1943, he was suffering from exhaustion and depression and took his own life.[31]

Hoare later claimed that between 1940 and 1944, his staff were able to help more than 30,000 refugees pass through the Iberian Peninsula to safety. In the vainglorious style that characterizes his memoirs, the ambassador claimed, 'It was well worth going to Madrid even if this result had been the only outcome of my mission.'[32]

To save so many men and women was indeed an exceptional achievement and the members of the British diplomatic corps in Madrid did play their part. However, the rescue of hundreds of fugitives from Nazi-occupied Europe was essentially due to the extraordinary courage of the Dutch, Belgian and French citizens who braved the tyranny of the Gestapo, and the Spanish guides that defied the Germans, the Vichy French and Franco.

Chapter 11

Violins of Autumn

In the post-war years the Gaullists sought to suggest that the French, with support from the 'Anglo-Saxons', had to a great extent liberated France (and specifically the capital) themselves. According to Robert Gildea, there is a Gaullist narrative of 'a straight line of resistance between 1940 and 1944'.[1] The British historian describes how the line excluded any detours (North Africa) and the role of any other leader (Admiral Darlan, General Giraud) that might undermine the myth that resistance began with de Gaulle's call to the nation from London in June 1940 and culminated in the liberation of Paris by indigenous forces loyal to him.

In 1940, stunned by unexpected and overwhelming military defeat, the mass of the French population had little choice but to adjust to the new conditions. While in the Vichy zone, at least for two years, the population enjoyed relative protection from the terrors of the SS and the Gestapo, those in the northern zone found themselves under the yoke of the brutal forces of repression of a totalitarian enemy more powerful and with greater tools of coercion than any regime seen before. A defenceless, unarmed population, demoralized by the shortcomings and failures of so many of its political and military leaders under the Third Republic and bereft of means and organization, was in no position to defy the occupying power.

The response in the south was complicated by the figure of Pétain. A national icon, the hero of Verdun, he had swept aside those who had advocated further resistance, made peace and restored order from the chaos of defeat. His National Revolution promised to right the mistakes of the failed Third Republic and to impose conservative, social (and French) standards on a society believed by so many to have been undermined by the modern values of the 1920s and 1930s. While the new circumstances in the south might have provided easier conditions in which to organize resistance, immunity from the brutality of German rule suffered in the north also made rebellion less imperative.

The gratitude of many French people towards the new 84-year-old president was understandably not shared by the Spanish Republican immigrants. They had been fighting the forces of Hitler and Mussolini since 1936 and argued that the crucial intervention of the Germans and Italians between 1936 and 1939 belied the idea that the struggle in Spain was a civil war. They now asserted that resistance in France was the next stage in a much wider war against fascism. The assumption was therefore that victory over the Axis would automatically lead to the liberation of Spain and the restoration of the Republic.

Resistance began with isolated acts of supreme courage and defiance. In the autumn of 1940, approximately 3,500 school and university students rebelled against an order that the 11th of November should no longer be a national holiday, and demonstrated in front of the Arc de Triomphe. The protesters were dispersed by German troops and later reports suggest eleven were killed and as many as 500 were deported. On 27 May 1941, miners in the Nord-Pas-de-Calais region called a strike in protest at deteriorating conditions. At least a hundred of the men and their wives were imprisoned and 270 deported. Many subsequently lost their lives (either by execution or in the infrahuman conditions of the German concentration camps). The Musée de L'Homme network was a small group of academics based on the Paris museum that collaborated in the work of the escape lines and produced four editions of a newspaper entitled *Résistance* before they were betrayed by a Gestapo agent who had infiltrated the group. Some managed to escape to the free zone, others were imprisoned and then deported to Germany. Seven were executed.[2]

At the grassroot level, the movement developed on the basis of uncoordinated actions carried out by individuals and groups: anti-Nazi slogans painted on walls (and the ubiquitous 'V' – for victory), the defacement of German propaganda, the distribution of newssheets, and sabotage in factories and installations controlled by the Germans. Throughout France, people listened to Radio Londres, broadcast by the BBC and the mouthpiece of de Gaulle's Free French, recognized by Churchill as the legitimate French authority (28 June 1940). The evening transmissions commenced at 2000 hours with the soon-familiar '*Ici Londres!*' and then '*Les Français parlent aux Français*' – 'London calling! The French speak to the French' – and a warning to listeners to lower the volume on their wireless sets to avoid the attention of the

Gestapo and their spies. The station was vital in countering the propaganda of the Nazi-controlled Radio Paris ('*Radio Paris ment, Radio Paris est allemand*' – 'Radio Paris lies, Radio Paris is German'). It also had a crucial code in transmitting messages to agents and Resistance leaders.

Among the first organized resistance groups were the small teams of Spaniards who developed a range of methods for acquiring weapons which included stealing them from the Germans. These incipient units grew from the Spanish workforce now employed in the *chantiers* – small enterprises which offered services in construction, demolition, mining and forestry, and provided cover and protection for those exiles in danger of internment and deportation. The *chantiers* played an essential role in the production of the charcoal which became a vital fuel source throughout the war – in particular in the widespread use of the *gazogène* vehicles.[3] One of the earliest guerrillas to enlist in the struggle, Luis Bermejo, would later write: 'Our hands were still warm from firing Spanish guns, when we had to take up arms again in France against the Germans.'[4]

In the first twelve months of the resistance movement, local leaders were loath to use violence against the occupying force for fear of the brutal reprisals that the Nazis threatened against civilians (the execution of fifty civilian hostages for every German killed). However, the invasion of the USSR led the French Communist Party to reappraise their attitude towards the resistance movement. As if to make up for lost time and their own duplicity, the Communists were less averse to attacks on German military personnel. The first of a series of admittedly sporadic assassinations took place in August 1941, and the subsequent mass reprisals by the Nazis exacerbated the situation of a French population that was desperately short of food, constantly anxious for the fate of the men held in Germany in POW and STO camps, and at the mercy of arbitrary German acts of barbarism. On 23 October, in a radio address to the nation, de Gaulle expressly ordered the Resistance to desist from such actions: 'It is absolutely natural and absolutely right that Germans should be killed by Frenchmen [...] But there are tactics in war. War must be conducted by those entrusted with the task [...] My orders to those in occupied territory are not to kill Germans there openly.'[5] In suggesting that the involvement of the Resistance was unwelcome, de Gaulle had also exposed his own fear that the Communists would ignore his leadership and seek to dominate the movement 'to permeate the whole of the resistance in order to make of it, if possible, the instrument of their ambition'.[6]

In the long term, if the resistance movement were to make any impact on the Nazi occupation of France, they needed organization, weapons and money. In London, and on Churchill's orders, the Special Operations Executive had been set up on 19 July 1940, with a mission, according to the oft-quoted command, 'to set Europe ablaze'. Indeed, until Hitler launched Operation *Barbarossa* against the USSR in June 1941 and declared war on the USA in December 1941, the only offensive options open to the British in Europe were incitement to guerrilla warfare and the strategic campaigns of Bomber Command. Hugh Dalton, Minister of Economic Warfare, and director of the new organization, described the SOE as a 'democratic international' designed 'to coordinate, inspire, control and assist the nationals of oppressed countries who must themselves be the direct participants'.[7] Between 1941 and 1944, operating out of its headquarters at 64, Baker Street, the SOE trained agents and supplied the Resistance with funds, arms, weapons instructors, military experts, and wireless operators.

Nevertheless, the ultimate success of the movement, in combination with an eventual Allied landing in northern Europe, also depended on the coordination of its various and diverse sections. The history of the Resistance is as fascinating as it is complex. It was never a single, monolithic movement but was divided ideologically (Christian Democrats, Socialists and Communists), geographically (not only between the occupied and the free zones, but also regionally within each), and at a lower level even between national groups. The growth of the Maquis was contingent on events and developments both at home and abroad. The *relève* and the subsequent STO order immediately swelled the ranks of the partisan movement. As many as 300,000 young Frenchmen, at risk of 'deportation' to work in Germany, took to the hills. Indeed, the situation of the *réfractoires* (STO-dodgers) was now little different from that of the Spanish, in which survival and resistance went hand in hand.

The victory of the British Eighth Army over Rommel's Afrikakorps and the success of Operation *Torch* (the Anglo-American landings in North Africa in November 1942) triggered the invasion of the unoccupied zone by the Wehrmacht in order to protect the German southern flank. The victories in Africa and the successes of the USSR on the Eastern

Front persuaded many across Europe that the tide had finally turned, and raised morale among the Free French and their supporters. The Germans and the Vichy authorities met the new optimism with ever more ruthless tactics which in turn inspired more support for the Resistance. On 30 January 1943, the Maréchal authorized the creation of the Milice (Militia), a brutal, paramilitary police force assigned the task of rooting out *résistants*, freemasons and Jews. By 1944, the Milice had between 25,000 and 30,000 agents, and while on the one hand they were was as vicious as the Gestapo, on the other, as French-speakers (and speakers of the regional dialects), they were considerably more effective among the local population. Their betrayal and their treatment of their fellow French inspired a new resentment towards Vichy, and pockets of southern France would eventually descend into civil war. The growing resistance to the Vichy regime in south-west France, encouraged in many areas by the example of the Spanish Republicans, was now to become an important factor in Allied planning for the invasion of Western Europe.

As more and more men and women joined the Resistance, so the SOE, the newly arrived American Office of Strategic Services (OSS), and the Free French became increasingly aware of the need for at least an umbrella organization to orchestrate strategies and military aims. De Gaulle's Comité National Français, recognized by the British as the de facto French government-in-exile, undertook negotiations for the unification of the movement. On New Year's Day 1942, the general dispatched his envoy Jean Moulin to France to establish a confederation of *maquisard* groups. His first success came with the formation of the Armée Secrète and the agreement in January 1943 between Combat, Libération and Francs-Tireurs to set up the Mouvements Unis de la Résistance (MUR) as its civilian arm.

His efforts culminated in the creation in May 1943 of the Conseil National de la Résistance (CNR) which included the MUR, five other groups including the Communist Francs-Tireurs et Partisans, representatives of the two main trade unions and the six mainstream parties of the Third Republic. The new grouping would soon become known as the Forces Françaises de l'Intérieur (FFI). Three weeks later Moulin was trapped by the Gestapo at a meeting in Lyon. He was delivered into the custody of the infamous Klaus Barbie but despite horrendous and unremitting torture he revealed nothing of the new organization. He died in transit to Germany. A symbol in today's France of the sacrifices made by so many men and women in the service of the Resistance, Moulin had paved the way for a coordinated partisan movement, in theory at least, at the orders of de Gaulle, which could now prepare for the eventual Allied invasion of Fortress Europe. In his memoirs, the general describes how in March 1944, he created the FFI 'obligatorily including all clandestine troops'.[8] He did not clarify whether the order extended to non-French partisans (including the Spanish) fighting alongside their fellow Resistance fighters; he simply failed to acknowledge them.

As D-Day approached it was agreed by Allied command and the Free French that apart from direct engagement with the enemy and specific raids on garrison towns, the Maquis was to disrupt the response of the Wehrmacht and SS to the landings through a carefully drafted plan of sabotage designed to prevent or at least delay the deployment of German reinforcements in Normandy. According to SOE archives, by May 1944, one month prior to *Overlord*, there were 35,000–40,000 'well-armed' men, 350,000 unarmed but committed members of the Armée Secrète, and 500,000 railway workers and 300,000 trade unionists who had pledged their support to the Resistance and were ready to obey whatever orders they received. The armed partisans had 74,131 Sten guns, 27,047 pistols, 16,595 rifles, 3,295 Bren guns, 572 bazookas and 160 mortars.[9]

The SOE/OSS had further deployed a total of 93 Jedburgh crews – 'the three-man, multinational teams comprised of an American or British officer/leader, a French officer, and a wireless operator (British, French, or American)'[10]. The Maquis was given orders to destroy the Germans' newly installed underground telephone lines, to disrupt railway services by wrecking both tracks and rolling stock, and to sabotage production and distribution of all supplies required by the German occupying force. In his memoirs, General Dwight Eisenhower (Supreme Commander Allied Expeditionary Force, or SCAEF), commander-in-chief of the Allied armies in Europe would later write:

> Throughout France the Free French had been of inestimable value in the campaign. [...] on every portion of the front we secured help from them in a multitude of ways. Without their great assistance the liberation of France and the defeat of the enemy in western Europe would have consumed a much longer time and meant greater losses to ourselves.[11]

In the latter decades of the twentieth century, historians both inside and outside France reappraised the reaction of the French people towards the occupying forces. Given the overwhelming nature of the military defeat and the ruthlessness of German rule, the population had little choice but to come to terms with the Nazi and Vichy authorities. The issue is not the response of what Gildea calls 'the conformist mass of the population',[12] but rather the dishonesty of those who later sought to understate the level of collaboration, to exaggerate popular participation in the Resistance, and to propagate the legend of 'self-deliverance' which ignored the part played by 'external' forces, including those thousands of Spanish Republicans who were impatient to take up arms against the invaders and their acolytes.

From the very beginning, those Spaniards trapped north of the Pyrenees were committed to the fight against the Germans. According to British historian Helen Graham, 'For most Republican refugees in France, the roads to resistance began with the imperatives of survival.' They lived on the margins of French society and created 'solidarity networks' that were the precursors of resistance units.[13] Jacques Poirier (aka *Capitaine Jack* and *Nestor*), a French SOE agent dispatched to the Midi to coordinate the disparate bands of Maquis, later described an encounter with Spanish partisans in the Pyrenees who were 'literally attempting to live off the land'. In an interview with Max Hastings, he told the British historian that,

> They seemed to exist chiefly on nuts and wild plants. They were desperately hungry and passionately eager to fight fascists. [...] For a long time, those who had least were the best *résistants*. The poor and the radical, those whom respectable citizens dismissed as troublemakers and drifters, sowed the seed of Resistance.[14]

Poirier also reported that at the end of the war, these same Spanish Republicans asked him, 'And now, *mon commandant*, will you ask Baker Street to begin their *parachutages** to us in Spain?' He claimed that he did indeed transmit the request to the SOE in London although he realized there was little point holding his breath. Initially, the Spanish Maquis had

---

* airdrop, parachute drops of weapons and other supplies

armed themselves by stealing guns from the Germans and purchasing weapons with money from the sale of tobacco they 'requisitioned' from smugglers using the same routes across the Pyrenees as the escape lines. Later however, they also intercepted *parachutages* intended for French resistance groups. Nearly eight years after the non-intervention agreement and several years too late to save the Second Republic in its struggle against fascism in Spain, the British had finally contrived (unwittingly) to arm Spanish Republicans. Nevertheless, there was no suggestion they might now extend the supply of armaments beyond the Pyrenees.

In his work on the Spanish Republicans in the Second World War, the historian Eduardo Pons Prades described the first recorded action of Spanish resistance workers – in the Haute-Savoie region where some 750 Spaniards were working in three GTE (514, 515 and 517) involved in road maintenance, stone quarries and forestry. They created 'solidarity and action groups' which immediately offered protection to anti-Nazi refugees (the majority of which were Jews). In the winter of 1940/1, a sabotage team in central France (GTE 643) partially destroyed a railway bridge at Saint-Brice-sur-Vienne. The actions of the Spanish partisans spread quickly throughout the Alps and central France, to Brittany and Normandy, and the west coast, where thousands of Spaniards had been conscripted to the Todt Organization and put to work on the Atlantic Wall and the submarine bases at Brest and La Rochelle.[15]

A number of Spanish Republicans who had been volunteered by the Vichy regime found themselves in the Channel Islands, the only territory of the British Isles occupied by the Nazis. In an interview recorded in 1987,[16] the Spanish Republican Vicente Gasculla Sole described how he arrived in Jersey in December 1941 as part of a team of 300 Spaniards deported to the islands to start work on the construction of labour camps. Over the course of the next three years, somewhere between 12,000 and 16,000 Todt Organization conscripts and slave workers from the east were transferred to the archipelago, where they were used in the building of a coastal wall and a series of bunkers, and in such projects as the underground military hospital at St. Lawrence. Of these as many as 2,000 were Spanish. However, despite the harshness of their conditions, as 'volunteers' their circumstances do not bear comparison with the brutal treatment reserved for the slave labour units transported across Europe to Jersey from the USSR and Poland.[17]

Nevertheless, some Spaniards were 're-deported' to the island of Alderney, which the German occupiers had rebranded Adolf Island. This particular destination was reserved for those the Nazis chose to identify as *untermenschen* and for those who had committed such misdemeanours as seeking to escape or stealing bread. Of the four camps on the tiny island, the most notorious was the Lager Sylt, a satellite of the Neuengamme camp (near Hamburg) run by the SS. The Nazi victims were put to work in inhuman conditions, and were starved, beaten and tortured. Many who became unable to comply with the demands of the work protocols set by their captors were executed.[18]

By some strange twist of fate, the island was close enough to mainland Normandy for the prisoners to see Allied shipping as it made for the French coast in support of the D-Day landings. However, another year passed before the Channel Islands were liberated, on 9 May 1945 (a week after the death of Adolf Hitler), by which time as many as 1,000 men had lost their lives on Alderney alone.

As the Nazis consolidated their control in France, so Spanish refugees became actively involved in raids against the German occupiers and the occupation infrastructure. They destroyed communications, demolished bridges, disrupted the railway network, and carried out collective and individual acts of sabotage in industry and military facilities. Federica Montseny (anarchist minister of health during the Civil War) would later publish a collection of oral testimonies describing and defining the fate of Spanish exiles in France. As an example of Spanish *picaresca* (guile), she recounts the story of one man pressganged into service at the U-boat pen at the Brest submarine facility. The Germans gave strict instructions to avoid all waste, and commanded workers to straighten bent nails rather than discard them. One man, obeying the order to the letter and to the evident bemusement of the guards, would spend up to one hour fixing a single damaged nail. However, when the guards turned their backs, he would simply pick up a box of nails (weighing a kilogram) and throw it into the sea.[19]

Spanish historian Secundino Serrano calculates that by D-Day, there were at least 10,000 Spanish *maquisards* in independent Resistance units.[20] In addition, there was a huge number of unarmed Republican men and women in and around Toulouse providing support (intelligence, refuge and logistics) to the Resistance movement.

While some Spaniards chose to join French partisan groups, the majority elected to fight in autonomous Spanish units. The XIV Corps was set up in April 1942 at a meeting near Foix in the Pyrenees. The name was taken in honour of the first XIV Corps founded as an initiative of Prime Minister Negrín in 1937 to continue the anti-*franquista* struggle behind enemy lines as the Nationalists slowly extended their conquests throughout Spain. Originally the corps was made up of units of fewer than 100 men but was eventually divided into two divisions allied to the Franc-Tireurs et Partisans (FTP), the Resistance group controlled by the Parti Communiste Français (PCF). As their war aims extended beyond the liberation of France, the Spanish resisted attempts to absorb them in the Main-d'œuvre immigrée (MOI), the group of non-French partisans (Jews, Poles, Rumanians, Bulgarians, Italians, Hungarians, Armenians etc.) 'affiliated' to the FTP. They retained their autonomous status as the military wing of the Unión Nacional Española (UNE) set up in November 1942 by the unofficial Spanish Communist leadership in Spain and France and designed to develop into a mass anti-*franquista* alliance capable of overthrowing the dictatorship. In May 1944, weeks before D-Day, given the rapid growth in recruits, the XIV Corps regrouped as the Agrupación de Guerrilleros Españoles (AGE, the Spanish Guerrilla Group).

Many of the Spanish Republican exiles were experienced fighters and expert in making the most of limited military resources. Indeed, their military expertise and sometimes almost reckless bravery earned them immediate respect. The New Zealand-born Australian, Nancy Fiocca (Nancy Wake), known to the Germans as '*die weiße Maus*' ('the White Mouse'), fought the early years of the war in Marseille with Ian Garrow and Pat O'Leary and after training with the SOE, was parachuted back into the Auvergne region in central France to fight with the Resistance. Days before the landings, she met a band of Spanish Maquis that was camped nearby and which supported her own unit when they came under attack from 6,000–7,000 German troops. She later told her biographer that they were 'a most impressive body of men'.[21] When it was determined that her notoriety among the Germans made it essential to provide her with bodyguards, she chose a team of six Spaniards who, she later insisted, 'regarded her as their complete equal as a soldier', but nevertheless treated her with 'the utmost gallantry'.[22] In her own autobiography, she recounts how on one occasion when they stopped at a village at mealtime, her bodyguards demanded to see the identity cards of two men eating in the restaurant because they did not like the way they were looking at her. She concluded, 'Never argue with battle-hardened soldiers who had fought in the Spanish Civil War.'[23]

Another SOE agent, Anne-Marie Walters, was parachuted into Gascony at the beginning of 1944 to act as liaison officer and courier for George Starr (Walters refers to him as 'the Patron') in the Wheelwright circuit (see chapter 18). She also worked closely with Republicans who had joined forces with the Resistance. In 1946, she wrote, 'They were hardened to guerrilla warfare and used to a tough life, being all veteran fighters of the Civil War.'[24] In Walters' own version, Starr insisted that she attach herself as assistant to the self-proclaimed commander of the Spanish partisans, the man she calls Alcazio, and whom she describes as 'an amazing character. He had lost a leg in the Civil War, but had nevertheless fought the 1940 campaign in France. He had been part of the Resistance since the defeat of France'. She claims that when she complained to Starr that she was wasting her time typing reports for Alcazio that nobody read, Starr replied, 'You must do what he wants. I want the Spaniards to stay with us. They are good fighters and very helpful. […] We need those people badly.'[25]

In his memoirs, Serge Ravanel, colonel of the FFI and commander in the Toulouse area, first recalled the 'shameful' reception given to the Spanish refugees in 1939:

> They were interned in camps behind barbed wire, treated like enemies: lack of food, no hygiene facilities, brutality of trigger-happy guards. Families were separated: women and children on one side, men on the other. The government never made the least gesture of republican solidarity, as if it had forgotten that General Franco, insurrectionist and Fascist, had only won power with the help of Mussolini and Hitler, our enemies.[26]

And then paid tribute to those that fought in the Resistance: 'Their courage was legendary. Their experience, forged in combat in the Spanish war, was absent in many of our [French] Maquis.'[27]

While the Resistance movement slowly took form inside France, de Gaulle was also anxious to create a regular army of men loyal to him and capable of finding a role in the wider conflict alongside the Allies. One man, Captain Philippe de Hauteclocque, was to play a huge role in de

Gaulle's plans, to lead an epic quest from central Africa to Hitler's Eagle's Nest in the Bavarian Alps, and to ensure that a company of Spanish Republican fighters entered the annals of military history. He was captured by the Germans twice in the course of the Battle of France and escaped both times. He eventually made his way to the *zone libre*, then across Spain to Lisbon where the British embassy arranged his transport to London aboard the SS *Hillary*. He immediately made contact with General de Gaulle, who claimed, 'when I saw what sort of man I was dealing with I settled his destination at once. It should be the Equator.'[28] Other versions suggest de Gaulle originally sent de Hauteclocque to join a unit of the Foreign Legion which was now based in Britain following the campaign in Norway and the French surrender, and that only when the posting was greeted with hostility – de Hauteclocque was a cavalry officer – did de Gaulle dispatch him to French Equatorial Africa.[29] The newly promoted major, took the precaution of adopting a nom de guerre in order to protect his wife and six children who were still in France. Henceforth he was known exclusively as Leclerc, and would become one of the three most famous and important leaders of the Free French (alongside de Gaulle and Jean Moulin).

With the support of the local colonial authorities, and in the name of de Gaulle, Leclerc secured control over Cameroun and then led a combined force of the 13e Demi-Brigade Légion Etrangère (with an undetermined number of Spanish recruits[30]) and Senegalese *Tirailleurs* (riflemen) against Gabon, where the colonial leaders were loyal to Vichy France. Libreville, the capital, was taken on 11 November. De Gaulle subsequently ordered Leclerc into Chad, which had already declared for the Free French, where he set up his HQ at the capital, Fort Lamy (today N'Djamena). Chad was directly in the war zone as it shared a Saharan frontier with Libya, a territory integrated in the Italian state (its coast became Mussolini's *Quarta Sponda* – Fourth Shore) and occupied by the Italian Army.

In January 1941, Leclerc sent a small force accompanied by a British Army Long Range Desert Group patrol to raid the Murzuk oasis in south-western Libya and the following month captured Kufra, an oasis/ settlement in the south-east. Having thus secured the first victory of the Free French against the Axis, Leclerc ordered his troops to take the Oath of Kufra: 'Swear that you will not lay down your arms until the day when our glorious colours fly over Strasbourg Cathedral'. For the Spanish soldiers among his troops, the oath did not extend to their own war aims; the liberation of France and indeed the final defeat of Mussolini and Hitler would be only the beginning of the end, or at the very least the end of the beginning. Their ultimate target was not Strasbourg, it was Madrid, and the overthrow of Franco.

In the meantime, the Brigade Française d'Orient (Free French Orient Brigade), including a unit of Spanish troops, set sail southward from Douala (Cameroun) on Christmas Eve 1940. In Durban, they were joined by a small expeditionary force of the Foreign Legion (according to Pons Prades, almost all Spanish[31]), which had been deployed from Britain. After a thirty-nine-day voyage around the continent, the troops finally disembarked at Port Sudan in mid-February 1941 and subsequently fought alongside the combined forces from Britain, Belgium, Kenya, British Somaliland, British West Africa, Ethiopia, India, Rhodesia, Nyasaland, Palestine, South Africa and Sudan in the East African Campaign which expelled Italy from her East African empire and concluded with the Battle of Gondar and the Italian surrender of November 1941.

Other Spaniards also fought in Operation *Exporter* (June–July 1941), the Australian/British-led invasion of Lebanon and Syria, French colonial territories under the control of the Vichy authorities. Had the Germans been enabled by Pétain to establish a military presence in the Levant, they would have been in a position to undermine Britain's hold on Egypt and to threaten the supply route through the Suez Canal. A combined British–French offensive (including troops of the 5th Indian Infantry Brigade Group and the 7th Australian Division) allowed the Free French to seize control of Damascus and Beirut and to raise their standard (which now included the Croix de Lorraine superimposed on the traditional tricolour) over the two Middle Eastern capitals. In skirmishes at Kissoué (south of Damascus) there was a brief fratricidal engagement between units of the Foreign Legion loyal to de Gaulle and others who had sworn allegiance to the Vichy regime.

In the early part of 1942, the British continued to suffer setbacks on the main stage of North Africa. The heroic defence by the Free French of the Bir Hakeim fort, in the centre of the Libyan desert at the southern tip of the Gazala defensive line, did at least divert enough Axis resources to delay the fall of Tobruk and eventually helped the British Eighth Army under General Auchinleck to regroup at Alamein and halt Rommel's advance on Cairo. The Free French troops, under the command of

General Kœnig, resisted the German–Italian offensive/siege for two weeks between 26 May and 11 June 1942, before making a surprise withdrawal and retreating to British lines. In the absence of exact official figures, Pons Prades claims that of the 3,500 men defending the oasis, approximately 1,000 were Spanish Republicans.[32] Following this first major battle with Axis forces, the *France libre* authorities adopted the name *France combattante* (Fighting French).

Finally, the victory of the Eighth Army at the second Battle of El Alamein in November 1942 was followed by a French advance northward en masse from Chad. The troops of the newly promoted General Leclerc occupied Fezzan (the south-western area of Libya) and took Sebha and Mizdah before reaching Tripoli on 26 January 1943. In return for 'food, petrol and clothing', he immediately put himself and his troops under the command of General Montgomery, who described him as, 'this remarkable man'.[33] Leclerc's troops, with a company of Greek reinforcements and now identified by the British as L Force, were ordered to cover the Eighth Army's left flank as it advanced into Tunisia and was instrumental in warding off German counter-attacks. They fought at the battle for the Mareth Line – the defensive system constructed by the French and reinforced by the Germans – when the combined forces under Montgomery's command overwhelmed Rommel's army. This breakthrough was critical and allowed Montgomery to join up with the American troops advancing east after the successful outcome of Operation *Torch*. When Rommel finally surrendered, the Allies took a quarter of a million Axis prisoners.

Leclerc's force now regrouped as the 2e Division Blindée (2e DB, the 2nd Armoured Division) and enlisted new recruits from the local population, including fugitives from the Vichy authorities, deserters from the Legion, French colonials, and Moroccan and Algerian troops. By 1944, the division consisted of approximately 15,000 men. It is impossible to determine how many of these troops were Spanish. There are no official figures for the composition of the division by nationality and Spanish Republicans had adopted the practice of assuming French names in order to protect their anonymity and the well-being of their families in Spain. Captain Raymond Dronne, the officer that Leclerc chose to command the 9th Company of the 3rd Battalion, later described how a number of Spanish soldiers refused to pose for the official regimental photographs taken in England, for fear that such pictorial evidence might facilitate their identification by the Francoist authorities.[34] The suggestion by Pons Prades that almost a fifth of the troops in the 2e DB were Spanish (at least in origin)[35] is not supported by published evidence. Nonetheless, Dronne described his 9th Company (which became known as *La Nueve*) as the Spanish company par excellence, in a battalion with many Spaniards and men of Spanish descent. Whether their numbers were to be counted in hundreds or thousands, the reality is that their war in Africa was now concluded. Their next engagement would be in northern France.

Chapter 12

The Devil, the Deep Blue Sea and the Rock

The fall of France in 1940 raised the issue of Spanish neutrality to the level of utmost strategic importance. Like France, Spain had both an Atlantic and a Mediterranean coast, but significantly she also controlled the European flank of the western entrance to *Mare Nostrum* – the Mediterranean – and was only separated from North Africa by the Straits of Gibraltar. In addition, she loudly proclaimed a longstanding political and military claim on the Rock, the site of a now vital British naval base on the southernmost tip of the peninsula. Sir Samuel Hoare, the ambassador in Madrid, found it difficult to disguise his dislike of Spain in general; in a memorandum to Churchill, he described it as 'this strange place'.[1] However, he was resolute in his mission to dissuade Franco from entering the fray. He was not the bravest of men – when he first arrived in Madrid, he refused to unpack and an aircraft was kept at his disposal in Madrid in case he needed to make a swift getaway[2] – and yet curiously he took up residence in a house next to that belonging to German Ambassador Eberhard von Stohrer in the Avenida Generalísimo Franco (today Paseo de la Castellana). In his own words, 'It was part of my plan of campaign to create an atmosphere of British indifference to alarms […]. I accordingly ignored the warnings of those who looked askance at the remarkable contiguity of the rival Embassies and we took the house.'[3] In his epistolary account of his own time in Portugal and Spain between 1939 and 1942, David Eccles of the Ministry of Economic Warfare described the ambassador as knowledgeable, socially adept and an excellent administrator, but prone to 'physical and moral cowardice'. He concluded, 'Hoare was an example of the exceptionally able man whose faults almost outweigh his virtues, but not quite.'[4]

In his first year in Madrid, Hoare lived on a 'knife's edge' that became ever 'thinner and sharper'.[5] He knew it was crucial to Britain's interests that Spain remain neutral in the conflict but was made abundantly aware of Franco's sympathy for the Axis cause and his debt to both Hitler and Mussolini, without whose help it is unlikely that his cause could have prospered. The ambassador's arch-enemy was Ramón Serrano Suñer, brother-in-law to Franco, chief of the Falange, minister of the interior, and from October 1940, also minister of foreign affairs. Fascist and fervently pro-German, he accumulated such influence that at one point he appeared to have at least as much power as Franco. Hoare was convinced that *el cuñadísimo** was intent on tightening relations with Hitler and Mussolini, and if there was no evidence that he actually favoured an early declaration of war, he did appear to support upgrading Spain's status to 'pre-belligerency' and contributing with all available resources to an Axis victory. Both Franco and Suñer were equally mindful that defeat for Germany and Italy would place Franco's regime in serious jeopardy.

Nevertheless, Franco was likewise alert to the fact that after three years of civil war, Spain was unprepared for a new military adventure against the British. The failure of the Luftwaffe to defeat the RAF and the suspension of *Unternehmen Seelöwe* (Operation *Sealion*, the invasion of Britain) also undermined the Caudillo's confidence in final victory. Moreover, he was wary of the dangers of challenging the Royal Navy, and the effects a blockade would have on the essential supplies of cereals and fuel without which the dictatorship might struggle to survive.

While Churchill's government recognized the importance of Britain's economic ties with Spain, there remained divisions on how best to weaponize Spain's urgent need for foreign goods. While the Labour Party and the Ministry of Economic Warfare in London argued that Franco should be treated at least as a potential enemy, and that strict sanctions should be applied to undermine his regime, Hoare and his staff in Madrid believed sanctions would be counter-productive and would definitively push the Spanish into the Axis camp. They urged that the supply of basic products be used as an incentive for neutrality, on the understanding that essential imports could be withheld whenever the regime swayed too close to the Axis. Hoare defined the policy in a memo to Churchill:

---

* Suñer was known popularly as the 'supreme brother-in-law' – he was married to the sister of Franco's wife.

> Our approach to Spain should offer regulated help on
> a generous scale, regulated because we must not allow
> the accumulation of stocks. The help should consist of
> (1) Necessities. (2) Shipping. (3) Credits. Our sanction is
> the power to stop it at any moment.[6]

Dalton at the MEW put his own case more succinctly: 'He [Hoare] wants
to keep them sweet; I want to keep them short.'[7] Ultimately, Hoare's
policy prevailed. Through the *navicerts* system, the British were able
to control overseas imports into Spain, and effectively to exercise a
carrot-and-stick approach to their relations with Madrid. Throughout the
duration of the war, Franco was never allowed to forget his dependency
on British (and later American) 'goodwill'.

If Hoare were to succeed in his 'special mission' to deter Franco
from declaring war on Britain, he also needed to be seen as neutral
in Spanish affairs. In other words, Britain could not act as an enemy
towards the dictatorship. He therefore lobbied fiercely against any
covert activities on Spanish territory that might be interpreted as hostile
or even provocative. As long as the regime in Spain felt tempted to
declare itself a belligerent, Hoare demanded that the SOE refrain from
taking any measures to undermine it. Should conditions change, if the
Germans crossed the Pyrenees, then the SOE would have carte blanche
to intervene. The policy, which was accepted in London, allowed the
secret services to make contingency plans for action, and even to place
units in a state of readiness, but also guaranteed Britain would not treat
Spain as an adversary (potential or otherwise) and would take no pre-
emptive steps towards the overthrow of the dictatorship.

Following Germany's declaration of war on the USA in December
1941, President Roosevelt appointed Carlton J.H. Hayes (1942–45) as
the new ambassador in Madrid. Hayes shared Hoare's distrust of the
secret services, and his reluctance to offend the regime and thus endanger
the delicate balance that allowed Franco to declare his solidarity with the
Axis without actually declaring war. He complained of the 'difficult and
time-consuming' task of making members of the OSS understand

> that we were in Spain not to fight Spaniards or overturn their
> government but to fight the Axis and to enlist all possible
> support for this purpose from both the Spanish people

117

and the Spanish Government. Over and over again I told members of the staff whose missionary zeal outstripped their judgement that they might entertain any ideas they wished about the existing Spanish regime, but they must preserve, in word and act, a strict neutrality. [...] No forceful overturn of the existing Spanish regime was likely or even possible, and the only result of our advocating it would have been our expulsion from the country and the surrender of strategic Spain to Germany.[8]

It is unlikely that Hitler's priority was to persuade Franco to commit the Spanish army to a full-scale intervention in the conflict. The Wehrmacht had taken mainland Western Europe in six weeks without the support of the Italians – the Italian army had not deployed until the battle for France was won – and after three years of bitter civil war, neither the Spanish people nor the armed forces were equipped to make a major contribution to the Axis war effort. Nevertheless, the key prize for the Germans was Gibraltar and given that the expulsion of the British from the Rock had been a cornerstone of Spanish foreign and domestic policy since the Treaty of Utrecht (1713), Hitler may well not have foreseen any serious Spanish objection to a German-led 'joint' operation against the colony. If they could expel the British from the Straits, the Italian Mediterranean submarine fleet would be able to disrupt Britain's supply lines and adventure more freely into the Atlantic. The Axis would also be in a far stronger position to take Malta, control the Middle East and consolidate their position in North Africa. In response, London made no attempt to disguise the likelihood of retaliation in the form of an invasion of the Canary Islands (Operation *Pilgrim*) and Spanish Equatorial Africa, should the Axis (with or without Spain) launch an offensive against Gibraltar.

In the opening months of the war, Franco made a series of gestures towards Hitler (see chapter 10) which included updating Spain's status from 'neutral' to 'non-belligerent' – on paper, a clear statement of his ideological bias, but in practical terms not even a declaration of intent. However, at the infamous summit at Hendaya in November 1940, both Hitler and Franco were left frustrated by their failure to reach an agreement. The train bringing the Spanish delegation was late – by one hour according to Hitler's interpreter Paul Schmidt, and by no more than a short delay according to Serrano Suñer.[9] While Hitler waited on the platform, he discussed Spain's ambitions in North Africa with his foreign minister. At this stage, his main concern was not to undermine the anti-British Vichy government by making concessions to Franco's imperial ambitions at the expense of French possessions in the Maghreb. Paul Schmidt later claimed to overhear him tell Ribbentrop:

> I want to try to induce the French to start active hostilities against Britain, so I cannot suggest to them such cessions of territory now. Quite apart from that, if such an agreement with the Spanish became known, the French colonial empire would probably go over bodily to de Gaulle.[10]

The Germans subsequently refused to make a firm offer on Franco's imperial demands. Nor could they guarantee alternative supplies of cereals and fuel. Hitler's offer to overcome the British forces at Gibraltar and return the colony to Spanish sovereignty was met with indifference. According to Serrano Suñer, he insisted that it was 'a question of honour for the Spanish people' that it be the fatherland (Spain) that expels the foreigners.[11] He no doubt also factored in the difficulties of removing a German force from the Iberian Peninsula once it had established a base. Franco was subsequently reduced to making empty promises on Spain's commitment to the Axis: 'Spain is joined to Germany by sincere and loyal friendship. In our war, Spanish soldiers fought side by side with Germans and Italians and forged an unbreakable alliance that will endure into the future.'[12] Serrano also claims that he was horrified when in a rare moment of emotional effusion Franco told the Führer: 'In spite of everything that has been said, if the day comes that Germany truly needs me, I will be unconditionally at her side, with no demands.' Serrano describes his relief when for some reason the German interpreter (Gross*) failed to translate into German this promise.[13] The next day, according to Schmidt, Ribbentrop described Franco as an 'ungrateful coward'.[14]

In Madrid, the senior staff at the British embassy worked tirelessly to gather intelligence, and to argue the case for neutrality with the few people

---

* The leading interpreter, Schmidt, did not speak Spanish. It is possible that the inexperienced Gross failed to understand the significance of the pledge.

in the upper echelons of Franco's regime who would listen. The British continued to take seriously the threat that changing circumstances might persuade Franco to commit to joining the Axis belligerents and Churchill consequently sanctioned the unofficially named *Knights of St. George* operation by which various Spanish generals would receive substantial amounts of foreign currency in return for taking a pro-neutrality stance. A joint MI6/Madrid embassy plan, inspired by Sir Stewart Menzies, chief of MI6, and Captain Alan Hillgarth, the naval attaché in Madrid, and authorized by Hugh Dalton, Minister of Economic Warfare (MEW), the operation was assisted by David Eccles (the MEW envoy in the Iberian Peninsula – who later described himself as 'an apostle of bribery'[15]) and the Spanish financier Juan March, who arranged for the deposit in the New York office of the Swiss Banking Corp. of some US$14 million. When the US treasury froze the account, the British prime minister was required to intervene personally and assure the authorities in Washington that the fund was not designed to support pro-Nazi activities. Various generals and the dictator's own brother, Nicolás Franco (ambassador in Lisbon), were the beneficiaries of the scheme. How effective the slush fund was in persuading key players in the dictatorship to argue against Hitler's demands that Spain declare war on Britain, and how far they were able to influence Franco is of course impossible to gauge. All that can be said is that it did not fail.

Throughout 1940, the British were facing a double dilemma. Even if they were successful in their campaign to dissuade Franco from declaring war, there was another threat: that Hitler would take unilateral action, invade Spain and lay siege to Gibraltar. After the British raid on the French Navy at Mers-el-Kébir (Operation *Catapult* – 3 July 1940), the tiny colony found itself in the sights of four hostile powers: Hitler's Germany, Mussolini's Italy, Franco's Spain and Pétain's Vichy France. The Italians and French indulged in occasional air raids against the Rock and later the Italians used their highly innovative *Maiale* (Pig) two-man human torpedo in a series of attacks on British shipping in the Algericas Bay. The Spanish meanwhile collaborated with the Germans in the construction of artillery batteries along the Spanish coast. There was also the constant fear of sabotage by both disaffected Gibraltarians and Spanish workers employed in the docks who crossed the border every day. However, there was no question that the real danger to the crown colony lay in a potential military operation, with or without Franco's assent, by the Wehrmacht.

The demarcation line between the occupied and 'free' zones of France had left the entire Atlantic coast under the control of the Germans. On 27 June, German troops were deployed at the western end of the Pyrenees on the Spanish border. Three days later the Madrid national newspaper *ABC* published the text of a speech given by General López Pinto at an event to celebrate the raising of the Swastika standard at Hendaya. In the presence of the commander of the German troops, General von Hauser, López Pinto declared that the arrival of the Wehrmacht reinforced the links between the two nations. He continued, 'The spiritual union has existed since our war of liberation, in which Germany, together with our other friends, Italy and Portugal, came to our assistance.'[16] The Spanish general finished with *vivas* to Hitler, Mussolini and Franco.

The embassy in Spain meanwhile continued to live in a permanent state of anxiety. In a letter to Lord Halifax on 8 August 1940, Sir Samuel Hoare wrote:

> The rumours grow in intensity every day. The night before last, for instance, the Military Attaché was rung up in the middle of the night by a member of the French Embassy, who said that he had just received a telephone message from San Sebastian from the French Consul, who had actually seen German units advancing through northern Spain.[17]

Although the report may have been exaggerated, it does appear that fraternization between the German troops camped on the border and enthusiastic members of the local Falange led to a number of incidents in which German troops were invited into Spain to participate in non-sanctioned victory parades, manoeuvres, or simply to enjoy the fabled Spanish hospitality. In her memoirs, the enigmatic British 'adventuress', Rosalinda Powell Fox, the lover of Spanish Foreign Minister Juan Luis Beigbeder, recounts an incursion on 29 June 1940. She was spending her summer holidays in San Sebastian with her son and younger sister, who rushed home and insisted that they had seen a German motorized column heading south towards Vitoria. When Fox looked through the window, she saw 'guns, tanks and heavily armed personnel with fixed bayonets. No bands were playing. No flags were flying. It was certainly no parade. And it had avoided the city itself and was moving south'.[18] She immediately phoned Beigbeder in Madrid. According to her version, within an hour, the minister sent orders inviting the Germans to return over the border. The local army commander who had authorized the expedition was subsequently suspended.

According to journalist and writer Nicholas Rankin, confirmation of the incursions was provided by Peter Kemp, a British agent working under the orders of Major Hugh Pollard for the Secret Intelligence Service (SIS – MI6). Kemp, who defined himself as 'anti-communist' but 'not pro-Fascist', was one of the few Britons to volunteer for Franco's Nationalists in the Civil War. Under cover as a holidaymaker on the Basque coast, he filed a report that fully armed German soldiers had recently taken part in a display of force in San Sebastian and that 'the surrounding country as far as Bilbao had been full of these troops'.[19] Although Kemp made no reference to this role in his own memoirs,[20] Fox describes how she met him for dinner at the Hotel Continental where he was staying and how they were later detained by the police when Kemp put an affectionate arm round her waist in public. They were 'upbraided for [their] unbridled lasciviousness'[21] but then released without a fine when they claimed to be married. Together they were also successful in persuading the consul in Bilbao to provide papers for three Scots and one French soldier who had been hiding out in the Basque countryside and escorted them to the boat in Bilbao that took them safely to Britain.

Sir Samuel Hoare was apparently unaware of Kemp's activities, but the Spanish press released ample details of the Hispano-German celebrations in the Basque Country and the ambassador made an unofficial, but no less vehement, protest to the Foreign Ministry against these German troop movements. Indeed, according to his version, it was his own intervention that 'secured the suspension of the military commander in San Sebastian'.[22]

British and Spanish concern at the proximity of the Wehrmacht was well founded. Hoare was concerned at the possibility of a German invasion of Spain by stealth. He later wrote: 'The German plan was based on the established Hitler technique, fraternization on a large scale with the local garrisons, a friendly infiltration of German troops, and the gradual occupation of the whole country.' If, he argued, a German presence on the Spanish side of the Pyrenees became accepted, it would be assumed that Franco had acknowledged the inevitability of a Nazi victory, and was ready to join the 'winning side'. Captain Hillgarth expressed his own concern at this 'trojan horse' approach[23] and few now questioned the peril of allowing Hitler any concessions. Hoare's conclusion was that eventually, 'The German Army, so far from being resisted, would have been welcomed as a triumphant victor'.[24]

In any case, it is unlikely that Spain alone would have been in a position to resist a hostile invasion by the Wehrmacht. In a memorandum from Captain Hillgarth to Churchill, the naval attaché in Madrid offered the following analysis of the state of the Spanish armed forces:

> Spain's Army is ill-equipped and nothing like mobilized. Her Air Force is rotten. An unadvertised attack along main roads by motorized divisions would soon overcome resistance. I calculate that the first German vehicles could reach Gibraltar in six or eight days, without heavy forces, of course.[25]

Nevertheless, Hillgarth also believed that the Germans would be unable to feed the population, would struggle to find fuel reserves and would be resisted by a people he described as 'tough, stiff-necked and cruel'. He concluded that if the Spaniards received aid from abroad, thirty German divisions would not be sufficient to pacify the country. He added, with a certain degree of Churchillian nonchalant bravado and unfounded optimism, that 'the corner embracing Gibraltar and Cadiz could be held if we lent a hand'.

Chapter 13

Golden Eyes

In the summer of 1940, as the frontline in the war in Europe was transferred to the skies above England, a small number of Spanish Republicans remained in Britain. Some had been evacuated with French troops after the fall of France and others had taken part in the Norway campaign. Most joined the Free French and departed for North Africa, but those who chose not to serve under de Gaulle were recruited to the Pioneer Corps of the Royal Engineers. British military law proscribed the deployment of foreign troops in a combat role and therefore the Spanish exiles had little choice but to join the Sappers (combat engineers).

Antonio Grande, the Spanish exile recruited by the Manchester Regiment in France to provide ancillary support, and one of the last men to be evacuated from the west coast, recalls in his memoirs the pleasant summer he spent in 1940 in an army-owned hotel in Westward Ho!. He had fought in the trenches at Madrid and following the defeat of the Republic, had been interned in a labour camp. Having escaped and found his way across the Pyrenees, he was confined to a French concentration camp before answering the call of two officers from the Manchester Regiment. After his tribulations, he was now safely ensconced in Britain, spoilt for female company and enjoying the pleasures of life thanks to donations made by the British troops based in Plymouth: 'with sixpence, you could buy twenty cigarettes, a pint of beer cost two and a half pence, and with a shilling you could go to the cinema or dancing.'[1]

In November he joined the newly formed No. 1 (Spanish) Company of the Royal Engineers and was almost immediately recruited for a commando training programme designed to prepare Spanish exiles for an eventual intervention in Spain should Franco bow to pressure to declare war on Britain or if the Germans invaded the Iberian Peninsula.

In August, Commander Ian Fleming of the Naval Intelligence Division (NID) launched Operation *Goldeneye* to coordinate military intelligence from the Iberian Peninsula, monitor German military preparations for intervention in Spain, draw up plans for a campaign of sabotage in the event of a Wehrmacht invasion (friendly or hostile), and to ensure the integrity of communications with Gibraltar. He worked closely with Captain Hillgarth, the naval attaché in Madrid, who enjoyed the confidence of the British prime minister and had made a series of proposals to the Joint Planning Committee in London in anticipation of a German occupation of the Iberian Peninsula.[2] After an intelligence summit in Lisbon, Fleming visited the colony in February 1941 to assess defence preparations and the arrangements for Operation *Relator* (see below). He held a meeting with William 'Wild Bill' Donovan, an American envoy touring the area on a fact-finding mission, who would later cofound and head the Office of Strategic Services (OSS, the predecessor of the CIA).

As a supplement to Fleming's initiative, Rear Admiral John Henry Godfrey, Director of NID, put forward a proposal – Operation *Tracer* – to construct a clandestine observation post in the Upper Rock area of Gibraltar. Should the crown colony fall to the Germans, a six-man team would be concealed in the cave with a radio and huge supplies of water and food, and would continue to transmit intelligence of naval traffic through the Straits.

The following year, Hillgarth drafted a memorandum which was presented to the Joint Planning Committee entitled 'Spain: Suggested Preparatory Measures', in which he outlined his vision of British-led military operations behind enemy lines, should the Germans indeed cross the Pyrenees. He even went so far as to propose the recruitment and training of Spanish pilots, a project that was apparently shelved. Nevertheless, a plan to create a forty-man team to infiltrate key areas of a German-occupied Spain did receive the go-ahead.[3]

The SOE set to work on two contingency plans: one in the case that Franco should grant the Wehrmacht access to Spanish territory (Operation *Sconce*) and the second in the case that Hitler launched a hostile incursion (Operation *Sprinkler*). They recruited approximately fifty Spanish nationals of different backgrounds and ideological persuasions. Antonio Grande later recalled his own experience with another eight of his compatriots who undertook commando training in twenty-three different paramilitary schools in England, Scotland and Wales. The basic fieldcraft base and the guerrilla training school were both located on the west coast of Scotland at Loch Ailort and Arisaig respectively. The men received instruction in explosives, weapons, unarmed combat and counter-espionage. Their final course was at the Parachute Training School at RAF Ringway (now part of Manchester Airport) where they were given their final preparation for an eventual drop into Spain.[4]

In his memoirs, Pablo de Azcárate, by now a close associate of Juan Negrín in exile in Britain, tells of a meeting in May 1941 with Manuel Mota of the Pioneer Corps who described the recruitment process. According to Mota, many of his fellow exiles were interrogated by British officers who asked questions on their ideology, political affiliation, military rank, and knowledge of railway and road systems and specific regions. Mota remarked on the unease of many of the trainees, who expressed a willingness to fight under Spanish officers in the cause of the Republic, but were reluctant to serve under British command in a campaign that might involve fighting against their compatriots.[5]

Another man recruited by the British for guerrilla training was Dr Martínez Alonso, the Francoist physician, who had supported the British embassy staff in rescuing escapers and evaders from Spanish prisons and internment camps and escorting them safely to Portugal or Gibraltar. He had fled to Britain before the Gestapo could detain him and was appointed as Senior Resident Surgeon at Queen Mary's Hospital (Roehampton).[6] He was approached by an anonymous colonel and agreed to join the operation on the condition that he would only take part if the Wehrmacht invaded Spain and Franco declared war on Germany. He was en route to the training camp when he was recognized on the platform of the Edinburgh railway station by a Polish officer whom he had helped in the Miranda de Ebro concentration camp. A British officer intervened to protect both men's identities. The next stop was Glasgow, which he described – in wartime and on a Sunday – as 'a morgue when the morticians are on holiday'.[7]

When he and his fellow recruits finally reached Camusdarach, they were given the 'finest scotch that [he had] ever had'. Their 'home' was part of a complex of shooting lodges near Arisaig, 'where there was plenty of admirably rough and secluded country'.[8] Next morning, they began with a pre-dawn ten-mile run in pyjamas and boots through the Scottish mist, which the doctor claimed was 'uphill both ways'. Apart from practice exercises on the moors, they received training in how 'to blow up things, kill the enemy from behind with knives, hand grenades,

Tommy guns, traps, kicks on the most delicate parts of a man's anatomy, and many other disgusting manoeuvres'. After one month, he was sent back to London to await further orders.

Peter Kemp also offered his services and was recruited to take part in Operation *Relator* (more commonly known as 'Ali Baba and the Forty Thieves'), a scheme run by Ian Fleming at Naval Intelligence. For the 'eighteen officers, and a number of NCO wireless operators and demolition experts' selected for the mission, training began at Loch Ailort in January 1941: 'forced marches over that rough country carrying fifty-pound rucksacks, pretending to blow up bridges [...], map-reading, pistol shooting and unarmed combat.'[9] Kemp found that the area around the shores of Loch Ailort and the Sound of Arisaig had 'a bleak, wild beauty of scoured grey rock and cold blue water, of light green bracken and shadowed pine, that was strangely inspiring in its stark simplicity and grandeur.'[10]

The instruction programme lasted three weeks during which Kemp came across a party of Spanish Republicans undergoing training on the shores of Loch Morar. Faced with men who had been the enemy two years before, he chose to ignore them. He later described the men as 'a villainous crowd of assassins'.[11] Harold 'Kim' Philby who met the same men at the Beaulieu 'Finishing School' for agents, was understandably more sympathetic. He concluded, 'My own feeling is that after being mucked around for a year or so by the British Government, they would cheerfully have killed anyone in the uniform of a British officer. But they exercised restraint.'[12] However, Kemp's label stuck; in a much later history of Beaulieu, the Spanish Republicans were still casually referred to as 'cut-throats' and 'frightful people'. They were found unfit for service as secret agents and eventually returned to duties in the Pioneer Corps – 'probably as labourers'.[13]

The members of the *Relator* mission left Liverpool for Gibraltar in mid-March 1941. They travelled aboard the same HMS *Fidelity* that would later be used for clandestine operations along the Spanish and French coasts. The ship now joined a convoy that sailed around the north of Ireland and west into the Atlantic until veering south and heading for Cape St. Vincent. According to Kemp, the '*Fidelity* was not a happy ship'. No provision had been made for the extra passengers, rations were scarcely sufficient, and the lower decks had not been adapted. To make matters worse, the captain – a Corsican by the name of Claude

André Michel Costa (Péri), inducted into the Royal Navy as 'Lieutenant Commander Jack Langlois RN'[14] – was a despot: in Kemp's own words, 'a stocky, black-bearded pirate'[15] who terrified his officers and crew.

Albert Guérisse's version is different[16]. Recruited under the nom de guerre Lieutenant Commander *Patrick O'Leary* RN, he agreed that the captain was prone to attacks of rage and brutality, and even to firing warning shots dangerously close to his own men, but also claims that ample arrangements had been made for the 'passengers' who alone 'remained unmoved by the wave of happiness that spread through the ship' as the crew embarked on their new adventure.

Costa's Royal Navy service record claimed: 'This officer displayed all the qualities of a leader – courage, energy, zeal, and a loyalty and enthusiasm which can only be termed as outstanding. He was an eminently competent naval officer. His methods of maintaining discipline were unorthodox [...] but he maintained discipline and obtained results.'[17] O'Leary also describes how the convoy came under attack from three Ju 88s, one of which he claims was brought down by fire from the guns of *Fidelity*. Furthermore, the vessel has a place in the annals of the Royal Navy as the first British fighting ship of the war to carry a woman as member of the crew: the enigmatic Madelaine Gueslin (*Barclay*), First Officer WRNS and a serving SOE agent.

When the 'forty thieves' finally reached the Rock, they discovered their training and miserable voyage had been in vain. From the embassy in Madrid, Hoare maintained his vehement refusal to sanction any undercover activity on Spanish territory that might be interpreted as hostile and might consequently provide Franco with a pretext for declaring war on Britain, and vetoed any contacts with opposition groups (in his own mind, the 'Reds'), though he did agree to low-profile discussions between diplomatic staff and disgruntled monarchists.

A disillusioned Kemp subsequently sought adventure in the Small-Scale Raiding Force (SSRF) in a series of cross-Channel raids, and then in postings in the Balkans, Poland and finally Asia. By the time Dr Martínez Alonso had finished his training, the Wehrmacht was embroiled in the battle for Stalingrad (Volgograd) and the Eighth Army had joined up with the Operation *Torch* forces and expelled Rommel from North Africa. Churchill had meanwhile made his famous speech claiming that victory at Alamein was 'maybe the end of the beginning'. By early 1943, the final and irrevocable defeat of the German Army in North

Africa and the setbacks on the Eastern Front diverted attention away from the Iberian Peninsula and Gibraltar ceased to represent a military priority. Martínez Alonso declined to pursue his commando career in other theatres and subsequently returned to his duties at Queen Mary's Hospital.

Antonio Grande and his fellow Spaniards were informed at the end of 1943 that the British authorities had determined that any possibility of Franco entering the war had disappeared. They ordered his unit disbanded and thus put an end to Grande's dream 'to return to Spain and liberate all the men and women from Franco's Fascist Dictatorship'.[18] Unfortunately for his team, this dream had never been shared by the British government or the SOE; 'regime change' was not part of their remit. At the beginning of the war, in his famous 'Blood, toil, tears, and sweat' address to Parliament, Churchill declared his policy was 'to wage war' and his aim 'Victory. Victory at all costs'. Just as the British prime minister had no compunction in dealing with Stalin, so he had no qualms about taking advantage of a fascist despot, whatever the price paid by the Spanish people. Newly promoted Sergeant Antonio Grande returned to the Royal Pioneer Corps and thus played his part in the build-up to D-Day and beyond.

In the end, the Germans did not launch an offensive against Gibraltar. Nevertheless, throughout the winter and spring months of 1941, the threat was real. As early as August 1940, Admiral Canaris (chief of the Abwehr) had begun a series of reconnaissance tours of the Algericas area in the company of General Agustín Muñoz Grandes, the commander of the Campo de Gibraltar military region. The Wehrmacht drew up detailed plans for the occupation of the Rock, which included a preliminary artillery attack in coordination with strategic bombing by a Stuka squadron, the landing of seaborne and airborne troops, and an infantry assault across the border with Spain. Muñoz Grandes is also understood to have delivered a Spanish plan of operations to Franco, in which the Germans would only supply support and reinforcements if the Spanish failed to take the objective themselves.[19] The British responded to the danger by evacuating all civilians not directly involved in vital supply and logistics services, and by reinforcing the garrison. They improved the anti-aircraft defence system and laid mines at the entrance to the colony. They also commissioned the Royal Canadian Engineer Company to complete work on a vast network of caves and tunnels within the Rock (approximately thirty miles in total – longer than the road system in the colony) to act as 'an alternative city, with power plant, water storage, hospital and living conditions for siege conditions'.[20] Nevertheless, it seems implausible that the forces deployed in Gibraltar could have successfully defended the colony against a full-scale attack by the Wehrmacht.

Muñoz Grandes's claim that his troops could take Gibraltar in twenty minutes was undoubtedly optimistic. The estimation of Major-General Mason-MacFarlane, the deputy-governor of the colony,[*] that enemy troops would have needed twenty hours to overpower the Rock's defences was probably more realistic.[21] Regardless of the precautionary measures taken to resist an assault, it was clear to the British government, and military and civil authorities, that given the overwhelming superiority of the enemy forces that Franco and Hitler would be able to deploy against Gibraltar, the only viable option to protect their position in the western Mediterranean was prevention. Aware that the British would be unable to offer anything but token support for Spain should the Germans launch a hostile invasion across the Pyrenees, Churchill nevertheless understood that it was strategically vital to convince Franco of the advantages of neutrality and of the dangers of military alignment with the Axis.

Hitler expected gratitude for his huge contribution to Franco's triumph in Spain, and insisted that the Caudillo's regime was unlikely to survive an Axis defeat. Franco, on the other hand, was a difficult leader to read. It was said of him that as a good *Gallego* (born in Ferrol, Galicia in 1892), if he was caught on a ladder, it was impossible to know whether he was going up or coming down. It is unlikely that he was swayed by one single factor when he opted for non-belligerency and then neutrality. He and his military hierarchy were aware of the devastation suffered by Spain during the Civil War and the state of unreadiness of the country and its armed forces for a new conflict. He was mindful of his dependency on Britain for essential imports and was made aware at Hendaya of the reluctance of Hitler to antagonize Vichy France by granting Spain new privileges in the Maghreb. His gratitude towards the Führer, and his sympathy with the Nazi movement were further tempered by the perils

---

[*] Lieutenant-General Mason-MacFarlane later returned to Gibraltar as governor (May 1942–February 1944).

of allowing a German garrison on Spanish territory. Finally, he could not fail to grasp the long-term consequences of the Battle of Britain.

Even after the failure of the Hendaya summit, Hitler continued to apply pressure on Franco and Serrano Suñer. On 12 November 1940, he issued *Führerbefehl* (Führer Directive) 18:

> Political measures to bring about the entry into the war of Spain in the near future have already been initiated. The aim of German intervention in the Iberian Peninsula (cover-name 'Felix') will be to drive the English from the Western Mediterranean. To this end – Gibraltar is to be captured and the Straits closed. The English are to be prevented from gaining a footing at any other point on the Iberian Peninsula or in the Atlantic Islands.

A week later he hosted Serrano Suñer at Berchtesgaden where he insisted that the Spanish government fix a date for Spain's declaration of war. In his memoirs, Serrano Suñer writes of his great discomfort as he reminded the Führer that at Hendaya, Spain had undertaken to enter the conflict when conditions allowed, not when Germany demanded. In response, he reports that Hitler told him that 'in any case, the joint operation against Gibraltar was essential […]. Just as he had said at Hendaya, the time had come for Spain to play her part'.[22]

In December, Hitler sent the enigmatic Admiral Canaris to Madrid to make a final bid to overcome Franco's refusal, and to inform him that the Germans were ready to cross the border into Spain on 10 January 1941. However, his choice of envoy was unwise: the Hispanophile admiral was disillusioned with developments inside Nazi Germany and reluctant to bully Spain into a war that he believed the Axis would not win.[23] Even when the initial date set for *Felix* had passed, the German leader still pressed Mussolini to intervene on his behalf when Il Duce met Franco and Serrano Suñer at Bordighera on 12 February 1941. In the aftermath of the meeting, the national daily newspaper *ABC* (15/02/1941) reminded its readers of the

> fraternal solidarity of Spain, Italy and Germany; the renovating and righteous nature of the Spanish revolution and the European war of liberation; and the fact that the

first clash between the new Europe and the old plutocratic democracies had taken place on the battlefields of Spain.

Nevertheless, this camaraderie and ideological unity were insufficient to persuade Franco to transition from words to actions.

In his memoirs, US Assistant Secretary of State Dean Acheson suggested that Hitler had 'wrung a promise from Franco [...] but had failed to pin him to a date'. He concluded, 'Franco continued to wriggle free, trading insults to the United States in place of fixed dates to fight Britain, moved to this as much by fear of his ally as of his enemy.'[24] Disgusted at the ingratitude of the new Spanish regime, Hitler might nevertheless have opted to ignore Franco, and to order a hostile incursion down the eastern side of Spain and the application of overwhelming force against the British colony. On three separate occasions between his capture (May 1945) and his suicide at Nuremberg (October 1946), Reichsmarschall Hermann Göring described his failure to do so as Hitler's 'greatest mistake'.[25] Nevertheless, the Führer's attention was now elsewhere. Italian failures in North Africa led, in February 1941, to *Unternehmen Sonnenblume* (Operation *Sunflower*), the deployment of a force that became known as the Afrikakorps under the command of General Erwin Rommel. Even more important for the Führer were the preparations for the ultimate test, the conquest of the USSR scheduled for the early summer.

Fears of a German attack through Spain did surface again in the planning stage of Operation *Torch* (November 1942). US strategists believed the Germans might counter the Allied landings in North Africa by deploying troops through mainland Spain and launching an offensive from the Spanish protectorate in Morocco. Indeed, General Kindelán informed Sir Samuel Hoare in the aftermath of the landings that Hitler had issued a request asking for 'the right of passage of German troops through Spain' but that Franco had refused. The Caudillo also resisted the temptation to order a general mobilization.[26]

In response to a possible German threat on either shore of the Straits of Gibraltar, the British had kept active the option of Operation *Pilgrim* (the invasion of the Canary Islands). The Allied command also sanctioned preparations for an invasion of the Moroccan protectorate and an area of southern Spain around the area of Gibraltar (Operation *Backbone*). In addition, the plan made provision for the infiltration of agents commissioned to gather intelligence and coordinate covert operations with local underground opposition units (Operation *Banana*). According to OSS officer Donald Downes, who was entrusted with enlisting operatives for the clandestine mission, *Banana* agents were to:

> Open contact with anti-Franco republican elements in Spain and in exile, with a view to organizing a partisan movement to operate behind Spanish–German lines as soon as the Germans enter Spain, prepare to sabotage railways, airfields, bridges, etc. etc., to impede the transfer of any great force into Africa.[27]

Downes also describes how, with the help of Julio Álvarez del Vayo (Negrín's foreign minister) and the Basque president-in-exile, José Antonio Aguirre, he had first recruited a number of Spanish Republican veterans in the USA. He subsequently transferred to North Africa and searched for more volunteers in the French concentration camps, which he denounced as 'torture holes which compared in horror and inhumanity with Buchenwald, Dachau and Mauthausen'.[28] Although various agents were successfully infiltrated and Downes was able to create a small clandestine network in southern Spain, the operation was swiftly dismantled by the Spanish secret service – six men were killed in a police raid and seven were detained and executed. According to Downes, Ambassador Hayes was forced to make an apology to Franco's government and to offer an undertaking that the Americans would desist from any further subversive activities on the Iberian Peninsula.[29] Operation *Backbone* would ultimately prove to be the closest the Allies ever came to military intervention in Spain.

Hitler's failure to occupy Spain and Gibraltar, especially before his invasion of Russia, proved to be a costly strategic mistake. Counter-factual history has focused on what might have happened had he implemented Operation *Felix*, and had the Germans expelled the British from the western end of the Mediterranean. Just as Göring claimed, there can be little doubt that such a development would have tipped the balance against Britain not only in North Africa but also in the naval war in both the Mediterranean and the Atlantic.

However, there is another question. Fortuitously or not, Franco cheated Hitler and by so doing secured Britain's position in a territory that the Spanish state claimed as its own and that was the single enclave on mainland Europe still hostile to the Axis. If Hitler had not intervened in support of the military insurgency in July 1936, it is quite possible that the Republic would have stifled the revolt and imprisoned Franco and his adherents. If so, when/if the Wehrmacht had reached the Pyrenees in 1940, instead of a pro-Axis fascist Spain, the military commanders would have been faced with a weakened, poorly armed, democratic country. It seems improbable that the Führer would have shown the same deference to the Second Republic as he did to the churlish Generalísimo.

Chapter 14

Con la camisa nueva

Hitler's approach to the conquest of Europe had been largely pragmatic and opportunistic, taking what he could when he could. He was able to rearm, reoccupy the Rhineland, carry out the Anschluss and take over Czechoslovakia without a war. Before launching his attack on Poland, he made an alliance with the Russians that forestalled any genuine attempt by the France and Britain to defend peace through collective security. Until July 1936, Spain had been peripheral to his ambitions, but the overthrow of the Soviet Union was central to his plans for a new world order and it is unlikely that he thought of the Molotov–Ribbentrop Pact of Non-Aggression as anything more than an expedient precaution until France and Britain had been defeated.

On 22 June 1941, the German armed forces launched Operation *Barbarossa* and crossed the border into the USSR. Apart from his almost mystical pursuit of *Lebensraum*, and his belief in the racial inferiority of the Slavs, the Führer despised Russia as the homeland of Marxism. However, Hitler had miscalculated; if defeat in the Battle of Britain proved to be a major setback in his plans for world domination, his attack on Russia was a pivotal point at which the ultimate defeat of Germany became viable. If the victory of the Eighth Army at El Alamein was 'the end of the beginning', Nazi defeats at Stalingrad and Kursk were almost certainly 'the beginning of the end'. The Germans had seriously underestimated the human, military and industrial capacity of the Soviets. Despite spectacular successes in the opening weeks and months, they failed to take Moscow (October 1941–January 1942) and Leningrad (1941–4), were driven back at Stalingrad (August 1942–February 1943), and were outmanoeuvred at the crucial tank battle at Kursk (summer of 1943).

Furthermore, Hitler had failed to eliminate his last enemy on the Western Front. Britain remained undefeated and available as a base for operations in the European theatre once, 'in God's good time', the USA intervened. After Pearl Harbor, Hitler compounded his error by declaring war on the Americans (11 December 1941) and providing Roosevelt with a justification for the 'Germany first' or 'Europe first' strategy.

Nevertheless, in the spring of 1941, Stalin, like Chamberlain before him, apparently believed he could trust Hitler, and as the Germans turned their military power against the Red Army, the Russian leader was thrown into a profound depression. But even more telling of Hitler's personality and strategy was his willingness to betray his own ideological allies. The Molotov–Ribbentrop non-aggression treaty had been a direct breach of the Anti-Comintern Pact negotiated by Germany and Japan in 1936, and signed by Italy (1937) and Spain (1937). If the deal between Nazi Germany and the Soviet Union proved traumatic and divisive for the Communist movement, it also bewildered many on the extreme right for whom Marxism was an abomination.

Operation *Barbarossa* restored the natural balance, and reassured those communists and fascists whose trust in their mission had been undermined. For Franco, it offered a providential low-risk opportunity to demonstrate his loyalty and gratitude to the Führer while avoiding a declaration of war on Britain. It also reignited the fervour of the Falange at home.

José Antonio Primo de Rivera, the founder of the movement, had distrusted Franco and suspected he was little more than an authoritarian ultra-conservative whose aim was to preserve traditionalist values at the expense of the Falange's plan for social revolution. According to George Orwell, Franco's aim was 'not so much to impose Fascism, as to restore feudalism'.[1] In a final interview with US journalist Jay Allen in the prison of Alicante, where he was held by the local Republican authorities, José Antonio claimed that if Franco won, he would probably find himself in another prison in a few months.[2] Franco was equally suspicious of a radical organization that threatened the privileges of the ruling elites and, determined to consolidate his own position, he resisted attempts to rescue José Antonio from gaol in Alicante, where he was subsequently executed in the early months of the Civil War. The Falange chief thus joined the list of Franco's rivals who came to untimely/timely deaths: General Balmes (shooting incident, a day before the military insurrection of July 1936), General Sanjurjo (aircraft accident, July 1936) and later General Mola (aircraft accident, June 1937).

Having rid himself of a potential opponent, the Caudillo was then able to tame the Falange, while taking full propaganda use of the José Antonio cult that arose after his death. He united the party with mainstream monarchists and Carlists in a new organization: the Falange Española Tradicionalista y de las Juntas de Ofensiva Nacional Sindicalista (FET y de las JONS – Traditionalist Spanish Phalanx and the Committees of National Syndicalist Offensive) which later became known as the *Movimiento* (the Movement). In one fell swoop Franco armed himself with a single party to articulate his policies, to integrate and thus dilute and manipulate the radical ideals of the Falange, and to establish a privileged political caste through which he could share the spoils of war and reward those loyal to him. In the aftermath of the Civil War, Franco took great pains to balance the power of the Falange, the armed forces, the Church and the Monarchists. The Falange diehards (especially the 'Old Shirts' – those who had joined before July 1936) were gradually side-lined in the political arena and their influence restricted to the media and social questions (education and welfare).

However, the invasion of the USSR restored faith in the anti-Bolshevik credentials of the Wehrmacht and provided ideologically committed fascists with a new quest and the opportunity to raise their profile and prestige at home. Ramón Serrano Suñer, minister of foreign affairs and president of the Falange, immediately seized his chance to put himself at the front of a wave of enthusiasm that swiftly mobilized the extreme right in Madrid. In an interview with German Ambassador von Stohrer, Suñer offered to send an expeditionary force of Spanish volunteers to fight side by side with their German comrades. On 24 June, he addressed a massive spontaneous demonstration from the balcony of the Falange headquarters in Calle de Alcalá and declared that 'Russia is guilty!' In his unscripted speech, he blamed the Russians for the Civil War, the execution of José Antonio and the deaths of countless Falange comrades.

In a BBC broadcast at 9 o'clock on 22 June, Churchill had reiterated his own anti-communism, but insisted that nothing should divert the struggle in which Britain had stood alone for one year:

> We have but one aim, one single, irrevocable purpose. We are resolved to destroy Hitler and every vestige of the Nazi régime. [...] Any man or state who fights on against Nazidom will have our aid. Any man or state who marches with Hitler is our foe. [...] It follows therefore that we shall give whatever help we can to Russia and the Russian people.

Sir Samuel Hoare summed up the British position in Spain: 'We had suddenly become the allies of the government that to almost every Spaniard who was not in prison or exile appeared as antichrist.'[3] Significant numbers of student activists at the Madrid demonstration abandoned the rally and marched on the British embassy in Calle Fernando el Santo where they repeatedly chanted '*Gibraltar español*' and stoned the delegation. The ambassador was understandably outraged by this 'carefully organized riot' – he claimed that the protestors were provided with a wagonful of stones as munitions, that a German film crew was in position to record the event, and that the Spanish police that had been entrusted with guarding the embassy compound had discreetly disappeared prior to the attack. He also describes how the British troops on guard duty were reinforced by the refugees who had been given asylum within the grounds and who were 'burning for the chance of a battle with the enemy'.[4] In his own memoirs, Serrano Suñer refutes the popular legend that when he offered the British ambassador greater protection, Hoare responded, 'Instead of sending me more guards, I'd rather you just sent me fewer students.'[5]

For both military and political reasons, the Spanish government opted for a volunteer force under the leadership of professional officers (above the rank of second lieutenant) and technical staff (sappers, signals corps, etc.) recruited from the Spanish Army. Franco thus sought to guarantee military competence while balancing the political rivalries and jealousies of the Falange and the army. As a further compromise, Franco selected General Agustín Muñoz Grandes as commander of the division, an anti-monarchist officer who sympathized with the ideals of the Falange. A bonus for the Caudillo was Múnoz Grandes's personal antagonism towards Serrano Suñer, whose thirst for power had unsettled his brother-in-law. The public announcement that a volunteer division force (División Española de Voluntarios, or DEV) was to be deployed in Russia was met with enthusiasm throughout Spain and recruitment centres opened immediately. Within days, the authorities had completed the initial call: 641 officers, 1,887 NCOs and technicians, and 15,918 infantrymen (total: 18,446).[6] As per Spanish military protocol, the division was divided into four regiments, each under the command of a colonel. Their uniforms consisted of a red beret (in honour of the Carlist movement), the blue shirt of the Falange, and the standard khaki shorts/trousers and black boots of the Spanish Army. The visual predominance of the Falange shirt meant that the DEV became known almost immediately as the División Azul (Blue Division).[7]

In the third week of July, officers and men were transported by train to the Grafenwöhr camp in Bavaria for military training. At some stations en route through France, the various convoys of recruits were greeted by hostile groups (including Spanish refugees) hurling insults and stones.[8] Once in Germany, the DEV set up a base camp at Hof, near Grafenwöhr, to coordinate supplies, medical services and reserves. The division was formally integrated into the German Army (Heer) as Division 250, and the four regiments were reduced to three in order to adjust to German organizational demands. They were provided with new, standard-issue Wehrmacht uniforms of field-grey with an identifying red and yellow patch under the legend *España* on the sleeve.

On 31 July, following a review of the division and a Mass, the officers and men of the DEV swore an oath of allegiance to the Führer. The only concession made by the Germans was that it should be clear that the loyalty to Hitler referred exclusively to the Eastern Front:

> Do you swear before God and on your honour as Spaniards, absolute obedience to the Supreme Commander of the German Armed Forces, Adolf Hitler, in the struggle against Bolshevism, and that you will fight as courageous soldiers, willing to lay down your lives at any point in the fulfillment of this oath?

General Franco had a reputation for being cautious, stubborn and yet at the same time unpredictable. He had resisted all efforts by the leaders of the Third Reich to persuade him to commit to war on the side of the Axis on their terms. The invasion of the USSR had now provided him with the means to establish a 'two-war' or 'two-front' policy, by which he could express his gratitude to Hitler and appease the most energetic Germanophiles at home by joining the great anti-Communist crusade while avoiding direct confrontation with the British. However, at the very moment that he seemed to have solved the conundrum of how to demonstrate his commitment to the Nazi cause on the Eastern Front without committing himself to a dangerous adventure against the British in the west, he chose to make an extraordinary gesture which once more threw into doubt his intentions.

On 17 July, to mark the fifth anniversary of the military uprising against the Republic, he delivered an address to the Consejo Nacional de la Falange (Falange National Council) in which he warned the USA against any intervention in Europe, and declared that the Allies had failed in their approach to the conflict and had lost the war. He congratulated the German Army on leading 'the battle for which Europe and Christianity have for so many years longed', and celebrated the fact that shortly 'the blood of our youth is to mingle with that of our comrades of the Axis as an expression of firm solidarity.'[9] At a stroke, he thus irritated the two 'Anglo-Saxon' powers on whose goodwill he depended for food and fuel supplies, and encouraged Hitler to reconsider the feasibility of greater Spanish participation in the Axis war effort.

On 21 August, the DEV commenced its journey to the front. They had been led to believe they were to link up with Army Group Centre and would take part in the Nazi's triumphant entry into Moscow. They were therefore anxious to set out as quickly as possible to ensure they arrived before the war was over. The division was transported by train to three major staging posts: Treuburg (in East Prussia, today Olecko in Poland), Suwalki (Poland) and Grodno (Poland, today Belarus)[10]. There were reports in Grodno of rising tension between Spanish and German troops and officers. The members of the DEV were particularly unhappy about the Wehrmacht diet which appeared to consist of cold meats, sausage and *sauerkraut*. The Germans were offended by the lack of discipline of their new comrades and their untidiness and lack of respect for the uniform. Worse was the Spaniards' refusal to adapt their behaviour to the strict protocols of Nazi racial policies: they continued to fraternize with Jewish and Polish women despite threats from the German officers and were antagonized by the brutality of the Nazis towards POWs, particularly the Poles, whom the Spanish did not identify as enemies.[11]

Either because the Wehrmacht lacked transport or because there were some in the German armed forces that questioned the Spaniards' readiness for combat, the non-motorized sections of the division were required to embark on the next stage of their quest on foot. They set out on a 1,000-kilometre march through Byelorussia (Belarus). However, having passed Minsk on the road to Smolensk, they received orders that they were no longer to support the 9th Army of Army Group Centre, but were instead to march north to reinforce the 16th Army of Army Group North under the command of Field Marshal Wilhelm Ritter von Leeb in the campaign against Leningrad (today St. Petersburg).

Hitler had reportedly scheduled a victory banquet at the Astoria Hotel (Saint Isaac's Square) which he planned to follow by issuing an order that the city of Leningrad be 'wiped off the face of the Earth'.

However, the Germans failed to break the defensive systems dug by the population and the Führer eventually decided to halt plans for an all-out offensive against the city. Instead, with the support of the Finnish Army that had attacked southward to regain territory lost in the Winter War of 1939/40, he ordered the Wehrmacht to lay siege to it, to starve and freeze its garrison and civilian population into surrender, and to raze the city to the ground by artillery and aerial bombardment.[12]

In the autumn of 1941, the DEV reached Novgorod and was deployed on a fifty-kilometre front along the River Volkhov and the banks of Lake Ilmen. Thus began their role in the near 900-day blockade of Leningrad – possibly the greatest test of human endurance of the entire war. On 12 October (*Día de la Raza/Día de la Hispanidad* – Columbus Day), the Spanish troops made their first contact with the enemy as the combined Spanish/German forces then launched an attack across the River Volkhov in order to establish a bridgehead on the eastern bank. The offensive failed, and on 19 December the 250 Division was ordered to retreat back across the river. Nevertheless, in the face of substantial Soviet superiority in numbers and weaponry, the Spanish impressed the Germans with their courage and discipline under fire. According to Martin Borman's records, on the night of 4 January 1942, Hitler told his special guest, Josef 'Sepp' Dietrich (commander of Leibstandarte SS Adolf Hitler – Hitler's personal guard):

> the Spanish are a crew of ragamuffins. They regard a rifle as an instrument that should not be cleaned under any pretext. Their sentries exist only in principle. They don't take up their posts, or, if they do take them up, they do so in their sleep. When the Russians arrive, the natives have to wake them up. But the Spaniards have never yielded an inch of ground. One can't imagine more fearless fellows. They scarcely take cover. They flout death. I know in any case, that our men are always glad to have Spaniards as neighbors in their sector.[13]

Indeed, the fighting resolve displayed by the DEV was a reminder to Hitler of what the Wehrmacht might expect should it undertake the invasion of Spain prior to an attack on Gibraltar without the consent of the regime.

Days later, the newly created ski-patrol unit performed the most heroic of the exploits of the DEV. A battalion of 543 German troops had been cut off by forces of the Red Army in Vsvad, at the southern end of Lake Ilmen, and on 10 January 1942, the company of 205 skiers under the command of Captain José Ordás was ordered to relieve them. Through blizzards, in temperatures of -50°C, and under constant attack from detachments of the Red Army, it took the patrol eleven days to cross the frozen lake to the Germans' position. Half the Spaniards suffered severe frostbite, and doctors were later forced to amputate both legs of some of the worst casualties. Nevertheless, on 21 January, the Spanish unit made contact with the German survivors and the combined force was able to fight its way back to base. Only twelve of the men who had set out on the mission remained.[14] The survivors were decorated by the Germans with the Iron Cross, Captain Ordás was awarded the Military Medal by Franco and his company received the Collective Military Medal.

In the context of Spain's position in the world war, it was impossible to separate military and political questions. The courage of the men of the DEV reflected on their commander, the Germanophile, pro-Falange General Muñoz Grandes. His involvement and engagement with his troops made him popular both at the front and at home, and the loyalty of his men and his prestige as an officer was quickly becoming a cause of anxiety for Franco. The situation was compounded by the growing respect of Hitler for a man who was an excellent leader of men in combat but also closely aligned with Nazi principles. The Führer had tired of Franco's ingratitude and had lost all faith in Serrano Suñer, who at the outset of the war had been identified as Germany's ally in Madrid, but had subsequently become as reluctant as his brother-in-law to commit to the Axis.

Hitler further despised the new regime's National Catholicism, a pale version of National Socialism, strongly linked to the Church, willing to compromise with the monarchists and deeply reactionary in its approach to social change. Indeed, it became increasingly clear that the Führer and the Caudillo were united only in their anti-communism, nationalism and brutal authoritarianism. Hitler quickly came to see in Muñoz Grandes a like-minded leader, a man who could overthrow the 'parson-ridden regime'[15] in Madrid, declare war on Britain (and the USA after December 1941) and deliver Gibraltar to the Wehrmacht.

The two men met first on 1 September 1941 when the Spanish officer made a courtesy visit to Hitler at the Wolfsschanze (Wolf's Lair) at Rastenburg before taking command of his troops on the ground. By the following summer, the deeds of the DEV had led Franco to the conclusion that the time had come to replace Muñoz Grandes with a less 'independent' officer. He subsequently announced the appointment of General Emilio Esteban Infantes as new commanding officer of the division. On 16 June, the general arrived at Hof and took the oath of loyalty to Hitler. However, the Führer requested the transfer be delayed and on 11 July held a second meeting with Muñoz Grandes at the Wolf's Lair where it appears the men conspired, if not to overthrow Franco, at least to wrest sufficient of his power to facilitate the implementation of pro-Nazi policies both in foreign and domestic affairs.

Once the Germans were satisfied that Muñoz Grandes could be more useful to them in Madrid than in Russia, they expedited the transfer of command to Esteban Infantes. At a final meeting in Rastenburg, on 13 December 1942, Hitler conferred on Muñoz Grandes the Oak Leaves to the Knight's Cross of the Iron Cross. His main anxiety now was the reaction of the Spanish government to the Allied landings in North Africa (Operation *Torch*, November 1942). According to the two US military historians Lewis A. Tambs and Gerald R. Kleinfeld, Muñoz Grandes assured Hitler that Spain would resist an Anglo-American invasion of the Iberian Peninsula but insisted that it was crucial that the Germans maintain their position in Tunisia.[16] Indeed, any attempts to manoeuvre Spain closer to Germany would depend on the capacity of the Wehrmacht to defend its position in North Africa and to launch a decisive offensive in Russia. Over the next few months, as the tide of war turned against the Reich, the pro-Nazi lobby in Spain would automatically become less influential. Significantly, Franco ordered the loosening of the iron grip the Falange held over the media, which had so offended Sir Samuel Hoare, and allowed the press to include press releases from London and Washington.

In August 1942, following a request from Muñoz Grande, the DEV had been transferred north to the Pushkin area on the outskirts of Leningrad to play an even more active role in resisting the attempts of the Red Army to lift the blockade. Esteban Infantes proved to be a highly competent staff officer, an able manager of supplies and logistics, who won the respect of the German high command, but lacked the charisma of his predecessor and failed to establish the same rapport with his troops. The surrender of the 6th Army at Stalingrad at the end of January 1943, meanwhile raised the morale of the Red Army and allowed for a new offensive in the north to relieve Leningrad. The DEV continued to fight with great distinction and in February played a crucial role in thwarting Operation *Polyarnaya Zvezda* (Operation *Polar Star*) – a pincer attack by the Northwestern, Volkhov and Leningrad Fronts of the Red Army against the German Army Group North designed to open road and rail communications between the besieged city and Moscow.

On 10 February, the Russians launched a fierce two-hour artillery bombardment on the Spanish lines at Krasny Bor, which were then overrun by tank and infantry divisions. Although outnumbered and despite appalling losses, the Spaniards were able to hold the southern area of the town and, using their genius for improvisation, attacked Russian tanks with hand grenades and Molotov cocktails. The Russians were eventually held, and after three days of vicious fighting the sector was stabilized and the offensive was suspended. At the Battle of Krasny Bor, the DEV lost 1,127 men killed, 1,035 wounded and 91 missing in action.[17] The Red Army had failed to make a breakthrough and the siege of Leningrad would last another year. However, elsewhere the Germans were losing ground.

In May 1943, the remaining Axis forces in North Africa were forced to surrender to the Allies. In July, the Red Army won the decisive tank battle at Kursk and an Anglo-American force invaded Sicily. Mussolini was deposed at the end of the month and the Allies landed in Italy in September. Franco now accepted that the most probable outcome of the war was an Allied victory, although he did not rule out the possibility of persuading the British and Americans to participate in a joint anti-Communist crusade against the USSR. In September he informed his government of his decision to bow to Allied pressure to withdraw the division and to replace it with the much smaller Legión Española de Voluntarios (Spanish Volunteer Legion). The gradual 'redeployment' began in the second week of October, and the last Spanish troops abandoned the Leningrad front on 17 October. The Legión Azul (Blue Legion), as it inevitably became known was designed to be the size of a regiment, with 103 officers, 530 NCOs and 1,500 men. It was assigned to the 121 Division in Liuban, but had little time to adjust to its new circumstances before a renewed Russian offensive in mid-January 1944 led to a generalized and desperate retreat. The legion was left without transport and was forced to fight westward through territory increasingly under the control of partisan groups.

On 20 February, aware that the legion had no role left to play in Russia and would be of greater use in Spain in the case of an Allied attack on the peninsula, Hitler preempted Franco's decision to withdraw the legion

Franco meets Hitler at Hendaya
(1940). (akg-images)

Franco and Hitler inspect
German troops at Hendaya.
(akg-images/ClassicStock)

Franco and Serrano (left) meet Mussolini (right) at Bordighera (1941). (akg-images/
Fototeca Gilardi)

Franco meets Pétain at Montpellier (1941). (akg-images/TT News Agency)

Chamberlain's war cabinet: Chamberlain (centre front), Sir Samuel Hoare (front, second from right), Churchill (back, middle) and Eden (back, second from right). (akg-images)

President Azaña (left) and Prime Minister Negrín of the Second Republic. (akg-images/World History Archive)

Figueres Castle. (Author)

Last HQ of the Republican government on Spanish soil – at Elda. (Author)

Memorial to Archibald Dickson, port of Alicante. (Author)

Former Casa Johnstone (large white building with pool) amidst new tourist development at Tossa de Mar. (Author)

The grave of Antonio Machado at Collioure. (Author)

Spanish refugees crossing the border at Le Perthus (1939). (akg-images/Album /Oronoz)

Spanish refugees in French concentration camp (1939). (akg-images/Album/Oronoz)

Beach at Argelès-sur-Mer today. (Author)

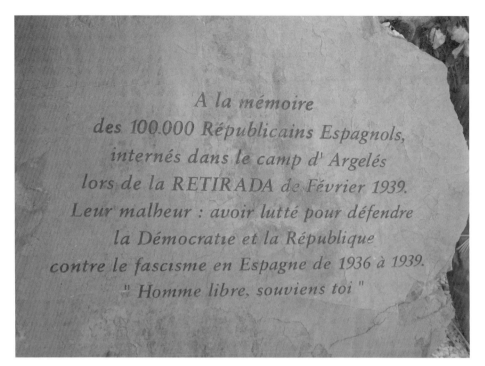

Above and below: Memorial at Argelès. (Author)

SS *Sinaia*, used to evacuate Spanish refugees from France. (akg-images/arkivi)

The Maternity Hospital at Elne. (Author)

Fraternization on the French border between Spanish and German officials. (akg-images/Sammlung Berliner Verlag/Archiv)

Survivors of the French garrison at Bir Hakeim approaching British lines (1942). (akg-images)

St. Michel Prison, Toulouse. (Author)

Enthusiastic support for the first volunteers of the Blue Division as they leave for the Eastern Front (1942). (akg-images/Sammlung Berliner Verlag/Archiv)

Leningrad war memorial marking the 900 days of the siege. (Author)

Juan Pujol García. *Garbo* – the super-agent. (Wikimedia commons)

(48008) WT.P.2250/2808 20,000 3/53 A.& E.W.LTD. Gp.685

LY.　　●　　**Graves Registration Report Form.**

COUNTRY: ITALY.

~~COMMUNE.~~

REPORT No. :　　　　　SCHEDULE No. : 22.

PLACE OF BURIAL : MILAN WAR CEMETERY

Land belongs to

Certified complete and correct.

The following are buried here :—

Signature _____　　　　Date _____

P.R.G.	No. and Rank	Initials, Name and Honours	Unit	Date of Death	For works use
4.E.12.	5438482　Pte.	W.C.　PETERS	1st Bn. Duke of Cornwall's Light Inf.	7. 3.43.	C.H.
4.E.13.	1105468　Gnr.	W.　BOWMAN	28th Fld.Rgt.R.A.	21.10.42.	C.H.
4.E.14.	868087　Gnr.	G.A.　TOMLINSON	2nd Royal Horse Art.	29.12.42.	C.H.
4.E.15.	T/267893 Dvr.	F.A.　BLANDFORD	R.A.S.C.	25.11.42.	C.H.
Jt.Gr. { 5.A.1. {	1192341　Sgt. (F/Eng)	W.G.　TROWBRIDGE	50 Sqdn.R.A.F.(VR)	16.7.43.	C.H.
	536891　Sgt. (A/G)	R.A.W.　WILKINSON	50 Sqdn. R.A.F.	16. 7.43.	C.H.
5.A.2.	1454431　Sgt. (A/G)	R.G.W.　GOFF	R.A.F. 50 Sqdn	16. 7.43.	C.H.
5.A.3.	ME/13041866 Pte.	R.　BRUCE	Pioneer Corps & Spec.Air Service Regt. A.A.C.	21. 4.45.	C.H.
5.A.4.	137803　Lt.	J.A.　RICCOMINI (M.B.E.,M.C.)	Spec.Air Service A.A.C.	27. 3.45.	C.H.
5.A.5.	328895V　Lt. (Pilot)	E.W.　ROSENSTEIN	185 Sqdn.S.A.A.F.	2. 4.45.	Jew. C.H.
5.A.6.	3316568　Cpl.	S.　BOLDEN (M.M.)	2nd S.A.S.Rgt.A.A.C.	27. 3.45.	C.H.
5.A.7.	1024879　Gnr.	J.G.M.　BURDETT	72nd Fld.Rgt.,R.A.	7.10.43.	C.H.
5.A.8.	147669　F/O. (Nav)	W.H.　ROGERS	23 Sqdn.R.A.F.(VR)	6. 2.44.	C.H.
5.A.9.	1473225　Gnr.	A.　HIND	81/25 Lt.A.A. Regt. R.A.	26. 4.43.	C.H.
5.A.10.		EMPTY GRAVE			

Grave report of Robert Bruce (Justo Balerdi). (with permission of Commonwealth War Graves Commission)

French Resistance ID card of Cristino Garcia. (Archivos Históricos del Partido Comunista de España)

US troops liberate the camp at Mauthausen. (Wikimedia commons: Cpl Donald R. Ornitz, US Army)

Citizens of Paris welcome La Nueve, the Spanish Republicans who spearheaded the liberation of the city (1944). (Wikimedia commons: blog's owner/CC BY-SA [https://creativecommons.org/licenses/by-sa/4.0])

The Pyrenees at the Bonaigua Pass with the Val d'Aran flag used today. (Author)

San Andreu church at Salardú, crucial in the fighting in the Val d'Aran. (Author)

Hospital Varsovia (today part of Hôpital Ducuing), Toulouse. (Author)

and ordered its repatriation. The most dedicated of the volunteers who still refused to abandon their mission enlisted in the Waffen-SS (the 'armed' or fighting units of the SS). Some who had already returned to Spain made their way back to occupied Western Europe and volunteered for service in the German Army. The most famous of this band of fervent anti-communists was Miquel Ezquerra who rose to the rank of *Hauptsturmführer* (captain) and together with some 300 other Spanish volunteers fought in Normandy, the Ardennes and once more against the Red Army in Berlin.

In a speech to his general staff and officers in Sevilla in February 1942, Franco had insisted in his faith in a German victory but boasted that should Berlin ever be threatened by the Red Army, it would not be a division of volunteers who went to fight alongside the Nazis, 'but that a million Spaniards would offer themselves'. The changing fortunes of war meant that in the end it was a few hundred.

The division and legion were not the only Spanish units that Franco committed to the Nazi cause on the Eastern Front. The Escuadrilla Azul (Blue Squadron) consisted of five rotating squadrons of pilots from the Spanish Air Force who volunteered for duty in the USSR (1941–3). Each squadron consisted of approximately twenty pilots, many of whom had seen service alongside the German Condor Legion during the Civil War. Flying Messerschmitt Bf 109s and Focke-Wulf fighter-bombers they provided support for Army Group Centre bombing campaigns. They shot down a total of 156 Soviet aircraft and lost twenty-two pilots killed or missing in action.[18] Approximately 150 members of the *Sección Feminina* (Women's Section) of the Falange also volunteered to provide nursing services to the wounded of the DEV.

Approximately 47,000 men saw service in the Blue Division/Legion between 1941 and 1943. Some 4,500 were killed and 8,000 wounded. Casualties include another 7,800 men suffering from various illness and 1,600 suffering from frostbite. Approximately 300 were taken prisoner by the Red Army and disappeared into the Gulag system (Soviet corrective camps). The survivors were not returned to Spain until 1954.[19]

The division played a not insignificant role in prolonging the siege of Leningrad over 900 days (September1941–January 1944). They also fought side by side with troops who actively applied the terms of the Barbarossa Decree – protocols defining how the Wehrmacht should deal with the civilian population in Russia – and were responsible for the extermination of Russian POWs and partisans, Jews, Romani people and mentally disabled patients. In the aftermath of the war, the USSR failed in its attempt to have General Muñoz Grandes indicted by the Nuremberg War Crimes Commission.

The city of Leningrad was finally liberated by the Red Army on 27 January 1944. At the Nuremberg trial, the USSR claimed 632,000 people died during the blockade – from the German bombardments but mainly from starvation, disease and hyperthermia. Alexander Werth, the *Sunday Times* and BBC war correspondent, who had been born in St. Petersburg and spent the war in the USSR, dismissed the figure as an underestimate. He later recalled that Shostakovich, whose Symphony No. 7 was taken as a tribute to the city, and its victory over fascism, claimed the figure was closer to 900,000.[20]

In the introduction to his own work on the siege, Harrison E. Salisbury, the *New York Times* correspondent, wrote:

> Each passing year deepens our realization of the triumph of man's spirit marked by the survival of the great city of Leningrad under the 900-day siege imposed by Hitler's legions in World War II. Nothing can diminish the achievement of the men and women who fought on despite hunger, cold, disease, bombs, shells, lack of heat or transportation in a city that seemed given over to death. The story of those days is an epic which will stir human hearts as long as mankind exists on earth.[21]

On the opposing side on the Eastern Front, although in far fewer numbers, were the exiled Republicans who found themselves in the USSR at the time of the Nazi invasion. Roque Serna Martínez, who fought for the USSR and was a member of the Comité de Veteranos de Guerra Españoles (Committee of Spanish War Veterans) estimated that approximately 800 Republicans took up arms in the 'Great Patriotic War' in defence of the one major power that had supported the Republic.[22] Anthony Beevor suggests the number was closer to 1,400.[23] Essentially these men and women were the 'war children' that had been sent to Russia during the Civil War, Communist Party loyalists who sought refuge at the end of the Civil War, party members who had been extricated from the French concentration camps, and military personnel (mostly pilots) who had been sent to the USSR for training and whose return to Spain had been precluded by the fascist victory.

The military authorities showed a certain reluctance towards Spaniards who volunteered to enlist in the regular forces of the Red Army. Apart from Soviet wariness of foreigners, there also appears to have been an understanding that Spanish personnel should be reserved for an eventual return to Spain. As a result, many of the Republican exiles chose to fight in partisan groups behind German lines.[24] Nevertheless, 125 Spanish paratroopers (119 men and six women) were accepted into the Multinational Battalion of the OMSBON (Independent Motorized Brigade for Special Operations) where they were organized as the 4th Spanish Company at the orders of Major Domingo Ungría and Capitan Pelegrín Pérez Galarza. Both men had served as officers in the Republican partisan XIV Corps during the Civil War. The company first saw action in the defence of Moscow in the winter of 1941/2. One unit was deployed as guards of the Kremlin, a mission of extraordinary significance and prestige. Once the German Army had been driven back from the Soviet capital, Spanish troops were then transferred to Ukraine and Georgia. Some saw action behind enemy lines in the siege of Stalingrad (Volgograd). Towards the end of the war, as the Wehrmacht retreated west, many joined the partisan units that were active in Poland, Czechoslovakia, Rumania, Hungary, Yugoslavia and finally in Austria and Germany.

At the outset of the German invasion, months before the División Azul was deployed on the Leningrad front, some seventy-four young Republicans in the city (many employed at the Elektrosila factory) spontaneously volunteered for service and were enlisted in the 3rd Leningrad People's Militia Regiment. By mid-September, only seven appear to have survived the initial onslaught.[25] The Soviet authorities refused to allow María Pardina Ramos (aka *Marusia*) to take part in combat missions, but she was attached to the militia as a nurse. A *madrileña*, she had served in the medical corps during the siege of the capital, before she and her brother were evacuated to the USSR. In the summer of 1941, she braved enemy fire to save the life of dozens of young men wounded in action and was ultimately awarded the Order of the Red Banner. She reportedly told a meeting of the Komsomol (Communist youth movement) that her concept of happiness was 'to have a beautiful ideal and to live and die for it'.[26] She was eventually reported missing in action in September 1941.

Captain Francisco Gullón, a veteran of the Civil War who had fought in Madrid, on the Ebro and in the final retreat from Catalonia, led a guerrilla detachment to the Novgorod Oblast in 1942 with orders to disrupt the railway services from the west which represented a vital supply route for the Wehrmacht forces besieging the city of Leningrad. The partisan force used TNT to wreck rolling stock and damage the rail infrastructure. Only three Spaniards returned from the mission, including Gullón, who died later of wounds he had received. In recognition of his service, he was awarded the Order of Lenin.

José Sandoval had joined the Fifth Regiment at the outbreak of the Civil War, and had also fought in the defence of Madrid, at the battle of the Ebro and during the withdrawal across the border in January 1939. Once in France, he was interned in the St. Cyprien concentration camp until the Communist Party arranged for his release and transfer to Moscow. In the summer of 1941, he joined a guerrilla unit and ended the war in the outskirts of Prague fighting for the liberation of Czechoslovakia (from the Nazis). He then spent the next fifteen years in exile in the USSR and Rumania working as a journalist, before the party ordered him to Madrid where he would replace the disgraced agent Jorge Semprún (aka *Federico Sánchez*) in the clandestine struggle against the dictatorship. He was detained by the secret police in April 1964, tortured and sentenced to fifteen years and three months' imprisonment. He was only released under the amnesty that followed the death of Franco.

Santiago de Paúl Nelken was the son of Margarita Nelken, art critic, feminist, writer and deputy in the Spanish Parliament (1931–9). He enlisted in the Republican Army and at the age of 18 fought at the Battle of the Ebro. Among the youngest of the officers in the defeated loyalist forces, he crossed into France in 1939, and was interned at St. Cyprien. His mother, who had been the only female deputy present at the last meeting of the Cortes in the castle at Figueres,[27] also escaped to France and was able to use her influence to secure his release. They were then safely evacuated to the USSR along with Santiago's sister, Magda. When the Germans launched Operation *Barbarossa*, he underwent artillery training and served as a lieutenant in the Red Army. He became a specialist in the use of the Katyusha, an easily transportable multiple-rocket launcher, ideal for relatively short-range saturation shelling. On 5 January 1944, at the age of 22, Nelken was killed in action in the small Ukrainian village of Mitrofanovka. His mother requested that the local authorities mark his grave with the inscription, 'Died for the USSR, for Spain and for the liberty of all peoples'.[28]

Another volunteer with a famous mother was Rubén Ruiz Ibárruri, the son of Dolores Ibárruri (La Pasionaria), who first travelled to the Soviet Union in 1935 in the company of his sister Amaya, and studied at a military aviation school. He then returned to Spain to fight for the Republic in the Civil War. In 1939, he crossed the Pyrenees and was interned at the Argelès-sur-Mer concentration camp. He was finally able to escape, and with local assistance was conveyed to the Soviet embassy in Paris where the diplomatic staff arranged for his evacuation to Moscow and a reunion with his mother and sister. Having graduated from military school, he was allowed to serve in the 1st Moscow Proletarian Division. In the early fighting that followed the Nazi invasion in July 1941, he took command of a machine-gun company near Borisov on the Berezina River and was awarded the Order of the Red Banner for his bravery in action. In the summer of 1942, having recovered from wounds suffered during the battle, he was transferred to the 35th Guards Rifle Division and returned to the front at Stalingrad. Once more in command of a machine-gun company and facing overwhelming odds, Ruiz Ibárruri was seriously wounded, but not before his men had repelled a series of enemy attacks. He died from his injuries on 3 September 1942. In 1956, he was posthumously awarded the title Hero of the Soviet Union.[29]

Three eminent officers of the Republic's high command were also allowed to serve in the Red Army, although they were restricted to non-combat roles. Enrique Lister, Juan Modesto and Antonio Cordón had exercised significant command responsibilities in the Civil War, in particular at the Battle of the Ebro. They were eventually extricated from the chaos of defeat and transferred to the USSR, where they joined the training staff at the Frunze and Voroshilov military academies. In 1943, they were promoted to the rank of general but were held in reserve for an eventual return to action in Spain. They were, however, used as advisors to Soviet forces in the Polish campaign and then to Tito's partisans in Yugoslavia.

Probably the most high-profile of the Republican cohorts who fought the Wehrmacht in the Soviet Union were the aviators. During the Civil War, several hundred pilots and navigators received training at the Kirovabad (Ganja) flying academy in Azerbaijan. The last class (of 1939) finished their course after the Civil War was over. Those that had seen active service in Spain had gained experience flying the Soviet Polikarpov I-15 biplane (Chato) and then the more modern I-16 (Mosca), the first single-seater fighter with retractable landing gear.

Nevertheless, the forty-six pilots that remained in the USSR in 1941 were denied the right to join the Soviet Air Force by military protocols, and many enlisted in the guerrilla units fighting the German rearguard. Their fortune changed however after an apparently gratuitous encounter between Alexander Osipenko and José María Bravo Fernández in Moscow in 1942. The two fighter pilots had met in Spain: Osipenko was awarded the title Hero of the Soviet Union in February 1939 for his service on behalf of the Republic. By this stage, he had been appointed commander of the fighter aircraft wing of the Soviet Air Defence Forces.

Bravo, on the other hand, had been rescued from the concentration camp at Gurs in 1939 and evacuated to the relative safety of the USSR. At the outbreak of war with Germany, he was unable to join the air force and had been fighting in a guerrilla unit in the area around the Sea of Azov. It appears he now persuaded Osipenko to reverse the ban on foreign pilots, and together with other Spanish aviators he was allowed to enlist in the Air Defence Command. The Spanish pilots did not form a separate wing or squadrons but were distributed across various fronts.

The most crucial contribution of Bravo in particular was in the air battle over Baku in defence of the Caucasus oilfields, which Hitler was so desperate to capture. Nevertheless, it is also true that his most conspicuous mission was as a member of the twenty-seven-fighter escort that accompanied Stalin to the Teheran Conference of the Big Three in November 1943. The general secretary of the Communist Party of the Soviet Union had consistently refused to fly, but was finally persuaded to take the 550-kilometre flight from Baku to the Iranian capital to meet Roosevelt and Churchill. Legend has it that on arrival at Teheran, he complained at the state of the fighter pilots' attire and asked why they were flying in their underwear. What is certainly true is that Stalin returned to the USSR by train and never flew again.

An estimated 207 Spaniards were killed in action in the service of the Soviet Union.[30] The fact that this figure appears insignificant within the context of the vast loss of life in the USSR between 1941 and 1945 (upwards of 24 million) does not diminish the courage and sacrifice of those individuals that refused to submit a second time to the forces of the Third Reich.[31]

Chapter 15

Back Entrances, Side Doors, Secret Elevators

Juan Pujol Garcia was born in Barcelona on 14 February 1912 and would become one of the most influential figures of the Allied campaign in Europe. Having taken up a post as manager of a poultry farm, he hid in Barcelona rather than enlist in the Republican Army when the Civil War broke out in July 1936. When he finally did join the ranks, he was posted to the Ebro front where he immediately deserted and fled to the Nationalist side. Apart from three weeks on the Teruel front, he then spent the rest of the Civil War in the rearguard, and in his own words, 'had managed not to fire a single bullet for either side by the time Madrid fell a few months later'.[1] He subsequently found employment as manager of the Hotel Majestic in the capital until he decided that he could not stand aside in the fight against 'the pyschopath Hitler and his band of acolytes'.[2] In his own description of Pujol, British intelligence officer Tomas Harris claimed he was also driven by a desire 'to leave Spain until the Franco regime had been overthrown'.[3] He approached the British embassy with a plan that he confessed was based 'on a medley of tangled ideas and fantasies going round and round in my head'.[4] The staff at the embassy were unimpressed by the exotic Catalan, and Pujol's attempts to speak to a senior official were rejected. According to the original records of Tomas Harris, it was in fact Pujol's wife, Araceli González, who made contact with the British consulate. The discrepancy is probably due to Pujol's later estrangement from his wife, who, in his own version, is no more than a shadowy figure who quickly disappears from the narrative. In Harris's account, she in fact played an active, even crucial, role in dealing with the British diplomatic corps.

Undeterred by the initial indifference of the British, the Pujols approached the German embassy and made contact with an Abwehr officer, named Federico. After a short stay in Lisbon, to register as a resident in Portugal and thus allow himself to travel in and out of Spain, Pujol persuaded his handler that he was due to make a visit to Britain where he would be able to gather intelligence. The Abwehr provided him with money, funds and invisible ink. However, when Pujol (or his wife) returned to the British embassy in Lisbon, armed with the evidence of their collaboration with German intelligence, their offer of help was rejected once more.

Undaunted (again), he bought a map and a Baedeker Guide of Britain and, having informed his German handler that he had settled in England, he retired to Cascais on the coast, near Estoril, with his wife and young son, Juan Fernando. He now launched his career as a freelance German spy, inventing intelligence reports from London and forwarding them to a safety deposit box in Lisbon via a 'KLM pilot' that he 'recruited' as his first agent. Prior to his departure from Lisbon, he posted the key to the box to the German embassy in Lisbon and asked them to forward his reports to Madrid.

During his short career in Portugal, working within the limits of his elementary English and almost total ignorance of British culture and traditions, he gradually established his position as an Abwehr agent. He later acknowledged that he did make mistakes. He once claimed that the diplomatic missions in London had abandoned the capital to avoid the stifling heat of an English August (1941) and were summering in Brighton. In another report, he wrote, 'There are men here (in Glasgow) who would do anything for a litre of wine.' His ignorance of the drinking habits of Scottish dockers somehow failed to alert the intelligence services in Berlin. According to MI5 records, it was fortunate 'that the Germans were equally unaware of Glaswegian drinking habits'.[5] However, they did at least begin to question the value of Pujol's information which, for obvious reasons, was lacking in detail.

Through the endeavours of the Bletchley Park network, MI5 was by now receiving decrypted ISOS (Intelligence School Oliver Strachey) German intelligence. Furthermore, committees B1(b) – responsible for intercepting enemy signals – and B1(g) – in charge of counter-espionage in the Iberian Peninsula and South America – were aware of the activities of a German agent working under the codename *Arabel*. They were particularly interested in a report transmitted to Madrid of a convoy that had left Liverpool for the beleaguered island of Malta. The Germans had taken the intelligence at face value and had deployed naval resources to hunt the ships down before they reached the Mediterranean.

Although MI5 gradually came to the conclusion that *Arabel* must be the agent that had tried to make contact through the embassies in Madrid and Lisbon, Section V (the Iberia desk) of MI6 was at first reluctant to take further measures to recruit him directly. At this point in the war, British intelligence had achieved huge successes both in terms of deciphering enemy signals and in turning German agents. It was initially thought that to work with an unknown source would mean jeopardizing the achievements of the previous months. Even among those sections of the intelligence services who did appreciate the potential of *Arabel*, inter-agency rivalries meant that while MI5 officers envisaged using him in Britain, MI6 (SIS) experts insisted he would be of more use in Portugal.

By now the Pujols had decided to try their luck with the Americans and after Germany's declaration of war on the USA (11 December 1941), they developed their contacts with the assistant naval attaché, Edward Rousseau, in Lisbon, who passed the information to his British counterparts. When, after months of prevarication, the British were finally convinced of the contribution that Pujol could make as a double agent in Britain, the question arose of how to transport Pujol and his family to London without breaking his cover. The Abwehr had established a huge presence in Lisbon and if an agent now identified Pujol leaving the country, when he claimed to have been in London since the previous July, it would undo the painstaking work of months. Gene Rossi-Gill, the top SIS agent in Portugal, made contact with the Spaniard and arranged for him to be smuggled on board a British merchant vessel on its way to Gibraltar. The newly recruited agent was received in the colony by Donald Darling (*Sunday*) who provided him with accommodation. In his memoirs, Darling provides details of the many people who stayed in his flat on the Rock, including Pat O'Leary, Jean-François Nothomb (*Franco*) of the Comète Line and the nephew of Franz von Papen (German ambassador to Turkey) who had defected from his post at the Istanbul consulate.[6] For obvious reasons, Darling makes no mention of Pujol, though he was later credited with giving him the codename *Bovril* – apparently his hot beverage of choice.

Pujol was flown on the next available Sunderland to Britain where he arrived on 25 April 1942 and was met in Plymouth by Cyril Mills of B1(a) and Tomas Harris of B1(g). Three days later, he was introduced to Desmond Bristow of MI6 who was to be responsible for his interrogation.

To his friends at V Division, Bristow described Pujol as 'a good chap with a phenomenal imagination, a good sense of humour and plenty of guts'.[7] He was finally approved by the Twenty (XX) Committee and assigned a case officer, Tomas Harris, a talented painter, art expert, and close friend of (Sir) Anthony Blunt, who was himself half-Spanish. Impressed by the acting skills with which Pujol had deceived the Germans, Mills proposed that Pujol should be rechristened *Garbo*. Over the next two years, Harris and Pujol (sometimes known collectively as *Garbo*) created and operated an extraordinary network of 22 fictitious agents around the United Kingdom which supplied the Abwehr with a vast quantity of misleading intelligence. *Garbo* was not strictly a double agent, as he had never been a bona fide German spy, but his contribution to the double-cross operations supervised by the Twenty Committee was vital to the war effort of the Allies. Throughout Operation *Torch* and the landings in Sicily and the Italian mainland, the Pujol–Harris–Twenty Committee team maintained a constant flow of apparently plausible disinformation to an ever-more-demanding Abwehr.

Garbo's work culminated in the wider Operation *Fortitude*, the vast plan of deception designed to persuade Hitler that the Allied landings in northern France (Operation *Overlord*) were to take place in the Pas de Calais, and thus draw troops and resources away from Normandy. By convincing the OKW (German High Command, Oberkommando der Wehrmacht) and Hitler that General George S. Patton's notional First US Army Group, theoretically based in Kent and Essex, would land south of Boulogne in July and lead the main thrust of the Allied forces, the intelligence services were able to disguise D-Day as a feint. Rather than send reinforcements to Normandy, Hitler held his armies east of the Seine, and by the time the Germans realized their mistake and mobilized reinforcements, the Allies had established a bridgehead. Eisenhower was then able to launch Operation *Cobra*, by which the US First Army led the breakout from Normandy in the west, while the British and Canadians engaged the brunt of the German counter-attack at Caen and contained 'the vast bulk of the German panzer formations and [...] the greatest concentration of 88mm anti-tank guns'.[8]

Garbo's role in the build-up to D-Day was to confirm the reports received in Berlin from a multitude of sources and to provide intelligence of the mustering of troops and the massing of tanks and landing craft in south-eastern England. In the first six months of 1944, the *Garbo* team sent some 500 radio messages to the Madrid offices of German intelligence.[9] They included a cocktail of information/disinformation and a series of fictionally leaked official reports on strategic planning for the liberation of Europe gathered by *Garbo*'s network of agents combined with supplementary logistics records, all suggesting the main assault on Fortress Europe would come in the Pas de Calais region in July. The most high-risk ploy was the attempt to warn Berlin of the invasion fleet on the night of 5/6 June 1944. Such intelligence was designed to consolidate *Garbo*'s credibility with the Abwehr. Unfortunately, the Madrid offices were closed and the messages were not received until next morning by which time German troops in Normandy had reported the first wave of the invasion. On D-Day+3, *Garbo* sent Madrid 'the most important report of his career'[10] in which he insisted:

> the present attack is a large-scale operation but diversionary in character for the purpose of establishing a strong bridgehead in order to draw the maximum of our reserves to the area of operations and to retain them there so as to be able to strike a blow somewhere else. [...] My opinion [...] is based on the belief that the whole of the present attack is set as a trap for the enemy to make us move all our reserves in a hurried strategical disposition which we would later regret.[11]

Fortunately, Hitler and the OKW found it easy to believe him. Not only was *Arabel* a trusted agent, but the information he transmitted appeared entirely credible and confirmed their expectations. The Pas de Calais area provided the most practical conditions for a cross-Channel offensive and if a landing were successful, the Allies would be considerably nearer the ultimate target of Berlin.

It is of course impossible to quantify exactly the impact of Operation *Fortitude*. It undoubtedly saved the lives of many thousands of US, British and Canadian servicemen. However, given the enormity of the undertaking and the huge logistic problems involved, it is even possible that without the deception plan, a more rapid response from the Germans may have foiled the invasion.

Extraordinarily, the Germans appeared to continue their trust in *Garbo* even when it became clear they had been deceived in northern France. They continued to use his network of agents to supply information on the V1 and V2 attacks on London – *Garbo* was asked to provide details of where the flying bombs landed, so that the Germans could adjust their settings in order to increase accuracy. British intelligence took advantage of the request to provide the Germans with misleading data in order to protect key targets.

For his wartime services Pujol was awarded the Iron Cross Second Class on 29 July 1944, and an MBE on 25 November 1944. The chairman of the Twenty Committee, J.C. Masterman, a keen cricketer, paid *Garbo* the greatest accolade he could when he described him as the 'Donald Bradman' of the double-cross world.[12]

Chapter 16

Ubique

On 24 August 1943 General Leclerc's Free French troops in North Africa were redeployed as the Deuxième Division Blindée (2nd Armoured Division). A light armoured division, the Deuxième was equipped by the US Army with Sherman tanks, half-tracks, armoured cars, bazookas and anti-tank weapons. According to the testimony of a recruit to the new unit, it attracted many 'spontaneous transfers' from Spaniards serving with the French Foreign Legion in North Africa who deserted rather than endure any further Legion discipline.[1] Other recruits included Republican veterans who escaped from the internment camps in Morocco and Algeria, where they had been held since 1940.

The 9th Company of the 3rd Battalion (Régiment de Marche du Tchad) was made up almost exclusively of Spanish soldiers. It was put under the command of Captain Raymond Dronne, who spoke a little Spanish and later claimed every other officer was too afraid of the Spanish to accept the post.[2] The company immediately became known as *La Nueve* (The Nine). Speaking of 'his Spaniards', Dronne later claimed that

> They lacked military spirit, some were even 'anti-military', but they were magnificent soldiers, brave and battle-hardened warriors. They (some at a very young age) had been thrown into the horrors and miseries of the Spanish War. They had suffered a lot, in Spain, then in France and in North Africa. They had committed themselves to us, they had spontaneously and voluntarily espoused our cause, because it was the cause of freedom. They were true freedom fighters.[3]

Other French officers told the Spanish journalist and writer, Evelyn Mesquida. '*La Nueve* could fight. They never retreated. They never gave up an inch of land they had taken. They always went first.'[4]

The Deuxième was transferred to Britain in April 1944 in preparation for the invasion of France, and posted to Pocklington in Yorkshire. However, to the considerable annoyance of Leclerc and de Gaulle alike, they were not to be involved in the D-Day landings.

Probably the first Spanish Republican to arrive in Normandy was Lucio Sauquillo (12th Yorkshire Parachute Battalion of the 6th Airborne Division) who parachuted into France minutes after midnight on the morning of 6 June. Sauquillo was one of the Basque children evacuated from Bilbao in 1937 on the *Habana*, and he somehow contrived to enlist in the British Army in November 1942. He took part in the heavy fighting around Ranville (Pegasus Bridge) against German forces – in particular the 21st Panzer Division – which had been ordered to lead the counter-attack against the British landings at Sword. He was killed in the Battle of Bréville on 13 June 1944 and is buried at the Hermanville War Cemetery (1. N. 19.).[5]

Alfredo Ruiz, another of the Basque refugee children, served in the Royal Navy, and at daybreak on 6 June 1944, he was aboard one of the motor launches that supported the Canadian invasion force at Juno. He had enlisted in July 1943 and as far as records show, was the only Spanish national in the fleet. He had trained as a radar operator and his first mission was patrolling the southern coast of Ireland in search of U-boats. A week and a half after D-Day, when King George VI visited Normandy to hold talks with Montgomery and meet some of the troops, Ruiz was part of the crew of one of the MLs that escorted his ship, HMS *Arethusa*.[6]

The first unit of Spanish Republicans to disembark in France were the sappers who had enlisted in the No. 1 (Spanish) Company of the Pioneer Corps. The company consisted of 250 Spanish Republicans with some 30 British officers and a combination of British and Spanish NCOs. Perhaps the most 'famous' of the men were known as the 'three Charlies'. Desmond Bristow of V Section interviewed them in London and later reported:

> These three Spanish longshoremen in Huelva had been given money by the Germans to load explosives on to English ships. They had consistently taken the money and dumped the explosives into the sea, thus saving British lives, ships and tons of supplies.[7]

When the Germans became suspicious of the men, they stowed away on a British ship and escaped to England. Having been cross-examined by V Section, they enlisted in the Engineers.

The company embarked in Portsmouth and landed in Arromanches a fortnight after D-Day. According to the account of Sergeant Antonio Grandes, they immediately set to work providing logistical support for the combat troops and organizing the distribution of supplies. He later recalled:

> Our small Number One Spanish Company was proud to be part of this vast Allied army, and that with our modest and humble help, we were contributing to the defeat of Nazi Germany, Fascist Italy and, if I tell the truth, we also believed of the dictator Franco: but it was not to be.[8]

They followed the advancing armies and finished the war in Belgium. On their return through France, they were posted to Le Neubour (fifty kilometres south-west of Rouen). When de Gaulle visited the village, and in the absence of any French troops, they were ordered to serve as the general's guard of honour. In the final weeks of their tour of duty, they were employed recovering British matériel, and cleaning the buildings the Allies had occupied and which were now to be returned to their French owners. They finally landed back in Britain in the autumn of 1945.[9]

Other Republicans who found themselves in Britain in 1940 also enlisted in the British armed forces. According to the Fighting Basques Project, along with Lucio Sauquillo, ten more of the children who reached Southampton aboard the *Habana*, served in the Home Guard, in the army and navy, or worked as ground crew in the RAF. José (Joe) Maria Irala was born in Bilbao in 1924. He enlisted in the Royal Armoured Corps in March 1944 and later volunteered for the airborne forces. He completed his parachute training at RAF Ringway in April 1944 and joined up with the 1st Airborne Reconnaissance Squadron. At the start of Montgomery's ill-fated Operation *Market Garden*, on 17 September 1944, he was dropped into Holland, near Heelsum. After four days endeavouring to break through German lines to reach the bridge at Arnhem, his squadron was waiting for orders near the Hartenstein Hotel at Oosterbeek, when they were warned of an impending artillery attack. They immediately sought to take evasive action in the few jeeps at their disposal but came under machine-gun fire and Irala was hit in the stomach as he tried to climb aboard one of the vehicles. He died of his wounds on 22 September at St. Elizabeth's Hospital in Arnhem and was buried in the Arnhem Oosterbeek War Cemetery (22. A. 5.). He was 20 years old.[10]

Another of the Basque exiles who fought in the British armed forces was Justo Balerdi

(ME/13041866). It appears that having escaped to France, he enlisted in the French Foreign Legion to escape the internment camps, was posted to the Middle East and deserted following the establishment of the Vichy regime. It also seems that recruitment protocols were less stringent in foreign theatres than in Britain. Balerdi enlisted in the 2nd Battalion of the Queen's Royal Regiment before undergoing commando training and joining a special forces unit that saw action on the Greek island of Castellorizo.

On his return to North Africa, he fought in the Desert War in various army groups including the Layforce and the Middle East Commando. Finally, at the end of 1943, he was 'badged' into the 2nd Regiment of the Special Air Service and in January 1944 received the Africa Star. As a member of the SAS he was encouraged to change his name and, as a Basque nationalist, opted for Robert Bruce. His friend and comrade, Rafael Ramos, apparently chose Francis Drake, but when his request was denied, insisted he would prefer to keep his Spanish name. Their mutual friend Francisco Gerónimo was given the more mundane name of Frank Williams.

Balerdi was transferred to Britain where he underwent parachute training at Ringway. In August he was dropped into eastern France, behind German lines, as part of the SOE Operation *Rupert*, a campaign of sabotage coordinated with the Maquis in the area between Nancy and Châlons-sur-Marne (today Châlons-en-Champagne). In early 1945, he was once more deployed behind enemy lines, this time in northern Italy alongside the local partisans (Operation *Galia*). Their mission was to harass enemy lines of communication and pin down German troops prior to the US Fifth Army offensive against the Gothic Line.

His final assignment was Operation *Tombola* (an extension of *Galia*), in the Reggio Emilia hills. In the course of the campaign, a transnational force of SAS troops, sixty escaped Russian POWs and deserters from the

Wehrmacht, and forty Italian freedom fighters, carried out a spectacular and unauthorized guerrilla raid on the German 14th Army headquarters at Botteghe d'Albinea. The battle was made famous by the role of David Kirkpatrick, a Scots piper of the Highland Light Infantry who parachuted into the area (in a kilt) specifically to take part in the assault. To persuade the Germans that the raid was a British operation and thus avoid reprisals against the local population, Kirkpatrick continued to play 'Highland Laddie' on his bagpipes throughout the fighting.[11]

Balerdi's compatriot Ramos was later awarded the Military Medal for his part in saving the life of Captain Michael Lees in the aftermath of the mission. Ramos and another member of the unit, Burke, strapped the 250-pound captain to a ladder and carried him for four days until they reached safety and arrangements could be made for his evacuation by light aircraft.[12] Balerdi, the only Basque to serve in the SAS, was killed in action on 21 April, in the final days of the last SAS operation in northern Italy. He was taking part in a raid on a German supply depot and in the words of his commanding officer, Major Roy Farran:

> two jeeps, guns ablaze, attacked this German position frontally. A German ammunitions truck was captured in addition to many prisoners, another large truck and trailer were set on fire and a quantity of petrol and anti-aircraft ammunition was destroyed. Unfortunately, Parachutist Bruce, one of our Spaniards, was killed by a stray enemy bullet during the action.[13]

Balerdi is buried in the Milan War Cemetery (V.A.3.), under the name Bruce, R (Private).[14] His 'Country of Service' is listed as United Kingdom.

Meanwhile, in the spring of 1944, the Deuxième had been attached to Patton's Third Army, and subsequently embarked in Southampton and landed at Utah Beach near Sainte-Mère-Église on 1 August 1944, eight weeks after D-Day. The brigade had been generously armed by the Americans with a range of tanks and anti-tank weaponry, a fact of which de Gaulle later needed reminding when he threatened to withdraw French forces from Allied command. Nonetheless, the symbol of their achievements was the 8–9-ton half-tracks with a maximum speed of over 75 kilometres an hour which accompanied the Sherman tanks.

Dronne recalls one of his NCOs (who served under the name 'Fábregas') bemoaning the arms embargo during the Civil War, 'If only we had had all this in Spain.'[15]

As Allied troops advanced out of Normandy through northern France, the Deuxième moved south through Avranches in the direction of Le Mans before turning north again towards the Falaise Gap and the German 7th Army. They liberated Ecouché after a fierce battle with elements of the 116th Panzer Division 'Windhund' and ground troops of the 2nd SS Panzer Division 'Das Reich' before sweeping back to Alençon, whence they advanced eastward in the direction of Paris.

In spite of their hard-fought military successes, the western Allies had serious disagreements on the immediate strategic priorities, and in particular regarding the liberation of the French capital. The Americans were anxious to press ahead towards Germany and feared a lengthy and violent campaign in the streets of Paris. Eisenhower was also reluctant to take over responsibility for the fuel and food needs of the Parisians. His dependence on the Normandy ports to supply his own armies was the cause of significant logistical challenges and the added burden of delivering vital stores to the people of Paris would seriously undermine plans for a swift advance on the Rhine and beyond. General Patton was particularly vociferous in his demands for the fuel his tanks needed if they were to deny the Wehrmacht time to regroup. The Allied command also assumed that by the time the Allies had occupied other key positions in France, the capital would simply fall without a struggle. The British, on the other hand, were anxious to take out the launch sites of the V1 missiles based along the coast that were wreaking havoc on the population of London.

General de Gaulle however, would not be swayed from his resolve to liberate Paris. A conservative autocrat, he mistrusted the political ambitions of the communist-led sections of the Resistance, and believed that it was essential to establish his own military control of the nation's capital and to seize the administrative structures of power, in order to pre-empt any moves to consolidate and institutionalize the growing support among the population for the partisans. Given his later claims that Paris liberated itself, it is worth recording his orders to the Gaullist sections of the Resistance to delay the popular rising on the streets of the capital until the Allied armies (spearheaded by the Deuxième Blindée) were in a position to guarantee his own military authority over all the Free

162

French forces. Indeed, following the German surrender in the capital, de Gaulle snubbed the Resistance leaders and immediately set about the task of disarming the French Forces of the Interior, dismantling their structures, and integrating them in the regular army where they served under military discipline.

With his attention focused firmly on the political future and the redemption of France, the general secured a promise from Eisenhower that whenever the time came, it should be French forces that entered Paris first and 'that it would be the Leclerc Division that he would assign to the operation'.[16] However, aware that Eisenhower had no interest in fighting for Paris at this stage of the war, de Gaulle threatened to circumvent the orders of the supreme commander and his staff:

> I acknowledged this promise, adding nevertheless that the matter was of such national importance in my eyes that I was ready to take action on my own responsibility and, if the Allied command delayed too long, would launch the Second Armoured Division toward Paris myself.[17]

In response to the breakout from Normandy of the US Third Army under General Patton and its march eastward, and following a series of strikes in key sectors in Paris (railways, police, postal services), the French Resistance also chose to assert its own autonomy. On 19 August, the communist Resistance leader Colonel Henri Rol-Tanguy, ignored the opposition of the Gaullist agents who pleaded caution, and issued the order for an uprising in the capital against the 20,000-strong German garrison under the command of General Dietrich von Choltitz. Rol-Tanguy was a veteran of the International Brigades and according to the historian Anthony Beevor, he based his strategy on the tactics used by the people of Barcelona against the military insurgency of July 1936.[18] By constructing barricades throughout the city, they were able to disrupt the deployment of troops and heavy weapons and thus undermine the superiority of regular military forces. However, it is also true that the French tradition of the barricades predated the Spanish Civil War.

The Resistance forced the hand of both de Gaulle, who was determined to prevent a new revolutionary Commune (Paris, 1871), and Eisenhower, who needed to keep the French under his command and who appreciated it would be a political mistake not to support the citizens of Paris. As the fighting on the streets of Paris intensified, the division embarked on a 'march' to the capital. With the approval of de Gaulle, Leclerc ignored a direct command from his superior, General Leonard T. Gerow, to recall his troops.[19] At this point, Eisenhower and Patton bowed to the inevitable, and released the Deuxième to advance on the capital. After slow progress through enthusiastic crowds, along roads that had not been designed for modern warfare, and skirmishes with retreating German forces, the vanguard of Leclerc's men reached the outskirts of the capital on 24 August. When Leclerc caught up with the 9th Company which, following the instructions of the Americans, had in fact turned back, Leclerc told Dronne not to obey stupid orders.[20] Leclerc now ordered the 9th Company to fight its way into the city centre, make contact with the Resistance, and hold their position until the arrival of the full division. They entered the city through the Porte d'Italie in the south in two separate columns, one under the command of Dronne and the other led by Lieutenant Amado Granell Mesado, one of the 2,600 Republicans who in March 1939 had escaped the Nationalists aboard the *Stanbrook* (passenger number 1928[21]). By 2130, the first half-trucks of Granell's section had reached the Hôtel de Ville.

Each half-track bore some reference to campaigns of the Civil War (Guadalajara, Ebro, Madrid, Teruel, Belchite, Guernica) that the Spanish troops had daubed in white paint on the front and sides of the vehicles. They also carried the flag of the Spanish Republic. The second column soon arrived, and the men took up defensive positions around the square, armed with sub-machine guns. As the news spread, the bells of Notre Dame and dozens of churches tolled to announce the liberation of Paris.

Granell and Dronne approached the town hall and were welcomed by the partisan leaders of the uprising. The next day, the newspaper *Libération* published a photograph of Granell with Georges Bidault (leader of the National Council of the Resistance) while joyfully announcing: '*Ils sont arrivés*' ('They've arrived'). The Deuxième Division Blindée entered Paris in force, together with the 4th US Infantry Division, and overcame the last pockets of enemy resistance. General von Choltitz, the German military governor, countermanded Hitler's orders to raze the city to the ground and officially surrendered to Leclerc at the Hôtel Meurice.

To the extreme irritation of de Gaulle, he was unable to prevent Colonel Henri Rol-Tanguy from gate-crashing the event and adding his signature to the document. The same day, the general made a radio broadcast to the nation. In perhaps the most histrionic speech delivered by any Allied leader, and ignoring the contribution of the fighting men of the US, Britain or Canada, he proclaimed:

> A violated Paris! A broken Paris! A martyred Paris! But …
> a liberated Paris! Liberated by itself, liberated by its people with the help of the armies of France, with the support and the assistance of all France, the fighting France, the only France, the real France, the eternal France!

It was apt therefore that the first troops into the centre of Paris should be Spanish. It is also pleasing to imagine the discomfort of Franco that those very troops should be carrying the flag of the Republic. This apparently minor triumph is a homage to the tens of thousands of Spaniards who were part of the Allied war effort. It went unrecognized for several decades – partly because the French had no interest in acknowledging the event and partly because the Spanish government had no desire to publicize the role of the Republicans in the victory over fascism. In 2004, a plaque was unveiled on the wall of the Hôtel de Ville in Paris (Quai Henri IV) and since then other plaques have appeared around the city. On 19 April 2017, the mayors of Madrid (Manuela Carmena) and Paris (Ana Hidalgo, daughter of Spanish Republicans) officially opened the Jardín de los Combatientes de La Nueve (Garden of the Combatants of the Ninth) in Madrid. In her speech to the assembled authorities and sympathizers, Carmena said, 'Freedom does not march alone, it must be cherished every day, and remembrance is vital for its preservation.' The writer Almudena Grandes added, 'today the warriors of *La Nueve* have not reached Paris, they have reached Madrid.'[22]

On 26 August 1944, General Leclerc gave the order that *La Nueve* should act as escort detail for de Gaulle in the victory parade along the Champs Élysées. The Deuxième was then dispatched to the Bois de Boulogne for a period of rest and recovery before embarking on a new campaign which culminated in the liberation of Strasbourg (as Leclerc had predicted years before in North Africa).

The Deuxième Blindée ended the war at Berchtesgaden. As the Russians approached Berlin, some of Hitler's entourage had mooted the possibility of establishing a mountain redoubt in the Berghof, the second seat of command of the Third Reich, and Hitler's private retreat.

The RAF therefore targetted the town in a massive air raid on 25 April by 359 bombers including sixteen Lancasters of 617 ('Dambusters') Squadron which delivered the last remaining sixteen Tallboy earthquake bombs. The aerial destruction of the town, and Hitler's suicide in Berlin on 30 April diminished the strategic significance of the complex but it remained an iconic Nazi outpost and one that various military units were vying to 'liberate'. Ten days after the raid, when the Deuxième arrived, Berchtesgaden had already been taken by members of the American 3rd Infantry Division (VI Corps). However, ignoring attempts by the Americans to establish their own control of the area, French and Spanish troops located the entrance to the Eagle's Nest and 'occupied' the Führer's private headquarters. There were only sixteen Spanish Republicans left in the corps to savour this final triumph and to stand where, four and a half years before, Serrano Suñer and Hitler had met to discuss Operation *Felix*. The Republican soldiers had been fighting fascism since July 1936, in Spain, Scandinavia, the Middle East and across Africa, France and Germany. News of the German surrender reached them in Berchtesgaden.

Nevertheless, none of the Spanish exiles who had fought with the Allies believed their own war was over. Between 1998 and 2006, the journalist Evelyn Mesquida was able to interview several of the men who had reached the Eagle's Nest. Daniel Hernández, who had 'liberated' a chess set from the Berghof, told her that as he and his comrades set off on the return journey to Paris, 'we were convinced the time had come to liberate Spain, and that France and the Allies would help us'. Sergeant Fermín Pujol recalled:

> We hoped to continue the struggle in Spain. We had been promised, we had been told that when the War ended we would return to Spain to finish the war there. Leclerc said so, and I believe he meant it, but they wouldn't let him. We Spaniards were ready, we had weapons and before we were demobilized, they kept telling us 'Soon we'll be in Spain, soon.'[23]

The last surviving Spanish Republican of *La Nueve*, Rafael Gómez Nieto, died at the age of 99 in March 2020, in a residence in Strasbourg, victim of the coronavirus. He had fought in the Battle of the Ebro, crossed the border into France at the end of the Civil War and had been interned in the St. Cyprien concentration camp. He managed to escape and in the company of his father made his way to North Africa where he joined the Free French. In May 1943, he enlisted in Leclerc's division, and travelled to Britain. In the summer of 1944, he landed at Utah Beach with Patton's army and was among those who entered Paris on 24 August, as co-driver of the half-track that carried the name *Guernica*. He later described to a journalist how they raised a Republican flag over the Spanish embassy in the French capital and celebrated by singing the Republican Army anthem *Ay Carmela* almost continuously throughout that evening. He too reached Berchtesgaden in 1945 and, as befitted a member of the elite group of soldiers who had been fighting Hitler longer than any other military force, he was able to claim his own spoils of war: a tea-set and a camera. Asked to describe his war-time experiences, he replied, 'People kill and people die. It's horrible.'[24]

The most appropriate homage to the men of *La Nueve* was paid by their leader, Captain Dronne:

> They were magnificent fighters. Many gave their lives and their graves mark the long route of hardship and glory that led them from Normandy to Paris, to Strasbourg and finally to the Eagle's Nest at Berchtesgaden. They were and still are a wonderful example of courage.[25]

Chapter 17

But Sometimes You Might Make the Wrong Decisions, Comrades

The only major power that stood by the Republic during the Civil War was the USSR. The fascist dictatorships swiftly deployed their military resources on the side of the insurgents and the British and French cynically imposed a policy of non-intervention which prevented the legitimate and democratically elected government in Madrid from buying weapons on the international market. The Soviet Union responded by sending tanks and aircraft supported by expert tank crews and pilots. The Comintern contributed to the cause through the creation of the legendary International Brigades and the recruitment of approximately 50,000 anti-fascist volunteers (2,500 from Britain and Ireland).[1] However, Stalin's support and sustenance came at a price.[2]

In the first place, the Republic was required to transfer much of its gold reserves to Moscow for 'safekeeping', as collateral and as down payment for the purchase of weapons that often turned out to be of inferior quality and in some cases even obsolete. More sinister was the influence that Stalin demanded in internal Spanish affairs. The events of May 1937 in Barcelona brought to a head the tensions between the Anarchists and the POUM on the one hand, who prioritized social revolution, and the Socialists and Communists on the other, who insisted all efforts should be directed towards military victory in the Civil War. From the outset of the Civil War, the Communist Party had taken the initiative in military organization and set up the legendary volunteer Fifth Regiment whose discipline and courage became an example for the new regular Popular Army. At the same time, the secretary-general of the party, José Díaz, defended a deliberately modest political programme of 'democracy with a social content', which included demolishing the semi-feudal economic and social structures that still dominated rural Spain, of revoking the privileges of the Church, of reforming the armed forces and of dismantling the financial oligarchies. However, he advised against 'experimenting with economic doctrines and theoretical systems, in seeking to build the future, while ignoring the present'. He warned that if the Republic failed to win the war, 'all the social achievements would be smashed like a house of cards under the jackboot of militarism and fascism'.[3]

The Communist Party prioritization of military efficiency over social change had the added bonus of curbing the violent excesses of the zealous application of revolutionary justice by the Anarchists. Nevertheless, however reasonable the Communist approach may have appeared, it was unfortunately also used as a cover for the brutal repression of 'renegade' factions on the Left opposed to Stalinist orthodoxy. The street fighting in the Catalan capital led to the restoration of Republican order over the revolutionary spirit so graphically described by Orwell, and the eventual outlawing of the POUM. The anti-Stalinist leader of the party, Andreu (Andrés) Nin, was detained, tortured and, in the words of the dissident Russian revolutionary Victor Serge, 'disappeared for ever into the shadows'.[4] In a campaign that typified the psychosis and cynicism of the Soviet dictator, Nin and his supporters were vilified as Trotskyists, spies, agents of Franco–Hitler–Mussolini, and enemies of the people. Given the Republic's dependence on the USSR, the new prime minister, Dr Juan Negrín, was reluctantly forced to turn a blind eye to the activities of the NKVD who were allowed to operate on Spanish territory with almost as much licence as they did at home. In 1940, it was intriguingly a Catalan agent of the same NKVD, Ramón Mercader, who was ordered by the highest authority in Moscow to carry out the murder of Leon Trotsky in Mexico with an ice pick. Stalin thus disposed of perhaps his greatest enemy and the man who inspired the Fourth International. Mercader spent twenty years in a Mexican prison, and on his release was awarded the highest decoration of the USSR, Hero of the Soviet Union.

Countless other anti-fascists also met their end working in the cause of the Republic. Probably the most notorious case was that of José Robles, John Dos Passos's translator, who had cancelled his return to his teaching post at Johns Hopkins University to serve the Republic, but vanished without trace in Valencia. Only later was it revealed to Ernest Hemingway that Robles had in fact been executed as a spy. When Dos Passos embarked on a mission to reveal the truth of his friend's disappearance, his erstwhile friend Hemingway insisted that the liquidation of one man should not be allowed to undermine the cause of the Republic. The disagreement led to open hostility.[5] No proof was ever forthcoming that Robles was a spy or fifth columnist, and his family were never notified of his execution; indeed, his widow was refused a death certificate and was therefore unable to claim a pension from his university. According to Serge, it was impossible to defeat fascism while murdering the 'most forceful and reliable anti-Fascists'; the tactics employed by the Stalinists in Spain 'destroyed the moral standing of democracy'.[6] W.H. Auden later claimed that, 'Nobody I know who went to Spain during the Civil War who was not a dyed-in-the-wool Stalinist returned from Spain with his illusions intact'.[7]

On the other hand, even the faith of the most loyal Stalinists was tested by the Non-Aggression Pact signed by Molotov and Ribbentrop in August 1939. Notwithstanding the faint-hearted duplicity of the British and French governments who hid behind the manifestly unfair policies of non-intervention and appeasement, Stalin's deal with Hitler destroyed the credentials of the Communist parties around the world as allies in the struggle against fascism.

Excluded from decision-making and any form of democratic control over the leadership, the greatest asset of the PCE remained its members, who had distinguished themselves throughout the Civil War and whose courage was expressed in their spirit of self-sacrifice and loyalty. Given their well-deserved reputation for discipline and organization, it is extraordinary that for the duration of the Second World War the official leadership of the Spanish Communist Party failed to offer a command structure either inside Spain or to the Communist community among the refugees in south-west France. At the end of the Civil War, the secretary-general, José Díaz, was receiving treatment for stomach cancer in Leningrad. He remained in the USSR for the next three years until he committed suicide in March 1942. During these years in exile, he wrote the self-serving *Las enseñanzas de Stalin, guía luminoso para los comunistas españoles* (*The Teachings of Stalin, a Shining Guide for Spanish Communists*) extolling the leadership qualities of the Soviet ruler and contributing to the personality cult.

He was replaced as secretary-general by Dolores Ibárruri (La Pasionaría) who had taken refuge in Moscow at the end of 1939, following her escape to Oran and a short exile in France. Her partner, Francisco Antón, did remain in France, but was arrested by the French authorities following the Molotov–Ribbentrop Pact and the ban on the activities of the Communist parties. He was detained at Le Vernet, the internment camp for 'undesirable foreigners' and hostile political activists. La Pasionaría ignored party protocols and used her influence with the Soviet government to persuade them to negotiate Antón's release with the Germans. He was thus saved by the intervention of the woman who loved him. Years later when Antón chose to end his relationship with Ibárruri, the process was reversed and rather than enjoy the benefits of her favour, he would suffer the consequences of her ire.

The Italian Communist leader, Palmiro Togliatti (*Ercoli*), was chief of the Spanish section of the Communist International during the Civil War and therefore responsible for liaising with Stalin and implementing his orders. He played a key role in policy and strategy and was one of the last of the Communist leadership to leave Spain in the final days of the Republic. He was detained for a short spell in Paris and then eventually settled in exile in Moscow where he dedicated his time to the Comintern and the affairs of the Italian Communist Party.

The last of the leading figures of the Spanish Communist hierarchy of the twentieth century was Santiago Carrillo (secretary-general 1960–82). Having manoeuvered a merger between the youth movements of the Socialist and Communist parties in March 1936, he subsequently became secretary-general of the new organization, the Juventudes Socialistas Unificadas. Towards the end of the Civil War, he made his escape to France and eventually to the Soviet Union. In June 1940, the party dispatched him to the Americas – USA, Cuba, Mexico and Argentina – to coordinate and develop the work of the Young Communist International.

In 1940, the PCE set up a secretariat in Mexico under Vicente Uribe, who had been minister of agriculture throughout the Civil War. The aim of the organization was to consolidate relations with exiled Republicans, American governments and potentially with the party cadres that remained in Spain and France. Uribe appointed Antón as his chief of organization and Joan Comorera i Soler as liaison officer with the PSUC. Carrillo was given special responsibility for the youth sections of the movement.

Meanwhile, the rank-and-file members of the PCE, PSUC and JSU in Spain and France were left to fend for themselves. Inside Spain, those who had in a first instance escaped execution, incarceration and the slave labour camps were prey to the brutal repression and increasingly effective work of the secret intelligence services who regularly infiltrated ad hoc opposition groups. However, the arrival of Heríberto Quiñones in Madrid in April 1941 did herald the first major attempt to reorganize the Communist bases. Born in Bessarabia, he was sent to Spain in the early 1930s as an agent of the Comintern. At the end of the Civil War, he was taken prisoner and held at the infamous concentration camp in Albatera. He then managed to escape and fled to Valencia, where he was arrested, tortured by Nazi agents seeking information on the Communist International and interned in the Porta Coeli detainment camp. He escaped once more at the end of 1940 and eventually made his way to the capital.

Despite his deteriorating health (he had been suffering from tuberculosis since 1936), he quickly took over the reins of power from the reorganizing commission that had been set up to coordinate those members of the PCE and JSU that remained at liberty. Quiñones established a politburo to which he coopted sympathizers and supporters and imposed his policy of autonomy for the movement inside Spain. He believed the leaders in exile could not grasp the realities of the new political, social and economic context of Franco's dictatorship and was enraged by the Molotov–Ribbentrop Pact. He refused to await orders from the Comintern leaders in Moscow and Latin America. Instead, he insisted that the party learn to act with an independent spirit, and was successful in expanding party structures to various provinces. He also advocated the strategy of 'national union' – the creation of a broad front of opposition groups, including even those who demanded the restoration of the monarchy – before it became the official policy of the Comintern after the Nazi invasion of the USSR in June 1941.

Quiñones was finally detained on 5 December 1941, and was submitted to months of torture in the dungeons of the Dirección General de Seguridad (DGS, the General Security Department) in the Plaza del Sol before he was sentenced to death. According to Paul Preston's account, such was the brutality of his treatment at the hands of Franco's secret police that only by tying him upright to a chair was the firing squad able to execute the sentence according to basic protocols.[8]

In spite of his courage, or perhaps because of it, he was disowned by the PCE. In his own memoirs, Santiago Carrillo denounced Quiñones as an 'ambitious adventurer', a *'provocateur'* or a 'Francoist agent'. He questions why Quiñones did not escape from Spain when the party gave him the opportunity in 1939, and claims that rather than escaping from the Albatera camp, he was in fact released by the compliant authorities. Only grudgingly does he admit that the execution of Quiñones by the dictatorship does appear to undermine the theory that he was a traitor.[9] Nevertheless, in the dogma of the PCE, *Quiñonismo* was denounced as a cardinal sin: a tendency to prioritize independence and local initiative over policies dictated by the leadership (however distant and disengaged the leaders might be).

In the meantime, the secretariat in Mexico was now ordered to dispatch a mission of their own to Spain to undertake the task of rebuilding the party. The team set off from Cuba and arrived in Lisbon on 19 May 1941. Two agents had been transferred earlier to Spain to establish contacts and to make preliminary arrangements for the infiltration of the remaining members of the group. However, they were detained by the Spanish police and one, under fierce interrogation, revealed the details of his mission. Those agents who had established their base in Galicia were subsequently captured and the Portuguese police arrested those who had not yet crossed the border. They were immediately extradited to Spain. The six main leaders, Jesús Larrañaga, Isidro Diéguez, Manuel Asarta, Jaime Girabau, Eladio Rodriguez and Francisco Barreiro were executed by firing squad on 21 January 1942. They did however manage to smuggle out of their prison a message to the Central Committee: 'In these last few moments that remain to us, we wish to insist that the enemy is still strong. Avoid unfounded optimism which leads only to the castration of our hopes.'[10] Their warning went unheeded.

The remoteness of the Central Committee and the mass incarceration of party members and sympathizers in the new Spain, meant that the PCE and PSUC exiles in France embodied the rump of the Spanish Communist movement. However, they also represented an expert and experienced fighting force. Inexplicably, as the leading figures of the party withdrew to the USSR, La Pasionaria's last trusted representative in France, Francisco Antón, 'appointed' Carmen de Pedro as the delegate of the Central Committee. Typist and former personal assistant to Togliatti, de Pedro was expected to play an administrative role (processing visa applications etc.) and eventually to provide support to Antón, interned in Camp Vernet. Manuel Azcárate, son of the last Republican ambassador in London and highest ranking of the young guard left behind, was promoted to the leadership of the JSU. In his memoirs, he recalls his first meeting with de Pedro, and condescendingly describes her as 'very young, cheerful, with intelligent, bright eyes'. Ignoring the circumstances of his own promotion, he claims that this encounter with the new party supervisor provided him with 'the final proof of the dissolution of the party in France'.[11]

However, at a subsequent meeting, de Pedro introduced Azcárate to her partner, Jesús Monzón Reparaz, who created a more favourable impression. Monzón was a qualified lawyer from Navarra, born into an upper-middle-class family. He had been civil governor of Alicante and then Cuenca during the Civil War. Although he had fled Spain from the small aerodrome at Monóvar (Alicante) on board the same aircraft as La Pasionaria, the fact that he had been overlooked when the Central Committee selected de Pedro as chief delegate in France, suggests he had lost the confidence of the party leadership. He was a man with a strong personality and great personal charm, but atypically for a Communist leader, he was also a man who placed social qualities (including friendship) above political criteria. According to his enemies, he was lacking in the proletarian virtue of austerity and a potential aesthete, unable to resist the temptations of bourgeois pleasures (especially good food). Worse was his spirit of independence and willingness to challenge party dogma. Released from the manacles of the Stalinist leadership style of the Central Committee, Monzón was free to improvise and to adapt policies to the demands of changing local conditions. Azcárate described him as 'very intelligent', someone who:

> Knows how to listen [...]: he considers various hypotheses, without taboos or narrow-minded prejudices, and then discards those he considers erroneous on the basis of common sense, with very few references to the ideological jokers that we communists so often tend to use in our political analysis.[12]

Monzón subsequently recruited Azcárate and together with Carmen de Pedro, Gabriel León Trilla (one of the founders of the PCE) and a trusted associate, Manuel Gimeno, he established an unofficial Delegación del Comité Central (Central Committee Commission). The team undertook the task of opening channels of communication between Spanish communist groups in France and coordinating strategies. The self-appointed chief of the Communist movement in France now proved extraordinarily successful in forging an effective leadership, organizing members and resources, recruiting support for the Resistance and raising the morale of party members who had been abandoned by the Comintern and the Central Committee. The work of his team would culminate in the formation of the Agrupación de Guerrilleros Españoles who played a significant part in the operations of the Resistance during the battle for Normandy and the liberation of France.

In the summer of 1941, following the German invasion of the USSR, the war entered a new stage. The restoration of the 'natural' hostilities between Nazi-ism and Communism swept aside any reservations harboured by the PCE as a result of the Ribbentrop–Molotov Pact. From their base in the South of France, Monzón and de Pedro promoted the policy of Unión Nacional Española (UNE), an attempt to bring together all those forces opposed to Franco and the Falange, and to prevent Franco fulfilling his promise to intervene in the war alongside his Axis allies. In August 1941, they launched a weekly bulletin, *Reconquista de España* (*Reconquest of Spain*), in which they made repeated calls on republicans, socialists, anarchists, monarchists, disillusioned catholics, masons, trade unionists, and Basque, Catalan and Galician nationalists to join forces with the communists in the struggle to defeat fascism and overthrow Franco. The message was also propagated by Radio España Independiente (Independent Spanish Radio), the 'clandestine' station known popularly as *La Pirenaica* (Radio Pyrenees), set up in Moscow in July 1941 to broadcast news and Communist propaganda to exiles and the population of the interior. The transmissions began with an instantly recognizable voice announcing: '*Aquí Radio España Independiente, estación pirenaica, la única radio sin censura de Franco*' (Here is Independent Radio Spain, Pyrenean Station, the only radio not censored by Franco). In fact, the *Pirenaica* was the only effective link with the politburo in the USSR available to the leadership in France. It seems that letters they dispatched via Switzerland and Mexico or through the PCF did reach members of the politburo, and there is some evidence to suggest they also received some replies.[13] However, the long delays between responses undermined the viability of effective communication. Indeed, so dependent did Monzón become on the information broadcast by the station, that he required Carmen de Pedro to transcribe the transmissions.

The Communist exiles also continued to publish editions of *Mundo Obrero,* the official press organ of the party, although it tended to focus attention on the activities of the UNE and to defend the line of unity with all socio-political groups opposed to the regime – including monarchists and dissident Catholics. At the top of the front page, above the hammer and sickle, the newspaper had traditionally included the slogan from the Communist Manifesto: '*Proletarios de todos los paises, uníos*' ('Workers of the world unite!'). Under the influence of Monzón (until 1945), the heading was changed to '*Unión Nacional, contra Franco y la Falange*' ('National Union, against Franco and the Falange').[14]

The UNE held its constitutional congress in Montauban, near Toulouse, in the summer of 1942 (codename *Congreso de Grenoble*). The strategy of national union had also been embraced as the official policy of the PCE and in an open letter to party activists and sympathizers (March/April 1942), the Central Committee called on Spanish patriots 'to join together in a broad national front [...] and to work towards the creation of a government of National Union at the service of Spain'.[15] The UNE issued a programme that included the formation of a broad coalition of forces opposed to Franco and the Falange, the removal of German influence in Madrid and the defence of Spain's independence, an end to the supply of raw materials to Nazi Germany, an amnesty for the victims of the Falange, democratic elections and freedom of expression and religion.[16]

In the spring of 1943, Monzón decided his organizational skills were of more use in Spain and he elected to return to Madrid to develop the clandestine activities of the surviving members of the PCE. He was joined by his ally Gabriel Trilla, whose skills developed in his liaison work in the French free zone made him an ideal partner in the campaign to reconstruct the party in occupied Spain, subjugated not by a foreign power, but by its own army. They established a Junta Suprema de Unión Nacional (National Union Supreme Council) in September 1943 and published a manifesto calling on the people of Spain to rise up against Franco and the Falange, to expel Axis agents from Spanish territory, and to disrupt the export of natural resources to Germany. Monzón also became romantically involved with Pilar Soler, a member of the JSU and early feminist who had been detained and tortured in the months following the end of the Civil War and had recently been released from gaol. When Monzón informed his former partner, Carmen de Pedro, who had remained in Toulouse, she in turn began a new relationship, with Agustín Zoroa, which would ultimately prove to be her salvation.

Believing that the overthrow of Franco depended upon the formation of a broad opposition front, Monzón embarked on a campaign to open the Communist movement towards groups from a wide ideological range. In a sense, he anticipated the strategies of the Western European communist parties in the final decades of the twentieth century, which sought first to distance themselves from the 'hegemony' of the Communist Party of the USSR and later to negotiate a new approach with other social movements.

The most significant opposition to Franco and the Falange within Spain, however, came from within the ranks of the regime itself and essentially from within the armed forces. Disenchanted monarchists who had rallied to the Nationalist cause in 1936 in order to defeat the Republic, were growing increasingly restless at Franco's refusal to make arrangements for the restoration of the monarchy. In the autumn of 1943, a group of generals presented the Caudillo with a petition to prepare for the eventual transfer of power to Don Juan, the sixth child of Alfonso XIII. In exile, Alfonso had abdicated shortly before his death at the beginning of 1941 in Rome, and Juan's two surviving elder brothers had both renounced their dynastic rights. Franco ignored the 'requests' that he relinquish his position as head of state, and told an ally that he would only abandon power in a coffin.[17] One leading advocate of the monarchy, General Kindelán, claimed the dictator was 'suffering from vertigo' and that he would cling to power 'by hook or by crook'. He had 'altitude sickness' and had risen beyond the limits of his own ability.[18]

The monarchists were by nature opposed to the 'social revolution' of the Falange, and their hostility to the fascist movement in Spain made them, if not completely pro-Allies, at least anti-Nazi. Unfortunately, if there was any development that would force the monarchists of both tendencies to rally once more around the figure of Franco, it would be fear of a possible restoration of the Republic based on the resurgence of the left (and particularly the PCE) as a military option.

It appears that Monzón had some limited success in contacts with José María Gil Robles (in Portugal). Head of the right-wing Confederación Española de Derechas Autónomas (CEDA, Spanish Confederation of Autonomous Right-Wing Parties) during the Republic and leader of the opposition during the Popular Front government until the outbreak of civil war, Gil Robles had now become the chief representative of the civilian monarchist movement. According to Spanish journalist Manuel Martorell, he agreed to preliminary talks with a view to a possible collaboration with the Supreme Council. Monzón was also able to attract some dissident religious and cultural leaders, including Victoria Kent,[19] and the Unión Nacional also gained the support of General Riquelme, a career officer who had remained loyal to the Republic and was forced into exile in France on the fall of Catalonia. However, Monzón's main effort was reserved for the development of a widespread and yet unified Maquis movement, including not only those in the rural areas but also new urban guerrilla groups in the major cities. Monzón travelled throughout Spain but at a national level he was unable to forge a coordinated movement and the Maquis failed to develop beyond the symbolic status they achieved as the only exponent of the armed struggle against the new regime. Indeed, local leaders appeared reluctant to forego their authority in favour of a centralized 'command'. The *huidos* (those who had 'fled to the hills' or '*se echaron al monte*' during and after the Civil War) were a highly disparate cohort, which included left-wing political activists committed to the armed struggle, deserters from the Nationalist Army, fugitives from prison facilities and common criminals. They had every reason to mistrust the Communist Party and little to gain from surrendering their autonomy to a clandestine authority that was unable to provide logistic support.

Nor did the UNE win the backing of the other major players on the left. The Socialists and Anarchists had witnessed the activities of the Communist Party and Communist International during the Civil War and were unwilling to submit to the PCE/PSUC leadership of a new anti-Franco front. The Communists took great pains to persuade potential allies that their aims did not include social revolution or a dictatorship of the proletariat. In their press – *Reconquista de España* and *Mundo Obrero* – they reiterated their aims to overthrow the Franco regime, to restore democracy, and to respect the role of the Catholic Church. Nevertheless, while individuals from different political groups collaborated with the UNE, the Communists failed to integrate other parties at an organizational level.

The libertarian Federica Montseny later acknowledged that there were anarchists in the National Union, but 'on a purely individual basis, not as representatives of the National Committee of the CNT'.[20] At the congress of the PSOE, held in Toulouse in September 1944, party representatives of local committees that were now being formed by exiled Socialists, specifically rejected the proposal to join the UNE.[21] While the Communists firmly believed that the people of Spain should actively participate in the liberation of their own country, many Socialists and centre-left Republicans remained confident that the Allies would eventually overthrow the regime in Madrid as a matter of course, and felt no compulsion to participate in a high-risk military quest to challenge the dictatorship.

Nevertheless, the most serious failing of the new leadership in Madrid was to underestimate the strength of Franco's dictatorship and the iron grip in which it held its own defeated people. In the conditions that prevailed in the Spain of 1943/4, it is difficult to understand how Monzón and Trilla might have 'misinterpreted' signs of a groundswell of popular opposition to Franco. The popular classes had been vanquished in war and were ruled by a tyrant who claimed legitimacy through the right of conquest. They lacked the most basic resources and the means and will to rise against the dictatorship. Countless thousands of their leaders, both at national and local level, were incarcerated or had disappeared into forced labour camps or exile. Families struggled to survive against the nightmare of hunger and disease. The repressive apparatus of the new regime, ably supported by the technical knowhow of Gestapo consultants, excluded the possibility of organized resistance to Franco and the Falange. Various reconnaissance groups infiltrated the north of Spain in the summer of 1944, including one group of 200 who crossed the border at Port Vell (Lleida/Lérida). They reported back that the population was neither on the brink of insurrection nor anxiously awaiting the arrival of Unión Nacional troops. The intelligence was ignored by the leaders in Toulouse.[22]

Instead, the party leadership chose to believe Spain had entered a 'pre-revolutionary' state and that the conditions favoured a popular uprising. Monzón appears to have persuaded himself that a series of isolated incidents provided a mandate for a new call to arms. His biographer, Martorell, claims he dispatched reports to Toulouse which included specific references to guerrilla acts; the sabotage of transport systems; strikes; an arson attack on a Falange newspaper in Sevilla; a mutiny by army conscripts in Malaga who feared they were to be deployed to fight alongside the Wehrmacht; attacks on Germans, Italians and *Falangistas*;

demonstrations in villages against the supply of their wheat crops to the Germans; protests by women against living conditions; raids on food stores; cuts in production in Barcelona and Bilbao industries to prevent the export of goods to Germany; the appearance of anti-fascist posters and leaflets; and so on.[23] However, to extrapolate from local outbursts of anger and courageous acts of defiance that the population would spontaneously join a war against the dictatorship was reckless optimism.

In the October/November 1943 edition of the *Reconquista de España*, the party issued a first call for national insurrection: 'It is vital then, that we understand that the hour has come to take up arms again in the streets, in the factories, in the mountains to liberate our homeland from the yoke of the Falange.' Despite their independence from the politburo of the PCE and the Comintern, Monzón and Trilla were clearly not immune to the Stalinist propensity towards denial and self-deception.

In fact, by the summer of 1944, the only favourable circumstance for the overthrow of Franco was the reality that the Allies were winning the war. As early as 1941, as Franco prevaricated over an eventual declaration of war against Britain, Hitler warned him that his fate was inextricably linked to that of the Axis: 'The battle which Germany and Italy are fighting will determine the destiny of Spain as well. Only in the case of our victory will your regime continue to exist.'[24] It was difficult to question Hitler's logic. Franco's regime had been installed with the direct intervention of Berlin and Rome, Franco had declared Spain 'non-belligerent' rather than 'neutral' in the war, the dictator and Spanish press made constant references to Spain's commitment to the Fascist cause, the Falange later dispatched nearly 50,000 volunteers to join the Wehrmacht on the Eastern Front, and the Spanish provided Germany and Italy with vital raw materials (wolfram), crucial naval logistic support and a free hand in espionage and counter-espionage activities throughout Spain. As the Allies advanced across Europe, it seemed unlikely they would tolerate the survival of a (pro-)fascist dictatorship in Spain.

Chapter 18

Une certaine idée de la France

In the weeks that followed D-Day, SCAEF General Eisenhower, acted on the understanding that his task was to defeat Germany, not to liberate France. As such, his priority was not to expel German troops from French towns, but rather to fight his way as urgently as possible to the Rhine and beyond. Nevertheless, by opening the second front in Normandy, the Allied strategy could hardly ignore the rising expectations of the French population and their demands for deliverance from the tyranny to which they had been submitted for four years.

The invasion of France was based on three operations: *Overlord* (the Normandy landings), *Fortitude* (the campaign of deception which aimed to persuade Hitler that the main assault force would land in the Pas de Calais) and *Dragoon* (the landings on the Mediterranean coast). In the early stages of planning, *Dragoon* (originally Operation *Anvil*) was timed to take place simultaneously with *Overlord*, but logistic and supply problems persuaded the Supreme Headquarters Allied Expeditionary Force (SHAEF) command to postpone the invasion of southern France and to concentrate all military resources in Normandy. However, two months after D-Day the Allies were ready to launch a second front in France, designed to relieve some of the pressure on the armies in the north, to neutralize German forces in the south, and to open new supply lines.

Operation *Dragoon* was launched from bases in North Africa, Italy, Corsica and Sardinia on 15 August 1944, four days before the uprising in Paris. The US Seventh Army was supported by the Free French, and American and British naval and air cover (Western Naval Task Force and Twelfth Tactical Air Force). Heavy bombardment of the German defences between Toulon and Cannes reduced the number of casualties of those disembarking on the beaches. Within two weeks, French troops had taken Toulon and Marseilles, and although the retreating Germans had inflicted serious damage on the dock facilities, the two ports would soon become an operative part of the supply chain to the Allied armies. The Americans meanwhile advanced north and by mid-September had linked up with the southern flank of Patton's Third Army. Now under the command of General Eisenhower, they participated in the defeat of the German Ardennes counter-offensive.

Significantly for this narrative, as the southern invasion force advanced rapidly to join the Allied expeditionary force in the north, the strategy left a substantial area of south-western France beyond the sphere of influence of the Allies and the regular French Army. In addition to their campaign of sabotage, the partisan groups thus launched their own offensive against those German garrisons that had not been ordered north. They also further intensified operations against the despised Milice, the Vichy paramilitary police force. In the words of author and OSS operative Ricardo Sicre: 'the Militia fought on without hope of quarter, and the Resistance without thought of mercy.'[1]

In June, at the age of 24, the leader of the Resistance in south-west France, Serge Ravanel, had been appointed colonel by General Kœnig (commander of the FFI), and following the landings on the Riviera, he ordered all the FFI forces in the area (including the 2nd Division of Spanish Guerrillas under the command of Luis Bermejo) to converge on Toulouse.

In the aftermath of D-Day, the infamous 2nd SS Panzer Division 'Das Reich' had meanwhile been withdrawn from its base at Montauban (fifty kilometres north of Toulouse). Its expedition north towards the beachheads of Normandy would come to symbolize the barbarism of the SS on the Western Front. The Resistance disrupted its advance through a series of ambushes and acts of sabotage against roads and bridges. In retaliation, the division left a trail of extraordinary cruelty against the civilian populations of the villages through which it passed, including the massacre that took place in Oradour-sur-Glane. A peaceful community, until this stage remarkably untouched by the war, the population of the small town was selected as the target for the worst single atrocity of the German occupation. On the afternoon of 10 June, some 645 civilians (virtually the entire population) were murdered by troops of Das Reich. According to writer Max Hastings, the victims included thirty Spaniards employed in manual labour, whom Hastings chillingly described as 'the flotsam of the Civil War'.[2]

However, the Germans no longer had the forces with which to defend Toulouse. On 19 August, as the Resistance launched the uprising in

Paris, so the people of Toulouse took to the streets and the barricades. The Gestapo and the rump of the German garrison set fire to their headquarters and sabotaged the city's communications before fleeing north. They were joined by those members of the Milice who were able to find transport. The Free French took control of the railway system and, with the assistance of a group of local women, released the members of the Resistance (including André Malraux) held by the Germans in the Saint-Michel Prison in the south of the city. By 20 August the final skirmishes had eliminated the last pockets of resistance and the liberation of Toulouse was complete. Spanish *guérilleros*, wearing the distinctive helmets they had requisitioned from German troops, joined the victory parade through the town centre. A total of thirty-five Resistance fighters died in the battle.[3]

According to Serge Vernal, by this stage of the conflict, some 4,000 Spanish partisans were active in south-west France[4] and they played a significant role in disrupting German troop movements and transport systems. British historian Robert Gildea reports that 'Spanish republicans were active from the Dordogne to the Pyrenees'.[5] The town of Foix, close to the border with Andorra, was liberated on 18 August before troops of the Agrupación de Guerrilleros Españoles (AGE) led by Colonel Vicente López Tovar liberated Périgueux on 19 August and Agen two days later. After fierce fighting at Rimont on 21 August, a small number of Spanish partisans took 1,200 German prisoners.

In her own memoirs, the SOE agent Anne-Marie Walters describes the role of the Republicans in the fighting in the Agen area north of Toulouse. In one particular incident at the outbreak of open hostilities, a squad of six Spaniards were surprised by a German column as they patrolled Agen. According to Walters' account they took cover and resisted the sixty-five-man German unit for ninety minutes before they were overcome, and the survivors of the skirmish brutally executed. Once the bodies of the men had been recovered, the leader of the Wheelwright circuit, George Starr, and his Spanish comrade-in-arms Alcazio (this is the name used by Walters) ordered a parade in their honour. A chastened Walters wrote: 'for the first time in our safe and secure maquis, death had been brought right before our eyes. We felt that the incalculable backwash of war was at our door.'[6] By the time the Wehrmacht and Milice eventually withdrew from the area, Walters claims the Germans had lost 248 men. The partisans on the other hand suffered nineteen fatal casualties.[7]

Elsewhere in southern France, Spanish Republicans played a significant part in the liberation of Avignon (25 August), Bordeaux (28 August), Angoulême (30 August), Montpellier (31 August) and Poitiers (5 September). The most spectacular victory of the Spanish partisans was at the Battle of La Madeleine in the Cevennes. On 24 or 25 August, as the battle to liberate Paris reached its climax, between thirty-two and thirty-six Spaniards and six to eight Frenchmen of the 3rd Spanish Division of the FTP ambushed a German column of more than 1,000 troops which had been ordered to evacuate eastward from Toulouse. In the absence of the commanding officer, Cristino García, who had been wounded in a raid on the prison at Nîmes (2–4 February), the unit was led by Miguel Arcas and Gabriel Pérez. In the early afternoon, having previously demolished a bridge over the main railway line between Lézan and Anduze, the partisans waited on the high ground on either side of the road. The enemy force consisted of two sidecars, sixty trucks, four half-tracks, and an unknown number of vehicles transporting anti-tank and anti-aircraft weapons. Once the column came to a halt, the guerrillas opened fire with Bren and Sten guns.

During a short truce, and desperate though their situation appeared to be, the Germans insisted they would surrender only to representatives of the regular armed forces. As the fighting resumed, the partisans constantly moved their positions to give the impression they were more numerous than in fact they were. They eventually received support from some 40 *gendarmes* and French FTP reinforcements and two RAF aircraft (possibly Mosquitos) which strafed the column, destroyed most of the German vehicles and caused heavy casualties. The Germans were eventually forced to lay down their arms at ten past eight in the evening. They surrendered to two officers, one British and one French, who were both attached to the Resistance but were also in uniform. More than 1,000 troops were taken prisoner. Unable to endure the humiliation, the commanding officer, Lieutenant-General Konrad Nietzsche, committed suicide. All those who took part in the battle were awarded the Croix de Guerre with a Silver Star, except apparently the two women who fought alongside the men but who remain unidentified to this day.[8]

Having established his own personal authority over the capital and the north, General de Gaulle then turned his attention to the Midi. Toulouse in particular was a cause of concern, as the absence of a regular army provided the Communist-dominated forces of the

Resistance with an opportunity to establish their own control. Indeed, the power vacuum that followed the defeat of the Germans and the Milice meant the Maquis was the only force of order in the region. Spanish Republicans took advantage of the circumstances to occupy Spanish consulates and to establish themselves as the de facto Spanish authorities in the region.

At this stage, the British ambassador in Madrid, Sir Samuel Hoare, made a short trip across the border into France to study the developing situation in the liberated areas. In his memoirs, he recounts an anecdote concerning a *pelota* match that was due to take place in Irun between teams from Spain and France:

> Owing to the nervousness over the movements of the Spanish Reds the frontier had been closed by the Spanish authorities. The national game of the Basques was not, however, to be stopped by officious guards. The French team, therefore, put themselves in the safe hands of the local contrabandistas and arrived on foot across the mountain passes in time for the match. In the team was the local chief of the Maquis who had escaped to South-west France from a German prison camp.[9]

The Gaullists denounced the Resistance leaders as warlords and complained that Toulouse was becoming the capital of a 'Spanish red Republic'. The general arrived in the city on 16 September with the intention of chastising those who had led the Resistance groups to victory, and of belittling their achievements, while still maintaining his version that the French had indeed largely liberated themselves.

He immediately questioned the ranks to which various of the leaders of the FFI (including Serge Ravanel) had been promoted and the medals they had been awarded. He informed them their role was now over and that they were to enlist in the regular army. His animosity was not limited to the French officers; he also indulged in an 'altercation' with the British agent, George Starr (alias *Hilaire*), who had been fighting with the Resistance for nearly two years. After his SOE training, Starr disembarked near Cassis in November 1942 and created the Wheelwright network in the areas of Bordeaux and Toulouse. The group then joined up with other forces (including the 35th Brigade of the Spanish AGE) to form the Armagnac Group which was responsible for numerous and substantial acts of sabotage before and after D-Day.

When de Gaulle arrived in Toulouse, Starr was among the most powerful military leaders of the area and his men controlled much of the territory around the city. Ravanel had himself had disputes with the agent but acknowledged the crucial role of the RAF *parachutages* (airdrops) and the part played by *Hilaire* and his radio operator, Yvonne Cormeau (codename *Annette*), in arming the Resistance in the Toulouse area. General de Gaulle was unimpressed by Starr's record, denied his right as a foreigner to organize or command military units, and ordered him to leave France with the Jedburgh teams and Allied missions for which he was responsible. The British agent responded by telling the General to 'go screw yourself' (*'je vous emmerde'*).[10] Although there was some semblance of reconciliation between the two men, Starr did indeed abandon his postion, and France, on 26 September.

Having established his authority over the Resistance and their British allies, de Gaulle turned his attention to the Spanish delegation in the victory parade in his honour. To the dismay of Ravanel, he watched them with evident distaste and demanded to know why they had been invited to take part. Ravanel later wrote, 'When a friend makes sacrifices for your cause, you show gratitude. You do not turn your back on him the moment you no longer need him.'[11] However, de Gaulle's plan of action was clear: emasculate the Resistance, restore the powers of the state, and establish a narrative in which the struggle of the French people against the German occupier was to be untainted by references to disreputable elements such as Spanish Republicans. For the next forty years, albeit for different motives, the Spanish and French authorities would passively collude in a denial by omission of the contribution of the Spanish Maquis in the liberation of France.

In an article entitled 'The Undefeated' published in *Collier's* (3 March 1945), Martha Gellhorn described her experiences among Spanish exiles in Toulouse. Gellhorn had spent time in Madrid during the Civil War and had lived in the famous Hotel Florida with her lover, and later husband, Ernest Hemingway. In the early spring of 1945, she wrote of the Spanish Republicans, 'You can shoot them and torture them, but you cannot break them.' Of a group of young people she met at a hostel, she reported, 'The Spanish make lovely children. And also they make brave children, for if you are a Spanish Republican you have to be brave or die.' Although she failed to disclose her sources, she claimed that the Spanish Maquis in France led 400 attacks on railway facilities, destroyed 58 locomotives and 35 railway bridges, cut 150 telephone lines, attacked 20 factories and sabotaged 15 coalmines. She further claimed they took 'several thousand' German prisoners and captured three tanks. Spanish historian Ferran Sánchez Agustí provided similar figures and also claimed that the Spanish guerrillas had released 190 members of the Resistance from ten different prisons and destroyed hundreds of sub-power stations and energy installations.[12]

In his memoirs published fifteen years later, de Gaulle admitted he had met Spaniards in Toulouse who had sought refuge in France after the Civil War, but disparaged their role by claiming that only recently had they joined the Maquis.[13] He insists however that he did acknowledge their involvement in the struggle: 'I informed the Spanish leaders that the French government would not forget the services they and their men had rendered in our maquis.'[14] On the other hand, British writer Rosemary Bailey recounts an episode in which the general misguidedly asked a Spanish Republican when he had joined the Resistance. The partisan replied: 'With all respect, General, before you.'[15]

Spanish fighters played a final part in the defeat of the Nazis in France in April 1945, three weeks before VE Day. Rather than wait for Germany's capitulation in Europe, de Gaulle ordered an offensive against the Wehrmacht stronghold in the Pointe de Grave pocket on the southern bank of the Gironde Estuary, north of Bordeaux. The German garrison had survived so long after the liberation of the rest of France partly through the provision of supplies via the Basque ports in northern Spain. Vicente López Tovar (*Coronel Albert*), commander of the Republican troops that invaded the Val d'Aran, refused to put his men at risk in order to flush out German units which were awaiting orders to surrender; in his words, 'so that some politician could win a medal'.[16]

However, a group of Basque *gudaris* (warriors) did participate in the attack. The Batallón Gernika, had dissociated themselves from the Communist-led sections of the Maquis and alongside a unit of anarchists (*Libertad*) were integrated in the Foreign and Moroccan Mixed Regiment. They joined the offensive through minefields, under constant bombardment by the German artillery and against seemingly impregnable fortifications. However, in a new experience for them, they were supported by aircraft from the US Army Air Forces – B17s and B24s of the Eighth USAF. The Germans surrendered on 19 April.[17] American historian Kurlansky describes the meeting between the Polish commander of the regiment, Jan Chodzko, and Basque president-in-exile Aguirre (once more on French soil) at the award ceremony of the Croix de Guerre to the *Ikurriña* (the Basque flag) in honour of the battalion's bravery. Chodzko apparently told the Basque leader: 'When we go liberate your country, I will meet you under the tree at Guernica.'[18]

On 22 April, de Gaulle inspected the victorious troops. In an interview given in 1977, Kepa Ordoki, the commanding officer of the Basque unit, claimed that as the general walked past him, he said, 'Commander, France will not forget the efforts made by the Basques in the liberation of our country.'[19] If his commendation was genuine, he was wrong. France did forget.

Chapter 19

¿qué gigantes? – dijo Sancho Panza

And so, with the battle against the Germans and the Milice in south-west France over, thousands of heavily armed, battle-hardened and expert fighters gathered for the next stage of their war: the reconquest or liberation of Spain. Against them, Franco was in a position to deploy a vast standing army, supported by the Guardia Civil (the paramilitary police force) and an air force. Although his armoured divisions lacked the new technological developments enjoyed by the Allies and Wehrmacht alike, they were still capable of obliterating unprotected infantry in a pitched battle.

Any possibility of a Maquis victory depended on two manifest conditions. The first was that an initial incursion in the north, and the raising of the Republican flag on Spanish territory should lead to a mass popular uprising and a flood of recruits to the anti-Franco standard. Secondly, that the Republicans receive the support of the Allies. The reasoning of the Communist command in France was that if they could establish a 'beachhead' south of the Pyrenees and if they could persuade the Spanish people to rise against the dictatorship, they would draw the Allied armies into an offensive against Hitler's last great ally in Western Europe.

An assumption that the population would rally to support renewed civil war was wildly irresponsible. The years that followed the victory of April 1939 were the best of times for high-ranking army officers and members of the Catholic Church hierarchy. They were the best of times for the landed classes, the industrialists, the speculators and the black marketeers. Crucially they were also the best of times for the members of the Falange, the ideological allies of the Nazis. The victors were rewarded with the spoils of war and the financial benefits of the spoliation of Republicans' assets.[1]

They were not the best of times for the vast majority of the population who suffered political and social repression and underwent years of appalling hardship and hunger caused by the destruction of the Civil War, drought, and the government's policy of autarky. Franco turned Spain into a vast prison/labour camp. Professionals who had sympathized with the Republic lost their jobs. Left-wingers were executed, imprisoned or condemned to forced labour. The population was deprived of all civil liberties and lived in a permanent state of intimidation. Babies were stolen from their incarcerated Republican mothers and gifted to politically deserving families. The Church imposed its own specialist brand of obscurantism and Falange bullies punished social undesirables.

The duration of the Civil War had been prolonged by Franco's military strategies and political ambitions and the conflict had provided cover for his ideological cleansing of the population in those areas occupied by the Nationalists. However, he had not finished: the defeat of the Republic did not herald the peace that most people on both sides had craved, but rather a state of victory that allowed the Caudillo to continue a relentless campaign to purge Spanish society of communists, socialists, anarchists, liberals, masons, Basque or Catalan nationalists, and any other individual or group he perceived as a threat.

The working people of Spain, both urban and rural, had not only been defeated militarily, they had been tyrannized and cowed by a brutal dictatorship. Their leaders were dead, in exile or in prison. They lived under a military occupation supported by huge garrisons in every major town and a range of police forces which recognized no constraints in their efforts to seek out potentially subversive and hostile elements. Those who might have sought to join a clandestine struggle against the dictatorship were also the victims of Franco's ruthless control of the press, radio and cinema. The Spanish people were starved of news. The media offered only the Falange's pro-Nazi vision of the unfolding events of the world war and Republican sympathizers had no information concerning the part played by Spanish exiles in France or any plans they might have to liberate their homeland.

The majority of the population dedicated their lives to their own survival and the survival of their families. In the post-Civil War years, tens of thousands of people who had escaped Franco's justice died of malnutrition and related diseases. According to British historian Mary Vincent, 'In the years of hunger, people "preferred eating to freedom-fighting".'[2] The fact that the majority of the people opposed the

190

dictatorship did not mean they were ready to risk another fratricidal war to overthrow it. In December 1943, the British ambassador in Madrid, Sir Samuel Hoare, dispatched a memorandum to London, urging the government to take measures to undermine Franco's iron grip on Spain, but warned: 'Whilst nine out of ten Spaniards are opposed to Falangism, they have shown themselves unwilling or unable to organise any effective opposition.' He also suggested that many remembered 'the horrors of Spanish history', and feared any initiative that might 'plunge the country into an orgy of massacre and chaos'.[3]

After a period of less than intense analysis, based not so much on the principles of dialectical and historical materialism, as on wishful thinking, the leadership of the Communist movement somehow judged the conditions optimum for a general strike and a popular uprising against the regime. However, efforts to trigger such a rebellion were at best naïve and at worst, politically and socially irresponsible. Any civil unrest would have further endangered the fragile well-being and lives of the most vulnerable. In 1943, Donald Downes of the OSS travelled to London to hold talks with Dr Negrín. In his memoirs, the American agent reports that the Socialist leader of the government-in-exile told him, 'The Spanish people are tired – they are sick of civil war – that is Franco's only real strength.'[4]

On the other hand, Franco had now been forced to come to terms with the unpalatable truth that an Allied victory was only a matter of time. The million Spanish soldiers he had promised to defend Berlin from the Bolshevik hordes failed to materialize. Instead, the Caudillo embarked on a policy of adjusting his domestic policies to establish at least an apparent breach with the Nazi regime in a process that American historian Stanley Payne would call 'deFascistization'. Franco's regime and his own brand of National Catholicism did vary significantly from the German model: Hitler dismissed it as diluted by the influence of the Church, it lacked the anti-Semite fervour of the Nazis and recoiled from radical socio-economic change. Franco was essentially an authoritarian ultra-conservative who sought to defend the privileges of the Church, the army and landowners, and to resist modernism. Furthermore, in spite of his despotism and initial attempts to install a totalitarian regime in Spain, Franco now understood the political expediency of making concessions to the democratic sensitivities of the Western Allies.

In March 1943, Franco presided over the inaugural session of a new Cortes – a pseudo-, single-chamber parliament designed to rubber-stamp the dictator's laws and to provide the dictatorship with a simulated form of popular representation through the 'natural' agencies and offices of the social relations of the new Spain. The establishment of the assembly, under the terms of the *Ley Constitutiva de las Cortes* – the second of his fundamental or constitutional laws – was a significant step in the institutionalization of Franco's rule. The *procuradores* (members) were nominated by the hierarchies (religious, economic, political, social and military) upon which the regime was built, or appointed by the dictator himself. They had no legislative powers and were required simply to 'legitimize' and approve proposals made by Franco; dissension was tantamount to ingratitude.

Later, in July 1945, the Cortes would ratify the *Fuero de los Españoles,* a charter outlining the rights and duties of the Spanish people. Although designed to project a less authoritarian image to the outside world, the *Fuero* established no effective limit to the powers of the dictatorship. Article 33 of Section Two stated that the exercise of those rights recognized in the charter was only authorized in so far as they did not endanger 'the spiritual, national and social unity of Spain'. Given the arbitrary nature of the justice system, the continued use of military courts, and the lack of any legal protection for those accused of political misdemeanours, the article neutralized any guarantee of individual liberty.

The new approach of cosmetic constitutional measures was intended to provide the regime with a less totalitarian gloss, and was therefore accompanied by the elimination of the paraphernalia and symbols associated with national socialism – including the straight arm fascist salute. The Fundamental Law of 1947 (ratified by referendum) declared Spain a kingdom (with an empty throne) and appointed Franco head of state for life. Ensconced in power, convinced of his own indispensability and impervious to foreign demands for genuine reform, the dictator chose to refer to the new Spain as an 'organic democracy' – a political system democratic in name only.

In 1944/5, the question that faced Franco was whether he had ingratiated himself sufficiently with Allied leaders and agents to counter any temptation to commit their armed forces to a military operation designed to impose regime change in a neutral/non-belligerent country.

Indeed, the level of Allied support for the liberation of Spain was an unknown factor and was not seriously discussed until the Potsdam Conference of July 1945, when Stalin urged his allies to 'help the democratic forces in Spain'.[5] However, in the autumn of 1944, the British, American, Canadian and French were involved in a desperate struggle with the Wehrmacht on the Western Front. Although the core of the German high command and civilian authorities were aware that they had lost the war, the Allies were equally aware that much bitter fighting remained before they could win it. The Germans fought with tenacity, and indeed fanaticism, to protect the fatherland from invasion, and Hitler continued to make references to new ('vengeance') weapons that would force his enemies to negotiate. Unsurprisingly, the British advocated the destruction of the enemy's V1 and V2 launch sites on the north-western coast of Europe and the Germans' capacity to wreak terror on the civilian population in England as a priority.

For their part, the Americans were determined to follow the most direct route to Berlin and unconditional surrender. The priority of the US government and military was to defeat Hitler as quickly as possible and then to turn their attention to the war in Asia. Although there were unsubstantiated rumours that General Eisenhower had issued a promise to Spanish recruits in the Allied armies that his plans included the liberation of Spain,[6] at this stage, no one in London or Washington would have seriously countenanced the possibility of diverting resources away from their main thrust in the north.

It did remain unclear whether or not Franco had made adequate concessions to the Allies on military and logistic issues to prevent an eventual intervention once Hitler had surrendered. Despite his vocal pro-Axis stance and a series of actions that undermined the Allies' war effort, it was also true that Franco had not declared war on Britain in 1940 and had resisted Hitler's attempts to launch an offensive against Gibraltar in 1941. Furthermore, he had done nothing to disrupt the Anglo-American plans for Operation *Torch*. Churchill later told the House of Commons (24 May 1944) that in the four weeks leading up to the invasion of North Africa in November 1942, the Allies had as many as 600 aircraft deployed on the Gibraltar airfield within range of the Spanish batteries. 'I can assure the House,' he said, 'that the passage of those critical days was very anxious indeed. However, the Spaniards continued absolutely friendly and tranquil. They asked no questions, they raised no inconveniences.'

In an ill-advised conclusion, he declared:

> As I am here to-day speaking kindly words about Spain, let me add that I hope she will be a strong influence for the peace of the Mediterranean after the war. Internal political problems in Spain are a matter for the Spaniards themselves. It is not for us – that is, the Government – to meddle in such affairs.[7]

The statement disappointed public opinion at home, the US government, Sir Samuel Hoare, the Spanish monarchists campaigning for the restoration of the Bourbon dynasty, and those Republicans who were fighting with the Allies on the Western Front. On the other hand, the Caudillo was delighted, and apparently took to carrying a translation of the speech in his pocket which he would produce when 'challenged' on his foreign and domestic policies.[8] It was perhaps disingenuous to expect the British and French to provide any more support to the anti-Franco cause than they had during the Civil War. The attitude of the Allies in 1944/5 was an extension of the policy of non-intervention which had optimized the conditions for Franco's victory. In a letter to the US president dated 4 June 1944, in which he sought to undo some of the damage caused by his Commons statement the previous month, the British prime minister told him:

> I do not care about Franco, but I do not wish to have the Iberian peninsula hostile to the British after the War [...]. We should not be able to agree here in attacking countries which have not molested us because we dislike their totalitarian form of government. I do not know whether there is more freedom in Stalin's Russia than in Franco's Spain. I have no intention to seek a quarrel with either.[9]

It is clear now that there was no will among British government and military command circles to open another front in the Iberian Peninsula. Nor did they forget that the people of Britain had been at war on different stages in three different continents for five years, and until the invasion of the USSR and the subsequent attack on Pearl Harbor, they had stood alone. They were war weary, anxious to bring their troops home and to make a new beginning with the promise of radical social change.

Despite his personal dislike for Franco, Churchill viewed him as a guarantee of stability in a troubled region. Nor is it beyond the realms of possibility that he had indeed negotiated with agents of the regime. He enjoyed a particularly close personal relationship with the 17th Duke of Alba, Franco's envoy to London during the Civil War and then ambassador for the duration of the world war. With his usual disregard for democratic proprieties, and even basic wartime secrecy protocols, Churchill enjoyed frequent lunches and 'brandy-laden get-togethers'[10] with the duke, which caused disquiet among the intelligence services in London. Kim Philby, in his capacity as British agent (Secret Intelligence Service – Section V [Iberia]), had access to the duke's dispatches and was aware that he was providing high-grade intelligence to the Spanish government, based presumably on the indiscretions of people in high places. Philby assumed this information would be passed on to the Germans. Given his friendship with Churchill, MI5 concluded that nothing could be done to stop the duke. Philby concluded: 'So there we had to leave it, cherishing a single hope. Alba's reports maintained a tone wholly friendly to Britain. It was possible that Hitler would dismiss him as an incurable Anglophile. After all, he was Duke of Berwick, too.'[11]

It does not seem implausible that the British prime minister may have explicitly suggested a quid pro quo either through the Alba conduit or Alan Hillgarth, the naval attaché in Madrid, who enjoyed both Churchill's confidence and good relations with many officers in the Spanish armed forces. In February 1941, 'Wild Bill' Donovan, in his pre-OSS days, travelled to Madrid on a fact-finding mission for Roosevelt. In an interview with the British ambassador, Sir Samuel Hoare reportedly told him that, 'there is a hope of keeping Spain out of the war' if Franco could be convinced that 'sooner or later we will win'. He also appeared to suggest that it might be necessary to overcome Franco and Serrano Suñer's assumption that 'a British victory would mean the end of all dictatorships in Europe, their own included'.[12] The British prime minister would undoubtedly have considered non-intervention in Spanish affairs a small price to pay in return for Spain's continuing neutrality/non-belligerency, and inaction over Gibraltar and the North Africa landings in the crucial years between 1940 and 1942.

In his intervention in Parliament in May 1944, he went so far as to refer to 'prolonged negotiations' on other questions – facilities provided to the Italian Navy, Tangier, wolfram exports to Germany – and told the House that he was glad that a 'better arrangement has been made with Spain'.[13]

President Roosevelt was, at least ideologically, a more resolute anti-fascist than Churchill, but the man he chose to represent the USA as ambassador in Madrid, Carlton J.H. Hayes, was not. Indeed, Hayes supported the statement made by Churchill to the House of Commons in May 1944[14] and believed Franco had done enough to distance himself from the Axis and to prove his worth as an ally of the USA. He expressed gratitude for Spain's 'benevolent neutrality' and claimed that the Caudillo's public declarations of support for the Third Reich were designed to appease Hitler 'with words rather than deeds'.[15] He concurred with Churchill's analysis that Franco had made a substantial contribution to the Allied war effort by refusing to declare war on Britain, by impeding Hitler's planned offensive against Gibraltar and by virtually turning a blind eye to the Anglo-American preparations for Operation *Torch*. He blamed the antagonism towards Franco in some governing circles in Washington and London on the 'leftist' press and Spanish Republican and Soviet propaganda, and with exquisite cynicism suggested that it was hardly the fault of the Allies if the population did not rise against the dictatorship: 'Surely they do not fear that France and Russia and England and China and the United States would interfere to *prevent* them from overthrowing Franco.'[16] He concluded that the absence of a revolt suggested there was greater popular support for Franco than was portrayed in the Allied media. The ambassador therefore counselled a 'policy of friendly relations' with the government in Madrid, in accordance with the principle of the non-interference in the internal affairs of European powers, as set out in the Monroe Doctrine (1823).

The only Allied power that therefore showed any real interest in regime change in Madrid was the USSR. Soviet military personnel had fought Franco's armies in the Civil War in Spain, and more significantly the División Azul had engaged with the Red Army on Russian soil at Leningrad. As a result, among the Big Three, Stalin had more motive to urge the overthrow of Franco than the other two. He first raised the issue at the Teheran Conference (November/December 1943) when he suggested the British and Americans might install a less hostile government in Madrid. Nevertheless, logistics ruled out any direct Soviet intervention.

There are no documented reports of approaches by the Republican authorities to the Anglo-American commands requesting military support for a campaign against Franco. Dr Negrín, the Prime Minister of the Republic, in exile in London, was largely ignored by the authorities and was denied any official status. In an interview with OSS agent Donald Downes on 12 April 1943 in his Grosvenor Square apartment (after Operation *Torch*), Negrín discussed the role of Spanish Republicans in North Africa and the conditions in which many had been held in French camps.[17] According to Downes, Negrín was enthusiastic about a campaign of sabotage and subversion among the armed forces, but excluded any possibility of a popular uprising. He apparently told the American:

> Our paths for the moment are parallel, our enemies we have in common, what will defeat Fascism and Nazism will in the long run help Spain. I cannot allow myself to believe that Franco will survive in a world of the victorious democracies ...[18]

Downes further reports that when he failed to reply, Negrín understood the significance of his silence: 'A deep Latin shrug of his shoulders and an elevation of his eyebrows made me understand that he too had serious doubts.'

The two men also mentioned the role of one of the more 'colourful' of Spanish participants in the struggle against fascism: Ricardo Sicre (although Negrín calls him Ricardo Sigro). Sicre had been a member of Esquerra Republicana (Republican Left – the Catalan socialist party) and was a veteran of the Civil War. He crossed the Pyrenees in 1939 and spent time in the camp at Argelès-sur-Mer. Through the services of an English volunteer nurse he was able to re-immigrate to Britain, where he worked as a hairdresser and joined the Local Defence Volunteers (LDV, or Home Guard) under the orders of Tom Wintringham, the former International Brigades officer. Alongside other veterans of the Civil War – both Spanish and from the International Brigades – Sicre was recruited to the staff of the Osterley Park Training School. Much of the military/guerrilla expertise the instructors imparted was based on the experience of the militias that defended Madrid in 1936.

However, Sicre soon opted to travel to the USA where he was detained as an illegal immigrant and offered the choice between repatriation to Spain or enlistment in the US secret services. His most daring feat in Washington was to break into the Spanish embassy and to steal a series of classified documents and codes. Once recruited by Downes, he travelled to North Africa and participated actively in the Operation *Backbone* preliminaries. In 1944, now an officer in the US Army, he returned to the South of France in the aftermath of Operation *Dragoon* with orders to root out Nazi agents left behind as the German forces retreated north. He also made contact with the Spanish Maquis who played such a significant role in the Midi.[19] After the war, Sicre married the British-Canadian Betty Ann Lussier – a former Air Transport Auxiliary pilot and fellow OSS operative – and finally settled in Spain, where he combined his espionage role as part of the new Central Intelligence Agency (CIA – successor to the OSS) with a highly lucrative import-export business. Once Franco was publicly recognized as an American ally in the global struggle against international communism in 1953, Sicre's position as a US agent and defender of both American and Spanish interests caused no embarrassment on either side of the Atlantic. He became an established figure in Spanish society and the friend of such celebrities as Ava Gardner, Salvador Dali, Hemingway and Orson Welles.[20]

Meanwhile, the 'authorities' in Mexico City enjoyed some access to the political lobby and to the media in the USA but its power to influence government and military authorities in Washington or London was negligible. The most active was Negrín's foreign minister, Julio Álvarez del Vayo. He collaborated with the *Free World Association*, the organization/journal committed to democratic reform and economic and social development beyond the military defeat of fascism, and was an effective mouthpiece for the principles of Vice-President Henry Wallace's vision of the *Century of the Common Man*.

Some dissident monarchists did also make tentative advances to the British diplomatic corps in Madrid and sought help in their intrigues against Franco. The fact that the British government chose to ignore intelligence emanating from the British embassy and declined to encourage even the right-wing opposition to Franco would appear to confirm the unlikelihood of any intervention on behalf of the Republicans.

It would seem safe to assume that the leadership of the PCE in exile in the USSR would have consulted directly or indirectly with Stalin's entourage on the possibility of Soviet involvement. However, Stalin's only option was to bring pressure on Roosevelt and Churchill. His own war aims, beyond the defeat of Hitler, were based on establishing 'friendly' regimes in those countries occupied by the Red Army. He was also keen to participate in the final struggle with Japan in order to bolster the position of the USSR in Asia and to limit US influence in the area. His ambitions were thwarted by Truman's orders to use the atom bomb. Stalin was enough of a realist to understand that to extend the new Soviet empire as far as the Iberian Peninsula without Red Army boots on the ground was not a viable project.

If it is true that the Allies had given no firm indication that they were prepared to commit themselves to a military operation in Spain, and that no objective criteria existed to suggest that Spain had entered a 'pre-revolutionary' stage, Spanish historian Secundino Serrano suggests that among the Republican troops in south-west France there was a momentum that was difficult to ignore.[21] A feeling of euphoria combined with a sense of destiny, that having fought the Nazis, history was now calling on them to liberate Spain. If Hitler, leader of the all-conquering and apparently invincible Wehrmacht had been defeated, then how could Franco hope to survive? It is further true that the Americans had made no public statement ruling out intervention if the Maquis gained a foothold in northern Spain. On the other hand, there was almost certainly a growing fear that, given de Gaulle's efforts to demobilize the Resistance, it was only a matter of time before he ordered the Spanish guerrillas to decommission their weapons and dismantle their organization. Indeed, the general later claimed that during his visit to Toulouse in September, he had already warned Spanish leaders that 'access to the Pyrenean frontier was forbidden them'.[22] In addition to this sense of 'now or never', it is difficult to imagine how the Republicans, who had finally tasted victory after eight years of fighting for the cause of anti-fascism, could now be expected to sit on their hands.

And so, in the last autumn of the Second World War, Jesús Monzón, de facto leader of the PCE of the interior, sent orders for his colleagues in France to launch Operation *Reconquista de España*: the mass infiltration of guerrilla forces across the Pyrenees into Spain – the first phase in the campaign to overthrow Franco and restore democracy in Spain.

199

Chapter 20

Republic Across the Mountains

Manuel Azcárate, son of Pablo de Azcárate (Republican ambassador in London during the Civil War) later wrote in his memoirs: 'We were free and armed, but just around the corner, across the border, was Spain where the people were oppressed and starving. We had to do something.'[1]

Azcárate was a co-opted member of the unofficial Delegación del Comité Central of the PCE in Toulouse. Since 1940, he had worked tirelessly with Carmen de Pedro to coordinate the Spanish Communist movement among the refugees in France. De Pedro had been the personal assistant of Togliatti and had been left in charge when the party leadership withdrew from Paris to the Soviet Union. She had been commissioned to facilitate the paperwork for cadres seeking to re-emigrate from France and to provide support for those left behind in prison camps. She had also been Monzón's partner until his departure for Madrid and her own for Switzerland.

The third associate was the slightly mysterious Manuel Gimeno, whose role has been largely ignored. Azcárate himself mentions him only once in his memoirs, claiming Gimeno had 'carried out some missions for Monzón in France'.[2] Santiago Carrillo, in his vast volume of memoirs, and Gregorio Morán, in his seminal work on the PCE, make only passing references to his position in the party, and both spell his name with a J instead of a G.[3] Spanish historian Daniel Arasa interviewed him for his own book on the Maquis and described his work in France in the JSU and in the Delegación del Comité Central in France. He had been captured at the end of the Civil War and detained in the notorious holding camp of Los Almendros in Alicante before being transferred to the no-less-notorious concentration camp at Albatera. Released through the intervention of family and friends, he escaped to France. He returned to Madrid in 1942 and was present in the meeting at which Monzón announced the creation of the Junta Suprema. Warned by a friend that the authorities were aware of his presence in Madrid, Gimeno escaped once more to France in October 1943. He was briefly in charge of party affairs when Monzón ordered Carmen de Pedro and Azacárate to neutral Switzerland in an attempt to establish communications with the party hierarchy in Russia and Latin America.

In his memoirs, Azacárate hints that Monzón may have tired of de Pedro and used their mission as a means to force a separation. Gregorio Morán suggests that the decision to send the two leaders to Switzerland was a response to the wave of arrests of Communist leaders in France.[4] In his own report of February 1945, Santiago Carrillo claims Monzón dispatched them to neutral territory in order to have time and space in which to impose his own control of the party structures in both Spain and France.[5] Once in Geneva, Azcárate was held in detention for several weeks until he obtained authorization to study at the International Institute for Higher Education. Carmen de Pedro meanwhile remained in the country illegally and was able to communicate with the politburo representatives in Mexico, to make contact with a correspondent of the TASS agency, and to transmit news of developments inside France and Spain to the central committee in the USSR.

More significantly, Azcárate and de Pedro were introduced to Noel Field, the representative of the Unitarian Service Committee, responsible for funding humanitarian missions to alleviate the suffering caused by the war in Europe. Field was a Soviet agent working inside the US State Department until the outbreak of the Spanish Civil War. He then gave up his post in Washington and went to work for the League of Nations in Spain, helping to repatriate volunteers from the International Brigades. He organized refugee relief missions in the South of France until the Nazis occupied the Vichy zone in 1942. He subsequently escaped to Switzerland and, at meetings with Azcárate and de Pedro, he agreed to provide substantial funds to support Republican exiles in France.

Nevertheless, as a determined anti-fascist, he also felt compelled to provide the US intelligence authorities (OSS) with information gathered during his work in France. At the end of the 1940s, the Soviet intelligence services denounced Field as an American double agent. In May 1949, he was abducted from the hotel where he was staying in Prague and removed to Budapest, where he was tortured and held in solitary confinement for over five years. His 'treachery' was used as the basis for a series of show trials in Eastern Europe designed to purge national communist leaders who proved too independent of Moscow. He was released after the death of Stalin, and remarkably opted to stay in

Hungary, where he died in 1970. Unfortunately for Monzón, Azcárate, de Pedro and Gimeno, as for all the other communist leaders who had, directly or indirectly, turned to Field for assistance, their contacts would eventually make them vulnerable to accusations of collaboration with US intelligence.

Meanwhile in 1944, in the weeks after D-Day, Azcárate and de Pedro left Switzerland separately, and were reunited in a liberated Toulouse. It was here that they received Monzón's missive and upon their shoulders fell the responsibility of either ignoring (or countermanding) the instructions that had arrived from Madrid, or ordering thousands of men into battle. In his memoirs, using the first-person plural without stipulating who that included, Azcárate records that the Delegación del Comité Central convened a meeting of guerrilla and party leaders. According to Gregorio Morán, the meeting was attended by Azcárate, de Pedro, Luis Fernández (*General Luis*), Juan Blázquez (*General César*), López Tovar (*Coronel Albert*) and Manuel Jimeno (*Gimeno*).[6] In his own description of the meeting, Gimeno claimed that the proposal to launch an invasion was accepted unanimously: 'There was no opposition and indeed the plan was greeted with the enthusiasm of all those present.'[7] The debate subsequently centred on where best to launch the attack. There is a suggestion that Monzón himself preferred an invasion of Andorra,[8] but the meeting was apparently swayed by the arguments of Juan Blázquez who was a native (and former mayor) of Bossòst in the Val d'Aran.[9] According to his wife, Lola Clavero, Blázquez was in fact opposed to the incursion but argued that if it were to go ahead, the most suitable target should be the Val d'Aran, 'because it was the only area of the Pyrenees [...] where it would be easy both to enter and to exit, with few risks and minimum loss of human lives'.[10] Another participant at the meeting, López Tovar, would also claim later that he had opposed the strategy from the beginning.

The Valle de Arán in Spanish/Castellano, Vall d'Aran in Catalan, and Val d'Aran in Aranés (the local language) is a mountainous zone of the central Pyrenees, of huge natural beauty and especially popular today with skiers. The surface area is a little over 600 square kilometres and in 1944, the population was approximately 4,000 inhabitants. It is a *comarca* (small region) of Catalonia, and it is bordered in the north by France, and in the south-west by Aragon. The capital, Viella in Castellano and Vielha in Catalan/Aranés, is approximately 160 kilometres (by road) to the west of Andorra, 170 kilometres to the south of Toulouse, and 160 kilometres to the north of Lleida (Lérida). In 1944, it was far more accessible from the north than it was from the south. The tunnel that would link the valley with the rest of Catalonia was still under construction and as winter was coming, it was assumed that snow would soon block the eastern road link with Catalonia at the Bonaigua Pass. The Republicans would thus be able to establish a bridgehead in Spain and hold it for several months.

Unsure of their own position, de Pedro and Azcárate decided to consult their comrades in the French Communist Party, not only as a courtesy to the Communist Party of the country in which they were based, but because they believed that the PCF might enjoy better communications with Moscow and might even offer valid advice. In his memoirs, Azcárate reports that they travelled to Paris after the meeting which approved the invasion. However, he appears to have told the historian Daniel Arasa that in fact they made the trip after receiving the letter from Monzón and prior to the conference.[11] Whichever the case, the journey to the capital in wartime France was not easy:

> American truck drivers gave us petrol which we swapped for brandy. A lot of bridges were still in ruins and we had to cross rivers on pontoons. There were huge queues and it could take hours to cross a river. We arrived in Paris at six o'clock as the lights were going out. The restrictions were still tight. We managed to get rooms at a hotel in the Rue Lafayette. Entering the headquarters of the PCF – they had repossessed the old building after the liberation – was like trying to get into a fortress.[12]

They were finally able to meet with Jacques Duclos, the leader of the PCF in the Resistance movement and André Marty, commander of the International Brigades during the Civil War. Neither man appeared to be particularly interested in *Operación Reconquista* and neither bothered to enquire about details of the plan. Duclos apparently stated that his priority was to confiscate the assets of those who had collaborated with the Germans. He claimed that as most of the capitalist classes had been collaborators, this would prove to be a short-cut to socialism. The Spaniards were left with the impression that the PCF considered the operation as a relatively minor and entirely Spanish diversion. Azcárate insists that he and de Pedro neither asked for, nor were offered, any material assistance. Daniel Arasa claimed that Azcárate told him later that he had secretly hoped that the PCF would intervene and demand the plans of invasion be aborted, as this would have freed him from responsibility.[13] In his own report to the party of 6 February 1945, Santiago Carrillo claimed that the French Communist Party had indeed opposed the operation[14] but failed to stipulate whether the leadership had expressed their disapproval before or after the campaign.

In the meantime, the leadership of the AGE, commenced the task of drawing up the military plans for the invasion. Commander-in-chief José Luis Fernández (*General Luis*) and his chief political commissar, Juan Blázquez Arroyo (*General César*) chose to move their headquarters from Toulouse to Montrejeau, some 28 kilometres from the border. The newly installed mayor invited them to occupy the castle, local school and a tower that was the property of his *collaborationniste* predecessor. Ramiro López (Mariano) was entrusted with the task of maintaining communications with the high command and the guerrilla leaders in the invasion force.

At this stage, *Mariano* found some resistance to the operation from local Maquis who questioned the wisdom of a large-scale attack that would provoke the response of Franco's army and would put at risk the survival of the partisan movement. Nor was everyone convinced that the Spanish people were ready for a popular uprising or that the Allies would provide support. The alternative strategy option was to embark on a sustained campaign of smaller incursions, infiltrating groups of partisans who could make contact with local Maquis (the *huidos*) throughout Spain. Through acts of sabotage and attacks on the repressive forces of Franco's state, they would then be able to undermine the morale of the Guardia Civil and police, incite the local population to action, and over time organize a coordinated popular response to the dictatorship.

Nevertheless, the military command insisted that the conditions for a more high-profile attack would never be more favourable. In particular, de Gaulle was unlikely to tolerate indefinitely the presence of autonomous, well-armed Spanish Maquis throughout the Midi. In his memoirs, Santiago Carrillo famously reported that when he finally arrived in Paris in the autumn of 1944, he was informed by party comrades that France was divided in two: 'As far south as the River Loire, the country was under the military authority of the North Americans; the area between the Loire and the Pyrenees was in the hands of the Spanish.'[15] Although the claim was an outrageous exaggeration, it was certainly true that the Spanish Republicans controlled much of the borderlands, apparently with the tacit consent of the Allies. Although de Gaulle was clearly unhappy at the role of the Spanish Republicans in the Midi and the occupation of Spanish consulates, at least for the time being, the priority of the French high command remained the expulsion of German troops and the definitive liberation of France.

In his memoirs, de Gaulle claimed that at an undisclosed date, he dispatched a unit of the First Army to the south 'to ensure the adequate patrolling of the Pyrenees passes'.[16] However, in October 1944, the Spanish still enjoyed a high level of autonomy in the area south of Toulouse and resolutely expressed their unwillingness to relinquish their own command independence. Daniel Arasa recounts a meeting between General Leclerc and members of the AGE general staff, at which the French general was persuaded to release some of the Spanish troops that had accompanied him through Africa and northern France, so they might join the Maquis army in the south (with their weapons).[17] Carrillo claims that during the German counter-offensive in the Ardennes (16 December 1944–25 January 1945), he resisted demands from the French Communist Party that the Spanish send reinforcements to support the French Army[18]. Finally, in April 1945, López Tovar himself refused to obey orders from the French general staff to take part in the assault on the German positions in Pointe de Grave, on the western coast. Given the impending surrender of the Wehrmacht, he argued that the action would lead to a needless sacrifice of the lives of his men.

It often appeared that de Gaulle, on the other hand, was almost as anxious to dismantle the Resistance as he was to defeat the Germans, and the new French military and civil authorities could hardly be expected to ignore the presence of a potentially destabilizing and independent force once the enemy had been expelled from French soil. In favour of an immediate and (relatively) large-scale offensive, *Mariano* also argued that the Allies were unlikely to intervene in Spain unless the Spanish people had demonstrated their own will to overthrow Franco, and, as a last resort, he insinuated that the invasion had been authorized by the party leadership and appealed to the discipline and the loyalty to the party which were the rudiments of the Communist creed.

The liberation of Toulouse brought the UNE a new ally: Radio Toulouse. The station, under the control of the local Resistance forces, offered substantial air time to the Spanish exiles, and specifically to the Communist leadership of the UNE. It proved to be a far more significant means of propaganda than *Reconquista de España* as it could be heard throughout south-western France and north-eastern Spain and was in a position to broadcast far more relevant news and instructions than Radio España Independiente operating under orders from the leadership in the USSR.

On 20 September, La Pasionaria issued a communiqué urging the Maquis to extend the struggle. She reminded the party that guerrilla warfare had been developed in Spain during the 'glorious war of independence' against the French occupiers (1808–14) and insisted:

> Our guerrillas must broaden their operations; the creation of new armed groups in the city and in the country is one of the essential tasks of the Junta Suprema and the committees of Unión Nacional throughout the country [...] Of course it is not enough to create isolated guerrilla groups which can easily be destroyed. What is necessary is to create [...] a guerrilla movement. [...] We must finish with Franco and the Falange; we must liberate Spain; we must fight to conquer the right to freedom, the right to be free and to live in freedom.[19]

However, according to the Spanish journalist and historian, Daniel Arasa, La Pasionaria later clarified both the role of the radio and the relations between the politburo in the Soviet Union and the party workers in France and Spain:

> We used the radio to broadcast manifestos, we made calls to join the struggle against Franco [...] but we did not order specific acts. How could we tell our comrades in France to do this or that if we had practically no contact [with them] and no knowledge of their specific problems? In Moscow we received practically no information, either from the Maquis or other circles. We had no relations with the rest of Europe, and communications were tremendously difficult. At that time, the governing bodies of the party in Spain and France were totally autonomous.[20]

In the early autumn of 1944, the UNE used Radio Toulouse to broadcast explicit calls to the exiles who had played such a significant role in the victory over the Nazis and the Milice in the south-west to muster in the Toulouse area in readiness for a military operation against the tyrant in Madrid, and repeatedly announced the imminent fall of the dictatorship. As a result, any slight element of surprise which may have existed was removed. The military command subsequently ordered a series of diversionary cross-border raids along the entire frontier from Girona (Catalonia) to Gipuzkoa (Basque Country) in order to draw attention away from the planned main thrust of the invasion, to make contact with Maquis groups inside Spain, and to gather intelligence. In the first week of September, some 800 men of the 153rd Brigade and the 54th Brigade launched attacks through the Roncesvalles and Roncal valleys (Navarra) respectively. They received virtually no support from the local population (many of whom were Carlist traditionalists) and were driven back by the Guardia Civil and Policia Armada.

Simultaneously, three brigades attacked targets in Aragón, but although the 21st Brigade enjoyed considerable success and in turn occupied thirteen villages, after a month on Spanish soil, the failure of the other two brigades forced a general retreat. Other incursions were ordered in Catalonia, but were all forced to withdraw. Tellingly, the Maquis did not appear to seek open hostilities with the *franquista* forces of order that opposed them, or to impose casualties, or to carry out reprisals against members of the Church or Falange. They appeared satisfied to make their presence felt, to collect intelligence, and to provide cover for the infiltration of individuals and small units deeper into the peninsula in order to coordinate operations with other guerrilla groups. If their reluctance to engage the enemy suggests their mission was in part a 'hearts and minds' operation rather than an attempt to convert the north-eastern region of Spain into a combat zone, it failed. Those local populations that were not overtly hostile, were clearly restrained by a dread of a resurgence of civil war or, at the very least, fear of retaliation by the *franquista* authorities when the Maquis withdrew.

While the raids were undoubtedly successful in masking the intended location for the initial attack of the main invasion force, the military outcomes and the response of the local population did not augur well. In one report, a guerrilla leader informed the high command that, 'Today we are treated more like foreigners in Spain than we are in France'.[21]

Nonetheless, by mid-September, approximately 10,000 well-armed fighters were ready to take the struggle to Franco. On 21 September, General Luis, from his headquarters in Montrejeau, issued the order which created the 204th Division, consisting of twelve brigades (of between 200 and 400 men), which would lead the invasion. He also designated Lieutenant-Colonel Vicente López Tovar as the commanding officer of the division.

López Tovar had been born in Madrid in 1909. He deserted from the army in 1932 and thus failed to complete his military service. He joined the Communist Party after the 1936 elections and at the outbreak of the Civil War, he participated in the ill-fated siege of the Alcazar of Toledo. He then joined the prestigious XV Corps of the Popular Army, and saw action in Madrid and at the Battle of the Ebro. He took part in the rearguard actions to support the *retirada* in January/February 1939 and was one of the last of the Communist Party hierarchy to abandon the government headquarters at Elda and fly out of the Monóvar aerodrome on 7 March 1939.

In France he went into hiding and found work as a woodcutter and charcoal burner. He also became actively involved in the coordination of the Republican units that were dispersed throughout the south-west, and his group was partly able to fund their activities by ambushing tobacco smugglers and taking possession of their wares. He later claimed that the life of the partisan was easier for Spanish Republicans because 'we had nothing to lose. We had no home, not even a suitcase, we had lost everything in Spain'.[22] Under the nom de guerre *Fernand*, he founded the 3rd Brigade of the Spanish Guerrillas, as part of the umbrella organization, the Main d'Oeuvre Immigrée (MOI) – the military structure sponsored by the French Communist Party. At the end of 1943, he was made head of the 5th Region MOI and given responsibility for coordinating the disparate forces in the Dordogne and the surrounding regions. He also developed a friendship with André Malraux (*Colonel Berger*), the man who had made a significant impact on the Republican air force during the Civil War and who was now in direct contact with de Gaulle. Although his close association with the French caused some distrust among his Spanish comrades, he was eventually appointed chief of the autonomous XV Division of the Agrupación de Guerrilleros Españoles.

A committed member of the Communist movement, he was perhaps too independently minded to be comfortable with some of the policy decisions of those above him in his own party. He would later claim that as he was opposed to the operation, he at first refused the posting and argued that the lack of heavy artillery made it unrealistic to suppose that a guerrilla force could defeat a regular army in a pitched battle.[23] According to his own version, he was finally persuaded by *Mariano* that as the PCE had ordered the invasion, it was his duty to take command of the division. His own men also suggested that whatever his misgivings, to allow a less competent leader to take command would increase the danger of a catastrophe and put at risk the lives of hundreds, even thousands, of brave Republican partisans.[24]

Once the reluctant military leader had come to terms with his 'duty', he commenced the strategic planning for the invasion. He later asserted, 'I drew up the General Order of Operations and made sure it was followed, but I was sure we would fail. So, at the same time as I prepared the attack and the occupation of the villages, I also laid plans for the retreat.'[25] By mid-October the Republican guerrillas were ready to launch what could either be the last battle of the Spanish Civil War, or the first battle of the Second Civil War: either a minor skirmish in a forgotten conflict, or the opening of a new front in the global struggle against fascism.

Chapter 21

For Courage Mixed with Prudence is not Foolish

By the second fortnight of October 1944, the British had been at war for five years (since September 1939), the Soviet Union for a little over three years (June 1941) and the USA a little under three years (December 1941). The Spanish Republicans had been fighting fascism for eight years (July 1936). The world war had entered a crucial stage. The Allied armies were approaching the German borders on both the eastern and the western fronts. On 14 October, Field Marshal Rommel had been forced to commit suicide as punishment for his involvement in the plot against the Führer. Soviet and Yugoslav forces entered Belgrade on 19 October. In Moscow, Churchill and Stalin had met to agree the distribution of spheres of influence in post-war Eastern Europe and the Balkans. In Asia, the USA had launched its offensive to liberate the Philippines and the greatest sea battle in history was about to begin in Leyte Gulf. The Japanese would respond with a new tactic, the *kamikaze* (the first mission took place on 25 October).

Nevertheless, like their allies the Japanese, the Nazis were unwilling to accept defeat. They launched the first V-2 rocket against England on 8 September 1944, and in the last year of the war almost 10,000 people were killed in Britain by Hitler's 'vengeance weapons'. Apart from terrorizing the civilian population in Britain, the V-2 was also used against such military targets as Antwerp on mainland Europe. Nor were the Nazis inclined to release their grip on the occupied and satellite territories in the east. In the face of the advance of the Red Army, they ruthlessly suppressed the Warsaw uprising of August and September (with Stalin's passive collusion).

In Budapest, they established their control over the government and Adolf Eichmann implemented the mass deportation of Hungarian Jews to Auschwitz. The commercial attaché at the Spanish embassy in the capital, Ángel Sanz Briz, who had been left in charge of diplomatic matters, subsequently embarked on a personal crusade to save the lives of as many Jews as possible. Acting independently and without the knowledge of the authorities in Madrid, he used the special status of Sephardic Jews as a smoke screen to issue thousands of passports and safe-conduct documents to those in imminent danger of deportation to Auschwitz. He also rented a number of apartments in which he sheltered hundreds more under consular protection. It is estimated he saved the lives of more than 5,000 Jews. He was recognized by the Israeli state as 'Righteous Among the Nations' in 1966.[1]

Given the extraordinary events on the world stage, it is unsurprising that the Battle of the Val d'Aran passed unnoticed and that it does not appear in any of the histories of the Second World War. The frontier that separates Spain and France, established by the Treaty of the Pyrenees in 1659, stretches for 656.3 kilometres between the Bay of Biscay and the Mediterranean, interrupted only by the principality of Andorra. The mountainous terrain, the deficient road communications and extreme weather conditions provided an optimum setting for a guerrilla offensive.

The aim of the military operation, as defined in López Tovar's plan of operations was simple: 'the Liberation of Spain'. The political issues were more complex. According to the same plan, 'the guerrillas would trigger a national insurrection'.[2] The 'reconquest' of Spain would thus require a popular uprising against the dictatorship and/or the intervention of the Allies. The Communist leadership believed that if they could establish a beachhead and raise the flag of the Republic on Spanish territory, the local population would respond and take to the barricades again, the army would split, other anti-Franco forces (including the monarchists) would join the struggle, and the Allies would have no choice but to intervene.

The leaders of the UNE even considered the possibility of setting up a government in Vielha (Viella), the capital of the valley, under the Socialist politicians Dr Juan Negrín (the last Prime Minister of the Republic), Julio Álvarez del Vayo (foreign minister under Largo Caballero and Negrín) and the Republican military leader General Riquelme.

Given the circumstances, the obvious lack of any census, and the very nature of the army that stood poised to launch the offensive against Franco's dictatorship, it is only possible to make an approximate estimation of the number of troops involved in the campaign. The research of leading Spanish experts – Daniel Arasa, Ferran Sánchez Agustí, Secundino Serrano, Luis Zaragoza Fernández[3] – suggests 10,000–12,000 men were under arms and waiting expectantly in the border area. Although there are no records of the political affiliation of the members of the partisan army, it is safe to assume that the vast majority were loyal to the PCE and the Unión Nacional Española. There were certainly some members of the PSUC and other Catalan parties, and also a number of anarchists who had fought alongside the communists in the Resistance. Federica Montseny, prominent member of the anarcho-syndicalist CNT, later acknowledged:

> There were anarchists who participated in the attack on the Pyrenees. [...] They were warned [by the National Committee] not to have any false hopes, that they were going to get themselves killed, as it was a hare-brained adventure, but they wanted to go.[4]

López Tovar signed the order for the invasion on 16 October and at six o'clock on the morning of 19 October, some 1,500 men of the expeditionary force of the 204th Division (out of 3,000) crossed the frontier on the first stage of the operation to liberate their country. They were armed with standard-issue pistols and rifles, Bren and Sten guns, and some light artillery (including mortars, bazookas and anti-tank guns). Many weapons had been provided by the British, in the build-up to D-Day, and the French Resistance who supported the invasion and willingly supplied their comrades-in-arms with guns, ammunition and food. Other weapons had been appropriated from the Wehrmacht or borrowed from the French Army.

However, the greatest asset of the invading guerrilla force was the element of surprise and in the opening phases of the campaign, and with few casualties, they were able to occupy a large section of territory and a significant number of villages including Bossòst, Les, Canejan and Es Bòrdes, in which they raised the tricolour flag of the Republic (red, yellow and purple). In the documentary film *Aqueth Dis I auie ua nôça,* various residents of Les recall that when the Maquis arrived, the village was celebrating the wedding of a local policeman, and that several villagers mistook the sound of gunfire for fireworks.[5] Locals also recall the eerie sight of Maquis appearing on mountainsides as they descended through the mist. The initial resistance to the invasion was provided by members of the Policia Armada, the Guardia Civil and men that the Maquis identified as *Carabineros* (frontier police) – although after the

Civil War they had officially been integrated in the Guardia Civil. On the first day of the invasion, the Guardia Civil defended Bossòst for some hours before withdrawing to Vielha. The 204th Division subsequently set up its command post in the Guardia Civil headquarters in the village.

Crucially they failed to dislodge the forces defending the capital. Indeed, the 204th failed even to launch a serious attack on the town. According to Sánchez Agustí, the fourteen-man garrison (*Guardias Civiles*) had inferior Russian guns and were clearly vulnerable to a determined offensive. In other words, if the highly experienced Maquis did not use their initial superiority in numbers to overpower the defenders, it was because they chose not to.[6]

There were more serious setbacks on the two flanks, where the invaders failed to capture the Vielha tunnel, or to take either the pass at Bonaigua or the village of Salardú. The latter occupied a key strategic point between the pass and the capital. It was garrisoned by members of the police and Guardia Civil and troops of the 1st Company of the Cazadores de Montaña (Mountain Light Infantry). When the village came under attack by members of the 9th Brigade, the defenders took up position in the bell tower of the Church of Sant Andreu with a single machine gun and were able to hold off the Maquis until infantry reinforcements arrived and forced the partisans to withdraw.[7] The machine gun was manned by two volunteers: Reixach, a taxi-driver from Barcelona, and Carmelo Solans Solanís, a watchmaker from Leida. Solans Solanís later said, 'I have never thought of myself as a hero. I remember closing my eyes and shooting and also feeling how close we were to death when a volley of guerrilla gunfire hit the belfry.'[8]

Meanwhile, east of the Bonaigua Pass, the 471st Brigade under Emilio Álvarez Canosa (aka *Pinocho*) met resistance at Esterri d'Aneu and witnessed the arrival of a long convoy of military trucks. According to some sources, the brigade withdrew across the border into France on 21 October having failed to achieve their objectives or to offer any resistance, and having suffered relatively minor losses.[9] This version was disputed by *Pinocho* who claims that his unit had in fact lost thirty-two men by the time they retreated.[10] In any case, in his own defence, *Pinocho* later declared:

> I believe that most units that entered Spain at the time
> did exactly the same as us: they returned to their bases in

France after the first important skirmishes with the enemy. In other words, once they saw that the odds were stacked substantially against us.[11]

As a result of these failures, the Maquis were unable to thwart the arrival of reinforcements and matériel from the east. Despite blizzards during the nights of 19 and 20 October, members of the 2nd Battalion of Franco's 41st Provisional Division were able to clear the snow each morning and keep the Bonaigua Pass open at least for some hours of daylight to allow the flow of reinforcements and artillery in the direction of Vielha.

Nevertheless, Franco greeted news of the offensive with alarm. His sister, Pilar, later recalled: 'I only remember having seen him jumpy once. In 1944, with the incident of the Maquis. Apparently, it was serious. The Generalísimo managed to hide it from the Spanish people so they didn't worry.'[12] It must be said that it is unlikely that Franco's decision to hide the news was based on his sensitivity towards the anxieties of his people and in fact the censors did allow some information regarding the events on the border to filter through to the readership of the national newspapers. The invasion coincided with the carefully choreographed elections of representatives in the vertical state trade unions that the regime had called as part of their campaign to present a less totalitarian image to the Allies, and the press coverage of the polls dominated the national news. However, on 22 October, the Barcelona-based newspaper *La Vanguardia Española* confirmed the continued infiltration of communist groups, and claimed that unnamed government forces had killed more than 100 Maquis in recent fighting. The article further claimed that, with the assistance of the armed forces of the USA, the French authorities had embarked on a campaign to disarm and intern those 'fugitives' who had re-entered France. Finally, the newspaper denounced the '*capitanes araña*'* who had persuaded their men to participate in a highly dangerous and hopeless mission. On 24 October, *ABC* carried a twelve-line item, claiming the French military authorities had removed most of the Maquis from the border area and had introduced a system of 'safe-conduct' documents. The article acknowledged that a few 'recalcitrant groups'

---

* captains who pressganged men on board their ships and then remained safely on dry land when the vessels set sail

remained, but also that 'the Spanish refugees themselves admit that the raids on Spanish frontier posts lacked any practical purpose and were useless and sanguinary'.

Two days later, *ABC* published reports that during the battle for France, the Maquis had refused to follow orders from the French Resistance chiefs and had appropriated weapons airdropped into the area by the Allies. The newspaper conceded that the Maquis controlled areas along the frontier and that the French civilian and military authorities were proving unequal to the task of pacifying them. On 28 October, both *ABC* and *La Vanguardia* carried reports from the official press agency EFE of a meeting between French and Spanish authorities at the Canfranc international railway station, at which the French representatives condemned the actions of the Spanish '*rojos*' and promised urgent measures to restore order. *ABC* also reported that the Republican exiles who had occupied Spanish consulates in the south of France had been mostly expelled and that the consulates were to come under the protection of the French forces.

On the other hand, if Pilar Franco had never seen her brother so anxious, it is also true that she was not with him when he realized the Spanish Navy had remained loyal to the Republic and that he was trapped in North Africa (July 1936). Or when the people of Madrid and Barcelona defeated the military uprising in the two most important cities in Spain (July 1936). Or when the Republican Army crossed the Ebro (July 1938). Or when the Wehrmacht reached the Pyrenees (June 1940). Nevertheless, he clearly took the threat seriously. Over the next week, 6,000 reinforcements were sent to the valley and more than 30,000 were ordered to the region, under the command of some of Franco's most senior officers including Lieutenant-Generals Monasterio, Yagüe, Garcia Valiño and Moscardó.

Moscardó was the hero of the siege of the Alcazar de Toledo (July–September 1936), when for sixty days, his hugely outnumbered troops and cadets resisted the attacks of the Republican forces that controlled the town. At the time of the Aran invasion, he was Captain-General of the IV Military Region (Catalonia) and was in Vielha to inspect the 'defences'. On two occasions he was within range of the Maquis and might easily have been taken prisoner had the invaders been aware of his presence. The vagaries of war meant that once more Moscardó and López Tovar faced each other on the battlefield. They had fought on opposite sides in the searing heat of a Castilian summer in the battle for Toledo (July–September 1939); they now met again in different circumstances and different conditions. It is not clear whether either man was aware of the presence of the other, at least not until much later.

Franco did not use his air force, in all likelihood because there was no need. It is also true that the meteorological conditions were hardly favourable, and as the battlefield was dangerously close to the frontier, the Caudillo would not have relished any cross-border incident. Finally, the roles of the Spanish Civil War had been reversed. Franco was no longer seeking to conquer enemy territory and populations, but rather to defend his own positions. He would therefore have been less willing to cause collateral damage.

Despite his reputation as a brilliant army officer – the youngest general in Europe when he was promoted in 1926, and triumphant victor of the Civil War – Franco was not an inspiring military leader. The Germans and Italians in particular became increasingly frustrated by his tactics in the war against the Republic. Rather than outmanoeuvre the adversary, the Generalísimo seemed to base his strategy on the principle of imposing the maximum damage on the enemy whatever the cost to his own troops. The conditions within the armed forces were poor considering the role they had played in the Civil War and the fact that they were the cornerstone of the regime. It is true that Franco took great care to ensure the loyalty of the officer class through a range of privileges. It is no less true that the military functioned merely as an army of occupation in a country where resistance had been all but eliminated. Nevertheless, it is remarkable that as a military dictator, Franco was satisfied with a poorly armed and poorly trained conscript army – many of whom concealed Republican sympathies.

Perhaps it is less remarkable that he showed little interest in the welfare of the foot soldiers. The men who were transferred to Aran were equipped with antiquated weapons and were unprepared for such warfare. They were fortunate that the Maquis maintained their policy of minimalizing casualties. Arasa describes an incident to the south of Vielha where members of the AGE 21st Brigade came across an enemy convoy. The regular army troops took shelter behind rocks unaware that other units of the Republican 3rd Brigade were also advancing on their position from a different angle. The conscripts found themselves trapped and exposed to crossfire from the Republican units. However, rather than use their advantage to inflict significant losses on Franco's army, the Maquis fired warning shots over the soldiers' heads and eventually withdrew from their positions. Arasa concluded that the reluctance to engage the enemy, to inflict casualties and fatalities, remains one of the great paradoxes of the entire military operation.[13]

On the other hand, and to compound the shortcomings in both weapons and training, the *franquista* military hierarchy was unable to organize an effective supply line, and infantrymen went days without adequate food rations in extreme weather conditions. During the night of 26 October, in the midst of snowstorms and freezing fog, the temperatures fell to -16°C in Viella and -20°C on the Bonaigua Pass.[14] Given that the Maquis were loath to fire on conscripts, Franco's troops had almost more to fear from the cold and hunger than they did from the enemy.

After the initial clashes, the military situation in the Val d'Aran was then reduced to stalemate. The Maquis had been fighting with the handbrake on; they now ground to a standstill. Crucially, and despite the best efforts of *Mariano*, the liaison officer between AGE headquarters in France and the military command in the Valley, López Tovar rejected demands from the general staff to launch an all-out attack on Vielha on the grounds that such a tactic would undermine his own plans for an orderly withdrawal should Franco's reinforcements threaten to surround the Maquis and cut off their retreat. According to his wife, Lola Clavero, Juan Blázquez (*General César*) also vehemently opposed a direct offensive against the capital and told his military superiors, 'I refuse, I will not lead my men there, it would be carnage, it's a death trap.'[15]

The invaders organized meetings in the villages they had occupied and sought to extend the message that they were the vanguard of a movement that would overthrow the dictatorship and restore freedom and democracy. In Bossòst, it was *General César* who addressed an assembly of the townspeople in the local cinema. Blázquez had been mayor in the early days of the Civil War before joining the Popular Army and fighting on various fronts in Aragon. After the retreat into France, he managed to avoid the first concentration camps and, with his wife, was given refuge in the Centre d'Accueil des Intelectuels Espagnoles (Welcome Centre for Spanish Intellectuals) in Toulouse. He later worked in a series of jobs, from labourer to bus driver. However, he was detained in December 1942 by the Vichy police and interned first in the Saint-Michel prison, and then in the Noé and Vernet camps. He was able to escape in the autumn of 1943 and joined the Resistance groups in the Pyrenees. In October 1944, he came home for the first time since 1937. It was also the last time.[16]

The Republicans were unable to persuade any but isolated members of the population to join their cause. The most demoralizing episode took place at the southern end of the Vielha tunnel, when members of the 21st Brigade sought to release a number of Republican prisoners enlisted in the 'redemption through forced labour scheme' of the dictatorship. They were employed in the construction of the tunnel and were accommodated in a compound known locally as 'the hospital'. When the guerrillas overpowered the guards, rather than rally to the cause of their liberators, the prisoners simply fled. If the Maquis were unable to recruit men who had been subjected to extreme levels of hardship and cruelty by their *franquista* masters, it did not appear likely they would win much support from the population as a whole.

Meanwhile, the guerrilla army continued to behave correctly towards the residents of the valley; they carried out no reprisals against members of the Falange, and appeared anxious to establish good relations with the local clergy. Blázquez reportedly ordered members of his own personal staff to stand guard outside the church in Bossòst to prevent any untimely interruptions during Mass.[17] The guerrillas shared their food supplies – including products that were not available in Spain such as white bread, chocolate and bacon.[18] They paid for the goods acquired from farmers and shops – although payment was often refused by those who, in all likelihood, erred on the side of generosity when attending men armed with sub-machine guns.

In the meantime, having survived the initial onslaught and having protected the access routes into the valley, Franco's army, police and paramilitary forces were content to await further reinforcements and heavy artillery in preparation for an eventual counter-offensive. At this stage, a new protagonist entered the drama. At the end of the Civil War, Santiago Carrillo had joined the other exiled upper cadres of the PCE in the Soviet Union. From Moscow, he was transferred to Latin America, and then ordered back to Western Europe, where he landed in Portugal at the end of June 1944. From Lisbon, he flew to Casablanca and then travelled on to Oran, now under US control. According to the account in his memoirs, as the new highest-ranking officer in the city, he dismissed the leading party representatives who were guilty of ignoring instructions to avoid any collaboration with the American services. He subsequently took charge of a planned insurgency in Andalucía. With the aid of dockers and drivers loyal to the party, his team was able to appropriate a US Army lorry with its consignment of weapons, canned food and medical supplies. They also acquired a number of motor launches and underwent a strict training routine in the Atlas Mountains. According to Carrillo, the operation involved the penetration of compact units of guerrillas whose mission was to make contact with the groups of *huidos* and to promote, facilitate and coordinate an armed uprising against the dictatorship.[19] As such, it was not unlike the mission sponsored the previous year by the American OSS, which had ended in tragedy and failure.

If the Val d'Aran offensive was based on false premises, the plan to raise an insurrection in the south of Spain was quixotic. Carrillo claims that he dispatched a letter via the offices of the French Communist Party to the PCE organization in Toulouse ordering them to desist from their plan of a mass invasion and to concentrate instead on the gradual infiltration of small guerrilla units along the lines of his plan for Andalucía, but admits that the letter apparently never arrived.[20] His strategy may indeed have been more effective in the north where maintaining supply routes and communications across the Pyrenees was a relatively simple operation, but supporting an operation from the other side of the Mediterranean presented huge difficulties. In addition to the logistical problems, Carrillo was adamant in his refusal to work with the Americans and as such his own scheme in the south was even less plausible than the *Reconquista* strategy. Moreover, he later acknowledged that the party had underestimated the effects and consequences of military defeat and dictatorship among the Spanish people. Casually ignoring his own refusal to work with the Americans, he also insisted that all Republican groups had misjudged the unwillingness of the western Allies to rally to Stalin's demands for intervention against Franco, or what he described as 'the contradictions that would soon appear at the heart of the anti-Hitler coalition'.[21]

According to his own version, Carrillo received orders from his secretary-general, La Pasionaria, to abandon his plans to lead the mission to Andalucía personally, and instead to make his way to France and to establish contact with the Delegación del Comité Central in Toulouse.

He stowed away on a French warship which had received orders to repatriate French Communist deputies who had been detained by the Vichy authorities in camps in Algeria. From Toulon, Carrillo travelled by train to Paris where he had a meeting first with officers of the PCF (including Jacques Duclos and André Marty) and then representatives of his own PCE. In his narrative, he claims that it was in the French capital that he learnt that the Val d'Aran offensive had already been launched. He subsequently returned south to Toulouse to consult with Carmen de Pedro and Manuel Azcárate, who insisted that in launching the invasion they had obeyed a direct order from the Junta Suprema de Unión Nacional, which, according to Carrillo, 'existed only in Monzón's imagination'.[22] He subsequently decided to hold urgent talks with the military commander López Tovar and set out for his headquarters in Bossòst for a meeting which would definitively settle the fate of the invasion.

By this point (28 October), it was clear the invasion had failed, either through the excessive caution of the commanders in the field, or flaws in the overall plan, or what is more plausible: the reluctance of the officers to engage the enemy as part of a plan in which they had no confidence and under the orders of superiors they did not trust.

In addition to the doubts concerning the military strategy of the Maquis, among many exiles and opposition groups of the interior, there remained a belief that the Allies would impose regime change in Madrid whether or not the Spanish people rebelled against the dictatorship. Franco had been in power for eight years (since he was appointed Generalísimo of the armed forces and head of state in Salamanca in September 1936). He had rid himself of his rivals, forced the various pro-Nationalist factions into a single party under his leadership, invited the friendship and military support of Hitler and Mussolini, and with their crucial intervention had won the Civil War. Through good fortune and miscalculation, he had stepped back from the brink of declaring war on Great Britain, but never hidden his contempt for the Allies and had repeatedly insisted that Spain would enter the conflict when the time was opportune. Without officially declaring war on the USSR, he had sent a division to fight alongside the Nazis struggling to overcome the epic defence of Leningrad. He had embraced the trappings of fascism, including the straight arm salute, and had purged communists, socialists, anarchists, republicans, and masons. Directly or indirectly, he was responsible for the execution of tens of thousands of Republicans, many after he had himself officially declared the Civil War over. Just as Hitler had warned him in 1940 that it was extremely unlikely that his regime could survive the defeat of the Axis, it seemed unthinkable that Roosevelt, Stalin and Churchill would fail to overthrow his regime once they had occupied Berlin and Rome. Indeed, in one of his famous 'Fireside Chats' (Number 25) on 28 July 1943, the US president had told the American people: 'We will have no truck with Fascism in any way, in any shape or manner. We will permit no vestige of Fascism to remain.'[23]

Chapter 22

Broma baisha

In the absence of official records, determining who attended the summit in Bossòst is akin to a jigsaw puzzle. According to Carrillo's account, he was accompanied by Manuel Azcárate and Luis Fernández (*General Luis*). According to Azcárate, the meeting was attended by military officers in command of units in the Valley. López Tovar later recalled that Carrillo was also accompanied by Ramiro López (*Mariano*). The historian Daniel Arasa claims that others present included Manuel Gimeno and Carmen de Pedro. López Tovar suggests that once those present had assembled, he invited Carrillo into his office so that they could speak in private.[1] Whatever the composition of the summit, at this stage of the operation there remained only one possible outcome. The offensive had failed. The Maquis had neither captured their main target, Vielha, nor isolated the valley from the rest of Spain. The failure to occupy strategically vital access points meant the plan to hold the bridgehead throughout the winter was no longer a viable option. Spanish Army reinforcements were arriving in substantial numbers and were equipped with potentially decisive artillery pieces. By 26 October, there were as many as 6,000 regular troops massed in the zone awaiting the next stage of the conflict. Already on 27 October, there was renewed and relatively heavy fighting as government forces prepared for a major counter-attack.

Santiago Carrillo claimed in his memoirs that he had opposed the Aran operation from the moment he was made aware of it. There is no hard evidence to refute his own self-serving narrative. His reaction may well have been different if he had been greeted in Toulouse and then in the valley with news of resounding military successes. But this was not the case. If, as López Tovar submits, the two men retired to consider the next step, there was little to discuss. Both were convinced that the Maquis had no choice but to withdraw across the border before the Spanish Army surrounded them. Carrillo also claims that he had been advised by representatives of the PCF that the French had dispatched a regiment of *Spahis* (North African troops integrated in the regular French Army) to the Pyrenees to cut off the retreat of the Maquis.[2] There is no other source to substantiate this suggestion and it seems highly improbable that the French authorities would take such measures against men who had fought so valiantly for their cause and still enjoyed the respect of the local population. López Tovar later denied that Carrillo had shared this 'intelligence' with him and declared that 'if the "*Spahis*" or *gendarmes* had blocked their retreat in order to enable the Spanish Army to eliminate them, it would have caused a civil war in the Midi. The Resistance would never have allowed it'.[3]

The controversy surrounding the meeting does not involve the outcome but rather on whose initiative the decision to retreat was made. In his memoirs, Azcárate recalls his own feelings when Carrillo arrived in Toulouse:

> I confess that I was hugely relieved because I was sure that at last we had someone who was much more capable and had more experience than the rest of us. But once we had explained the operation, he immediately declared it was madness; he saw it from a perspective that differed from our own clouded viewpoint. Immediate withdrawal was crucial.[4]

However, according to López Tovar's account published by Daniel Arasa, and repeated in two televised interviews,[5] he had already decided to evacuate the valley. While Carrillo claims that it was not difficult to persuade the military leaders to organize a retreat, López Tovar, the man who insists he had expressed serious misgivings about the operation, even at the planning stage, and had refused to allow his men to launch an attack on Vielha because such an engagement would jeopardize their capacity to carry out a swift and orderly withdrawal, simply contends he had already organized the retreat when Carrillo arrived. In his own words:

> I explained that we had obeyed all orders except the one to attack Vielha, as the enemy forces were too strong and we could not fight them in open battle. When Carrillo asked my opinion about what to do, I told him, 'I'm going back to France,' to which he responded, 'I agree': I added that the Division was his to command and that I would obey

whatever orders he gave. He asked me, 'How long do you need for the retreat?' My answer was, 'Just give me the order.' He did so immediately and I informed the various units. At nine o'clock the next morning (28 October) we and our prisoners were in France having not fired a shot.[6]

He was fully aware of the consequences of rebelling against the orders of the party in France as transmitted by *Mariano* and completed his account by describing the relief he felt on the arrival of an eminent member of the politburo to assume responsibility. However, he also maintains that, 'Even if Carrillo had not come, I would still have retreated, because I had already taken the decision'. In an interview with Ferran Sánchez Agustí, months before his death in Toulouse in 1998, he went further. Insisting that his great fear was that his men should be trapped in the valley by the enemy, he concluded:

> from the very first day that, acting on the orders of the party, I took responsibility for the invasion, my first concern was to prepare for a retreat with the minimum number of casualties. When Santiago Carrillo arrived, I had already given the order to retreat.

Although the truth of who actually opted to withdraw the Maquis from the Val d'Aran might appear a relatively insignificant detail, it was crucially important to Santiago Carrillo in his eventual ascension to the post of secretary-general of the PCE. As the first member of the exiled politburo to be 'parachuted' back into Free French territory, he seized his opportunity to establish himself as the de facto leader of the party in the field. To consolidate his position, he embarked on a campaign to discredit the influence of Jesús Monzón and his team by undermining their achievements and challenging their judgement. Critically, he highlighted his own initiative and decisive action in ordering the withdrawal of the Maquis from their positions in the Val d'Aran. In his report to the party of February 1945, Carrillo repeated that the military leaders in the field intended to continue with the mission and that he alone had persuaded them that their loyalty to the party leadership in Madrid was misplaced and that it was essential to retreat before the Spanish Army launched their counter-offensive.

He thereby claimed credit for avoiding a slaughter and for saving thousands of Republican lives.[7]

The evacuation proved to be most successful manoeuvre of the entire operation, a fact which supports the López Tovar case that preparations were already at hand. Moscardó ordered the counter-offensive on the night of 27/28 October, but as his troops approached enemy 'lines', they found no one. The Maquis had simply vanished. On 31 October, in a four-inch item hidden at the bottom of page 16 and under the headline 'The last Spanish "Red" has crossed the border back into France', *ABC* reported a press conference by Moscardó in Barcelona. The general informed journalists that following an offensive launched three days earlier, the army had forced the Maquis to retreat into France, had taken a large number of prisoners and recovered significant quantities of weapons. The article concluded: 'The Valle de Arán has been cleansed of *maquis*.' Meanwhile, in its edition of 28 October, the *Reconquista de España* displayed a reckless disregard for timing by running the headline: 'National Insurrection in Spain begins'. Claiming that more than 20,000 Maquis were involved, the article outlined operations in Lleida, Girona, Figueres and Tremp and reported other acts of sabotage, protest or rebellion in Madrid, Asturias, Navarra and throughout Andalucía.

In his history of the invasion, Ferran Sánchez Agustí claims the retreat was executed calmly, without haste, and the Maquis returned to their bases in France with a number of prisoners, with all their weapons intact and with other arms they had captured from the enemy. According to López Tovar, in the course of the mission, they took 300 prisoners.[8] Most were released unharmed before the retreat, others accompanied their captors across the border and were almost immediately repatriated. Over the course of the next twelve months, twenty prisoners who had been injured during the fighting were escorted to the border and released following hospital treatment.[9]

Sánchez Agustí also reveals that, according to his research, in the Val d'Aran, the AGE lost twenty-seven men, while on the government side, a total of thirty-six men were killed (the Spanish Army twenty-nine, the Guardia Civil three and the armed police four). Four civilians died. In fighting in the surrounding areas, the Maquis lost sixty-seven men in Lleida and twenty-six in Girona, while the government forces lost forty-four and seven respectively. In the course of the campaign following the liberation of France, he also estimates that government forces killed twenty-nine Maquis in the province of Barcelona, four in Tarragona, seventy-three in Aragón and seventy-nine in Navarra.[10] Finally Sánchez Agustí breaks down the figures on all fronts in Spain of what he describes as 'the great invasion' (1944–5). According to his research, guerrilla losses totalled 323, the government forces lost ninety-one men and nineteen civilian non-combatants were killed.[11]

Within the context of the Second World War, it may be an exaggeration to describe the invasion, and in particular the battle in the Val d'Aran, as even a 'skirmish'. It did little or nothing to persuade the Allies that they should open a new front in the Iberian Peninsula and had no impact on the lives of the population of Spain who remained largely unaware of the activities of the guerrillas. The Maquis were unable to establish a bridgehead and were not welcomed as conquering heroes or national liberators.

Some attempts were made to disseminate news of the raid and to raise the morale of disenchanted exiles. The Toulouse section of the Central Committee of the PCE published an open letter in the January edition of the party journal *Nuestra Bandera* analysing the international situation and commending the role of the Maquis inside Spain.

> For ten days the towns of Valle de Arán were liberated by the Catalan section of the guerrillas who inflicted hundreds of casualties on the repressive *franquista* forces, which, despite their superiority in numbers and weapons, were defeated and forced to retreat. During those 10 days in the Valle de Arán, the Unión Nacional set up its own organs of power; the people took charge of their own affairs. There were no reprisals, nor persecutions of any type; the Unión Nacional town councils operated normally, even with the participation of the clergy. Prisoners were treated with respect including a lieutenant of the Guardia Civil who surrendered to the guerrillas. Churches were kept open, nobody hindered religious activities.[12]

Nevertheless, what was intended as the first phase of the overthrow of Franco became an empty (albeit heroic) gesture of little propaganda value because few people outside the region of the Pyrenees were listening.

The American ambassador in Madrid, Carlton J.H. Hayes, dismissed the incursion of the Maquis as a minor nuisance:

> A few hundred of these [Maquis] did attempt to get over and to incite popular uprisings in Catalonia and Aragon. They didn't get very far, however, and they failed utterly to enlist recruits on Spanish soil. They only managed to be killed or taken prisoner or to escape back to France with some cattle and sheep pilfered from peaceable peasants. The reaction within Spain was, at first, one of alarm and fear; then, of annoyance and disgust, and finally, of relief. This was not limited to the Government and its supporters. It was shared by the majority of 'Leftists,' who were equally opposed to any resumption of civil war.[13]

Hayes did not clarify which 'Leftists' he consulted or was even in contact with. On the other hand, Franco was able to use the external threat as a means to consolidate his own position and restore unity among the high-ranking officers of his armed forces. The very existence of a danger, however small, of a resurgence of left-wing and Republican politics was enough to persuade dissident *franquistas* that the Caudillo was 'the devil you know'. Once the imminent danger had passed, the regime had no qualms about exaggerating the magnitude of the peril. Franco's sister Pilar later recalled:

> It was all kept secret, even I didn't find out until it was all over. Apparently, it was very serious; it was the first stage of an all-out invasion. An organized army that crossed the French border. They said there were more than 100,000 men. The leaders of the Popular Front were behind it, from the other side of the Pyrenees.[14]

Notwithstanding the flaws in the overall political strategy of the Junta Suprema, the outcome in the Val d'Aran was a military defeat. It is probable that if the commanders in the field had wholeheartedly embraced the operation and had proved more resolute in the pursuit of their aims, and if substantially more troops had been thrust into battle from the very beginning, then the Maquis would have overwhelmed the government forces defending the valley and successfully isolated it from the rest of Spain by establishing strongholds at the points of access. If they had, they could have tested the viability of maintaining their presence throughout the winter against the vast superiority in numbers and weaponry of Franco's armed forces.

But they did not, and defeat in the Val d'Aran would prove to be more than a setback. It was a decisive battle that finally precluded any possibility that the Spanish people would be able to liberate themselves. Nevertheless, so long as the world remained at war with Nazi Germany, the Republican exiles themselves were not ready to accept defeat. In her article published in *Collier's* in March 1945, Martha Gellhorn misguidedly dismissed the '*Val Daran*' episode as a 'commando raid, purely and simply'. She described the Spanish Maquis as 'intact in spirit' and 'armed with a transcendent faith' and insisted that after listening to them, it was easy to believe that 'there will be a republic across the mountains and that they will live to return to it'.[15] Nevertheless, the decision on the overthrow of Franco and the liberation of Spain now depended not on the Spanish people or the exiles, but on the military priorities of the Allied commanders and on political developments in London, Moscow, Washington and Paris.

The only significant monument to the guerrillas who fought in the Val d'Aran campaign is the castle-like mansion which housed the Hospital Varsovia, opened in the Saint-Cyprien district of Toulouse in October 1944 to treat those wounded in the fighting and to provide care for other Republicans suffering the sequelae of their incarceration in French and German concentration camps. Named not after the Polish city of Warsaw, but after the street in which the mansion stood (at number 15), the centre had between fifty and sixty beds when it opened, distributed between five wards. In the first three months the medical staff treated approximately 200 patients. Unable to deal with the demands on the health services in Toulouse, the French authorities chose to allow exiled doctors and nurses to practise medicine among their compatriots even though their qualifications could not be validated in France. They also provided supplies that had been requisitioned from the retreating Nazi military hospital services.

The hospital was supported by donations from a range of sources that were known simply as 'friends' of the hospital, and included the

Anti-Fascist Refugee Committee (JAFRC) and the Unitarian Service Committee (USC) in the USA, the Toulouse Faculty of Medicine, and a series of local aid commissions set up in Mexico, Cuba, Vancouver, Geneva, Glasgow and Toulouse itself.[16] Although the hospital offered care services to all Republican exiles, it was identified by the Spanish and French governments alike as a communist organization. In the USA, pressure from the House Un-American Activities Committee eventually truncated the steady supply of donations to the Varsovia. The escalation of the Cold War and the fear of Soviet expansion encouraged the French police to launch Operation *Bolero-Paprika* in September 1950 against PCE representatives in France who were considered as potential fifth columnists in the event of an invasion threat from the Red Army. Fifty arrests were made in Toulouse and the entire staff of physicians of the Hospital Varsovia was detained.

In order to save the hospital from closure, a team of French health professionals agreed to take over responsibility for its services. The centre was subsequently renamed the Hôpital Ducuing, after Dr Joseph Ducuing, who had inspired the rescue scheme. Today the original hospital building still stands although it is hidden behind the more modern facilities of the new clinic. There is however a plaque which reads in French and Spanish:

> In honour of the Spanish Republican guerrillas who fought Franco's dictatorship and Nazism.
> Many of them, in particular the communists, contributed to the establishment of the Hospital 'Varsovia' today 'Joseph Ducuing'.

Chapter 23

Veil of Oblivion

In the decade that followed the incursion at the Val d'Aran, the Maquis were gradually relegated to the shadows of history. They did remain active in many parts of Spain – particularly Andalucía, Aragon, Levante and Asturias – until 1947 and Paul Preston describes the *guerrilleros* as 'a considerable irritant to the regime'. He calculates that between 1945 and 1948, there were probably as many as 7,000 men involved in operations against Franco's dictatorship.[1] Their favourite targets were the Guardia Civil, and railway and energy installations. In reprisal, the Guardia Civil made generous use of the *Ley de Fugas* (Flight Law – April 1921), which sanctioned the paralegal execution of felons seeking to avoid arrest or escape custody. Franco also introduced the *Ley de Bandidaje y Terrorismo* (Banditry and Terrorism Law – April 1947), which tightened the already draconian measures against the opposition, extended the use of courts martial in the case of unlawful political activity, and increased the number of offences punishable by death.

In 1948, at a meeting with Carrillo, Antón and La Pasionaria in the Kremlin, Stalin hinted the PCE might abandon the armed struggle and instead advocated a variation on the Trotskyist policy of 'entryism', whereby Communist representatives would participate in Franco's official 'vertical' trade union in order to establish a new power base. The party subsequently withdrew its support from the *guerrilleros*, cut off supplies and funding, and abandoned those who persisted in the armed struggle to their fate. Many found their way to France. Those who chose to stay in Spain became involved in a battle for their own survival. All hope of overthrowing Franco's regime was lost and the rural populations increasingly considered the *guerrilleros* a liability that disrupted their lives and put them in danger of reprisals from the Guardia Civil. Daniel Arasa makes the interesting point that symptomatic of the failure of the Maquis to garner popular support was the fact that despite the existence in Spanish of the word *guerrilla*, which has been borrowed by the

English language and is still widely used today, the Spanish (allies and enemies of the Maquis alike) continued to use a French word (derived from the Corsican Italian *macchia*) to describe their own *guerrilleros*. [2]

The retreat from the Val d'Aran was a crucial step for Santiago Carrillo on his long rise to power. Claiming that his decisive intervention had saved the lives of thousands of guerrilla fighters, he established his leadership of the PCE in France and, ipso facto, in Spain. In Moscow, he had learnt the Stalinist principle of 'revolutionary vigilance' and subsequently embarked on a campaign to discredit Jesús Monzón and his team. At first his recalcitrant rivals were described as misguided or lacking in discipline. In his report to the party, he warned that Monzón was following a dangerous path of self-sufficiency, vanity and confrontation with the party. He further accused him of ignoring criticism, refusing to implement party policy and seeking to forge a leadership clique with Pilar Soler and Trilla designed to defy the instructions of the politburo and ignore all guidance. Claiming to have the support of de Pedro, Azcárate and Gimeno, Carrillo outlined his plan to invite Monzón and his team to France to defend their position and suggested that failure to do so would lead to expulsion from the party. He added that the party would not hesitate to take whatever measures were necessary and that the responsibility of the party to the people trumped all other considerations.[3]

Gabriel León Trilla, Monzón's closest collaborator in Madrid, declined the invitation from Carrillo's team to submit to interrogation in Toulouse. Cristino Garcia, the Resistance hero now based in the Spanish capital, was subsequently ordered to eliminate him. Garcia refused to participate personally, but nevertheless dispatched members of his unit to carry out the order. In September 1945, Trilla was lured to the Campo de las Calaveras (Field of Skulls), the site of a former cemetery in the Chamberí district, where he was stabbed to death. His executioners took his belongings in an attempt to disguise the attack as a robbery. On 15 October 1945, Alberto Pérez Ayala, who had worked closely with Trilla, was shot dead in the centre of Madrid. Pere Canals, who had been Monzón's representative in Barcelona, did agree to travel to Toulouse, but was murdered on his way there.

In one of the most famous programmes ever broadcast by Spanish Television (RTVE), an edition of a weekly debate show *La Clave* on 10 November 1979, Carrillo was confronted by the young French philosopher

Bernard-Henri Lévy. The Communist leader dismissed accusations that he had ordered the murder of Trilla and claimed that Lévy was too young to appreciate the conditions under the dictatorship and the perils facing PCE agents in Spain. Of Trilla, Manuel Azcárate wrote in 1994:

> for a long time, I rejected the Francoist claim that the communists were responsible for his death. Today, after a process that began in my final years in the party, I have come to the completely opposite opinion. It was a time of terrible repression. The arrests of communist cadres was increasing and the temptation to blame them on the presence of a traitor was overwhelming.[4]

In his own memoirs, Carrillo claims that once Trilla refused to travel to France to confer with the leadership in Toulouse, it was obvious to the party that he was concealing a dark secret and represented a threat to the security of his comrades in the clandestine struggle. In a veiled attempt to deny his own direct implication in the crime, he concluded: 'In those days, it was not necessary to give orders, whoever challenged party discipline while under cover in Spain was treated as a danger. [...] The harsh realities of our struggle did not allow margins.'[5]

In October 1945, Cristino Garcia was detained by the Spanish police in Madrid while working to re-establish guerrilla operations in the central zone. He had participated actively in the Resistance movement against the Germans in France – most famously the attack on the prison in Nîmes, in which the Resistance liberated seventy-six prisoners due for deportation to Germany. At the summary court martial, he refused efforts to mitigate his actions and declared:

> We are not bandits, we are the vanguard in the struggle of the people for their freedom. The crooks are those that accuse us, who torment and starve the people [...] Even if we lose our lives in this quest, Franco will never be able to claim victory [...] You are in a hurry to be rid of us. You do not want the world to see our tortured bodies.[6]

In response to a suggestion by the defence that he had been misled and his actions were misguided, he responded:

We are convinced anti-francoist patriots, who have not given up the struggle against the murderers who oppress our people. I have been wounded five times in the fight against the nazis and their *falangista* lackeys. I know what is in store for me, but I can state with pride that if I had a thousand lives, I would dedicate them all to the cause of my people and my country.[7]

Garcia was executed, alongside other members of his unit in February 1946. In protest, the French government closed the border between the two countries.

In his biography of Santiago Carrillo, Fernando Claudín (whom Carrillo had expelled from the PCE) later described the real fears and suspicions of PCE agents in Spain and how the cells were infiltrated by Francoist agents or betrayed by members turned by the security forces through brutal torture or threats to their family. On his arrival in France, Claudín, who had spent the war in Mexico, was recruited by Carrillo to assist in the work of purging the party of hostile elements, which included anybody too close to Monzón or López Tovar and any party members who had survived internment in the camps of Nazi Germany. Claudín enigmatically described his work as a 'Sisyphean task'.[8] The error of some, and the cynical dishonesty of others, was to see a Francoist agent in every member who challenged the Stalinist perception of the party.

Jesús Monzón, whose personal charm and organizational genius was responsible for rebuilding the PCE both in Spain and France, and who had inspired the Val d'Aran operation, finally agreed to obey Carrillo's order to travel to France, in the company of his new partner, Pilar Soler. Fortunately for him, he fell ill in Barcelona and sought refuge in the house of a member of the PSUC, where he was discovered and detained by Franco's police. Pilar Soler managed to escape, and to make her way to Toulouse. Monzón was held in the Ocaña Prison until his court martial in 1948. Interventions from family and friends from Pamplona saved him from the death penalty. Enrique Lister, communist hero of the Civil War later wrote that if Monzón survived, 'he owed it to the fact he was arrested by the Spanish police on his way to meet the agent who was supposed to get him to France but who in fact was under instructions to deliver him for execution'.[9] Monzón was sentenced to thirty years' imprisonment of which he served nearly half. In the El Dueso Prison, his fellow communist prisoners ostracized him and in 1948, he was expelled from the PCE.

Following the arrest of Noel Field in 1949, and Azcárate's subsequent 'confession' that on Monzón's orders, he had contacted the 'American/ Soviet' agent in Switzerland in 1943/4, Carrillo further denounced Monzón as a US spy. In his work on the PCE and Carrillo, Enrique Lister wrote that Monzón committed two crimes that the politburo could never absolve: 'having stayed in France to fulfil his duty and then having returned to Spain to continue fulfilling it. Courage was a felony that Carrillo and company always detested.'[10]

Once released from prison, Monzón moved to Mexico where he was reunited with his wife, Aurora Gómez Urrutia. They had separated at the beginning of the war, when Monzón had insisted their infant son, Sergio, be evacuated to the USSR. Years later, they discovered he had died of scarlet fever during the journey east.[11] In the last years of the dictatorship, they returned to Spain and bizarrely Monzón worked in a business school in Mallorca. He died in Pamplona in October 1973.

Joan Comorera i Soler, secretary-general of the PSUC, survived politically until 1949, when he was dismissed from his post and subsequently expelled from the party. The following year, he chose to return to Spain but according to Enrique Lister, Santiago Carrillo – and presumably La Pasionaria – ordered his 'physical liquidation'.[12] A six-man hit team was deployed near the border to intercept him but, after waiting three weeks, they abandoned their mission. Lister claims that Comorera had become aware of the danger to his life and had simply entered Catalonia at a different point. In an article published in *Mundo Obrero* in September 1951, Carrillo denounced him as a traitor, police spy and enemy of the working class and the Catalan people. Comorera continued his clandestine struggle against Franco until he was arrested by the police in 1954. He was sentenced to thirty years' imprisonment by court martial in 1957 and died in prison in 1958.

After lengthy and brutal interrogation by Carrillo and his acolytes, Manuel Azcárate, Pilar Soler and Carmen de Pedro (temporarily) survived the politburo offensive by distancing themselves from the policies and strategies of Jesús Monzón and by confessing to their own errors of judgement. Carmen de Pedro was ably defended by her new partner, Agustín Zoroa, staunchest of Carrillo's allies who enthusiastically, and opportunely, became Monzón's greatest detractor. Zoroa later returned to Madrid as undercover agent, was detained by the police in October 1946 and executed in December 1947. Carmen de Pedro, was eventually expelled from the party after the Field show trials. In the 1970s, Carrillo refused even to support her application for a pension from the French state. The intervention of Luis Fernández (*General Luis*, one of the military leaders of the Val d'Aran operation) eventually ensured the pension to which she was entitled for her service in the Resistance.[13]

These were not the only communist faithful who suffered the wrath and Stalinist zeal of Carrillo and his team. The purges in the PCE were not limited to the upper echelons of the party. There are no records of the many unreliable elements among the loyal rank-and-file communists who were eliminated in the South of France. During the Spanish Civil War, Soviet intelligence agents in Spain felt no compunction in ridding the movement of non-orthodox, non-Stalinist volunteers who had been brave and generous enough to risk their lives in the fight against fascism. Similarly, at the end of the Second World War, the politburo of the PCE that reassembled in France felt compelled to eradicate potentially disloyal elements from the party. Carrillo was joined by La Pasionaría, who returned from the USSR in April 1945, and Vicente Uribe who arrived from Mexico the next year. The communist leaders who had watched the world conflict from behind the lines in the USSR and Latin America now endeavoured to wrest their power and moral authority back from those who had fought the Nazis and those who had suffered the degradation of the German camps. The Stalinist rationalization for the directive to discredit and eliminate the party faithful who had endured the Nazi terror was chillingly simple: those who had emerged alive from the hell on Earth created by the Germans could only have survived by reneging on their communist ideals and collaborating with the enemy.

The most graphic example of what Spanish historian Gregorio Moran described as the 'misery, grandeur and agony' of the PCE was the case of Luis Montero Álvarez (alias *Sabugo*), a railway worker who joined the UGT in 1931 and the PCE in 1936. During the Civil War, he served in the Batallón Ferroviario (Railways Battalion) and joined the exodus into France when the Republic was finally defeated. He spent time in an internment camp (Gus), before his release to work in the 184th Compagnie de travailleurs étrangers in the Loire Valley. When the French Army surrendered, he walked south to Bordeaux and made contact with agents of the PCE. He joined the FTP–MOI and took part in sabotage missions before his detention by the French police in November 1942. He was tortured and then transferred to the custody of the Gestapo and eventually to Mauthausen, the destination of so many *Rotspanier*.

He played an active part in the organization of party members within the camp and in the national and international committees set up to prepare for an eventual battle with their SS guards when liberation became imminent. According to Spanish historian Luis Antonio Vilanovas, the prisoners were able to gather a collection of 'knives, axes, picks and whatever else could serve as a weapon on the day of reckoning'.[14] Lister describes how, in addition to coordinating plans to neutralize those SS units threatening a mass slaughter of inmates as the Americans approached, he was even able to appropriate weapons from the camp arsenal.[15]

On his return to France, Montero was not perceived by the politburo as a welcome addition to the PCE community. Nor did it help that he was decorated by the French Republic for his wartime service. Carrillo had by now developed a strategy to deal with comrades whose presence in France he took as a constant reminder of his own war record. Despite his poor health, caused by the years of detention and abuse in Mauthausen, and the primary factor that he was known to the Francoist authorities, in March 1948, the party requested Montero undertake a short turn of duty in his native Asturias to help coordinate the clandestine activities of party operatives and Maquis in the north of Spain. In November the party ordered him back for a five-month mission in Asturias. From his base in Spain, he appealed to the party to recall him on grounds of illness and exhaustion, but his request was ignored, and the mission was extended by more than a year. He was finally detained by the Guardia Civil in Gijón in January 1950.

There are different versions of what ensued. According to the report received from Horacio Fernández Inguanzo (aka *El Paisano*), head of the PCE in Asturias, Montero 'put himself at the service of the police'.[16] Paul Preston believes that in spite of his weakened physical condition, Montero resisted his torturers the standard length of time to allow the local Maquis group to escape. He was however finally broken and revealed the whereabouts of their refuge. Tragically, for reasons unknown, the guerrillas had failed to relocate, and the police were able to dismantle the entire guerrilla operation.[17]

Secundino Serrano acknowledges this version may be correct, but offers the alternative possibility that the Maquis were in fact betrayed by a Guardia Civil agent who had infiltrated the group.[18] As Montero was never allowed to record his own version of events, it is impossible to know which is closer to the truth. Enrique Lister, on the other hand, claims there is a wider issue:

> Even if [Montero] had had a moment of weakness at the hands of the Guardia Civil, who was to blame? There is only one response: those that sent a man who had recently emerged from the Nazi hell back and forth to Spain, while they – first in Toulouse and then in Paris – lived a life of luxury, with chauffeurs, servants, bodyguards, 'secretaries' and the like. None would dare to accuse me of lying. I can give the names of these chauffeurs, servants, bodyguards, 'secretaries'. And the hotels on the banks of the Marne, in Saint-Gemain-en-Laye or Champigny, where Dolores Ibárruri sunbathed while Party activists suffered the calamities of the time.[19]

Montero was released from custody and chose to travel back to Spain to explain his actions to the party. However, he was intercepted and executed by a hit squad. For many years, his family sought to uncover the truth of his death and to recover his remains. In a letter to the family, Carrillo definitively stated: 'I never knew who executed Luis Montero; the unwritten law of the clandestine struggle was applied in the interior [i.e. Spain]. I have no idea where he might be buried.'[20]

By 1950, the Spanish Republicans in south-west France had accepted defeat and had resigned themselves to a lengthy, even 'permanent' exile. They established Toulouse as their capital and integrated effectively in French society. They had little problem assimilating the French language and French culture and were accepted by the indigenous populations. Spanish surnames became commonplace in all areas of life and first, second and third generation immigrants have had an important impact on French life. Luis Miguel Fernández, a midfielder who played for Paris St. Germain, won sixty caps for France and was a member of the team that won the European Championships of 1984, beating Spain 2–0 in the final. Raphaël Ibáñez played 98 times as hooker for the French national rugby team between 1996 and 2007 during which time France won the Six Nations four times. Manuel Valls (Parti Socialiste) was prime minister of France between 2014 and 2016, during the presidency of François Hollande. Anne (Ana) Hidalgo (Parti Socialiste) won the municipal elections of March 2014 – and became the first woman to be elected mayor of Paris. In his second successful presidential campaign, François Mitterrand famously included an image of Pablo Picasso in a video montage dedicated to the grandeur and unity of France.

The death of Franco and the legalization of the Spanish Communist Party during the Easter holidays of 1977 propelled Santiago Carrillo into a new role and he became one of the key players in the democratic transition. Nevertheless, history caught up with him eventually. Defined by Paul Preston as 'the last Stalinist', he failed to stem the tide of the young renovators within his party. Poor election results forced him to stand down as secretary-general in 1982 and he was replaced as secretary-general by Gerardo Iglesias, a young miner from Asturias.

The writer Jorge Semprún – member of the French Resistance, survivor of Buchenwald, long-term undercover agent of the PCE inside Spain (aka *Federico Sánchez*) – had been expelled from the PCE in 1964. In an article in *El País* of 23 April 1980, he wrote: 'The time has come to listen to the dead communists, not just their executioners.' In April 1986, Gerardo Iglesias announced the official rehabilitation of Monzón, Quiñones and Comorera, previously denounced as traitors, now rebranded as 'heroic fighters for freedom'. The epitaph is no less valid for the many thousands of Republican exiles (of all ideological persuasions) whose courage and sacrifices have been forgotten, ignored and often denied. Of those who fled across the border into France in the early winter of 1939, Pablo Casals wrote, 'in that exodus were the best and noblest people of Spain – the soldiers and poets, workers and university professors, jurists and peasants who had championed freedom and would not bow to tyranny.'[21]

Chapter 24

Die Welt des freien Menschen

If the Maquis failed on the ground, the options for the overthrow of the Franco dictatorship were ultimately quashed by the Allies and by international developments in the post-war era. Churchill had revealed his own intentions towards the Caudillo (and ultimately those of the western Allies collectively) in two interventions. The first was his statement to the House of Commons in May 1944 when he expressed his gratitude to Franco and announced his reluctance to intervene in the internal affairs of Spain. The second was a reply to a letter from Franco to the Duke of Alba, the content of which was transmitted to the British leader. The letter was dated 18 October, the day before the main Maquis offensive into the Val d'Aran. The Caudillo first referred to the 'noble words which the prime minister recently spoke regarding our nation',[1] and then graciously stated he was willing to ignore Britain's wartime hostility towards Spain and the misdeeds of British intelligence agents on Spanish territory. Moreover, he insinuated that Spain would support an alliance against the Soviet Union.

It would appear that Churchill had come to regret his 'kindly words' speech. In his own response to Franco's missive, he reminded the Caudillo that the USSR was an ally of Great Britain (under the terms of the Anglo-Soviet Treaty 1942) and rebuked him for the speeches, 'in which your Excellency contemptuously referred to this country [Britain] and other members of the United Nations and spoke of their defeat as desirable and unavoidable'. He then warned the general that 'his Majesty's Government cannot overlook the past record of the Spanish Government nor the consistently hostile activity of the Falangist Party [...], nor the fact that Falange has maintained a close relationship with the Nazi dictatorial party in Germany and with the Italian Fascists'. He concluded: 'it is out of the question for His Majesty's Government to support Spanish aspirations to participate in the future peace settlements. Neither do I think it likely that Spain will be invited to join the future world organization [United Nations].'[2]

Nevertheless, the prime minister refused to reconsider his determination not to intervene in Spanish domestic affairs. Curiously, he now came into conflict with Sir Samuel Hoare, the ambassador in Madrid, who had dedicated the first years of his term to his mission to dissuade Franco from declaring war on Great Britain. To this end, he lobbied against any open interference or even provocation (either by the authorities in London, or by the SOE on the ground in Spain or even by the American OSS). However, by 1944, Allied successes in North Africa and on the Eastern Front had made the issue of Spanish neutrality less critical. Antagonized by Franco's hubris, Hoare increasingly advocated support for the military–monarchist opposition to the regime. He joined forces with the Foreign Office to propose measures (sanctions) that would undermine the Caudillo's authority and would pave the way for a monarchist coup and the restoration of the Bourbon dynasty.

In a memorandum to 'London', he wrote, 'the present Spanish government with Franco at its head is fundamentally hostile to the Allies and the aims for which we are fighting.' He argued that Anglo-Spanish relations could never be satisfactory while Franco was in power and insisted, 'the sooner he and his Falange machine disappear, the better it will be, not only for ourselves but for the whole of Europe'.[3] Churchill, however, would not be moved from his appeasement of Franco. He refused to countenance any type of intervention that he apparently and disingenuously believed would somehow favour the communists now gathered on the French side of the Pyrenees. Nor did he authorize the ambassador to deliver any type of threat or ultimatum to the Caudillo at their farewell audience (December 1944) before Hoare's final return to London.[4] Ignoring the wishes of his prime minister, Hoare did in fact reprimand Franco although he later acknowledged that he failed to shake Franco's complacency. Hoare had the minor satisfaction of refusing the offer of a 'high Spanish decoration' (presumably the Gran Cruz de la Orden de Isabel la Católica) but later confessed that the only evidence he could see that Franco was prepared to make concessions was that 'photographs of the Pope and President Carmona of Portugal had been substituted for those of Hitler and Mussolini in the place of honour on Franco's writing table'.[5]

Stalin on the other hand did expect more. Without declaring war on the USSR, Franco had sent troops to fight alongside the Nazis, an action which had played a not insignificant role in the prolongation of the suffering of the people of Leningrad. At the Potsdam Conference (May 1945), Stalin demanded his allies break off diplomatic relations with the government in Madrid and provide support to those democratic forces seeking regime change. By this stage President Roosevelt was dead and had been replaced by Harry S. Truman. As a mason and a Protestant (and a Democrat), Truman had developed a deep personal dislike of 'Franco and Catholic obscurantism in Spain'[6] and throughout his terms in office (1945–53), he maintained his hostility. However, in light of the Cold War, the Department of State undertook an adjustment to US foreign policy and enforced a new approach to Spain in line with their notions of the developing geopolitical realities of the post-war world.

At Potsdam, the new president agreed with Churchill that the Allies should not interfere in the internal affairs of a sovereign state (even though the regime had largely been established through the military intervention of Nazi Germany and Fascist Italy). He concluded: 'I have no love for Franco. I have no desire to get into a Spanish Civil War. We would be most happy to recognize another government. But Spain must settle it.'[7] In November 1945, the Spanish ambassador in Washington, Juan Francisco de Cárdenas, informed the Ministry of Foreign Affairs in Madrid that the US government was considering a more hostile policy towards Franco's regime. He quoted a report in *Newsweek* that while Truman was still resolved to avoid a second full-scale civil war in Spain, he would nevertheless take firm measures to support the overthrow of the dictatorship. In a second telegram, one week later, the embassy in Washington provided details of a letter to Truman from Scottish-born labour leader Philip Murray (of the Congress of Industrial Organization) which had deeply impressed the president and had been released to the press. Murray demanded the US government recognize the Spanish government-in-exile in Mexico and denounced the failure of the USA to support the Republic in its struggle against fascism during the Civil War. He insisted that America recognize 'the debt of gratitude it owed to those heroes' and that 'democracy in the world could not exist so long as they innocent victims continued to suffer'.[8] On the basis of these two telegrams, the American historian W.H. Bowen concluded that Truman would have supported the Republican exiles had they 'seized and held appreciable territory within Spain'.[9]

On 16 December 1945, Under-Secretary of State Dean Acheson held a brief 'private' meeting with Juan Negrín in Washington,[10] at which, according to Pablo de Azcárate, he told the former prime minister: 'We want to get rid of Franco,' but then acknowledged that they did not know how to.[11]

Given his oft-repeated public statements on socialism and communism, it is unsurprising that Churchill ignored the plight of those in the opposition to Franco. In his memoirs, he acknowledges Stalin's demands at Potsdam that the Allies intervene in Spain, and writes: 'I resisted this suggestion, and eventually the subject was dismissed.'[12]

More disconcerting was the reaction of Clement Attlee, leader of the Labour Party, whose victory in the general election was declared in the course of the last of the great wartime summits. In his memoirs, Attlee recalls the criticism he suffered in Britain for giving the clenched fist salute to Republican troops while on a visit to the front during the Spanish Civil War.[13] However, once elected prime minister, he did little more than his predecessor to support those seeking to overthrow Franco, and simply maintained the policy of diplomatic sanctions. His only reference to the Spanish question at Potsdam in his autobiography concerns a conversation with Stalin: to Attlee's question on a possible venue for the next hypothetical summit, the Soviet leader replied, 'Well, why not Madrid?'[14]

On 28 August 1945, the new foreign secretary, Ernest Bevin, made a statement to the House of Commons in which he showed how little had changed in British policy towards Spain, since the election of the new Labour government:

> I am satisfied that intervention by foreign Powers in the internal affairs of Spain would have the opposite effect to that desired, and would probably strengthen General Franco's position. It is obvious from what I have said that we shall take a favourable view if steps are taken by the Spanish people to change their régime, but His Majesty's Government are not prepared to take any steps which would promote or encourage civil war in that country. In this, I know, I am voicing the views not only of myself but of many ardent Spanish Republicans.[15]

Six weeks before the Val d'Aran offensive, the French writer and philosopher Albert Camus published an editorial in the journal *Combat* demanding Allied support for the Republican cause:

> The European war which began in Spain eight years ago,
> cannot be ended without Spain. [...] The struggle transcends
> our borders and [...] we will never achieve victory as long
> as the cause of freedom continues to be crushed in long-
> suffering Spain.[16]

However, Charles de Gaulle, the new leader of France, was (like Franco)
a military leader to whom political parties were anathema. It has even
been suggested that he was tempted by some of the ideological premises
and social and economic policies of Pétain's Vichy regime.[17] In terms
of his ideology and approach to constitutional theory, he was certainly
closer to the Caudillo than he was to the Maquis. Indeed, together with
the other forces within the Resistance, the Spanish Republicans were
perceived by de Gaulle to represent a threat to the political stability of
France and were a far greater nuisance than Franco and his regime. The
new government in Paris felt little compulsion to honour promises made
by military and Resistance commanders in the heat of battle to support
an operation to liberate their neighbour.

In short, the Americans and British revoked their pledge to eradicate
dictatorships from Western Europe, the French restored the policy of
non-intervention, and Stalin resigned himself to making forlorn protests.
The Americans invested huge volumes of money and effort in the
reconstruction of the economies and the consolidation of the democratic
structures of their erstwhile enemies, German, Italy and Austria, and yet
elected to abandon the Spanish people to poverty and tyranny.

However, despite their timid approach to the Spanish question, the
British, French and Americans did at least agree that Franco's Spain
should be excluded both from the United Nations, set up at the San
Francisco Conference (April–June 1945), and the European Recovery
Program (Marshall Plan). The opposition inside Spain, having seen the
prospect of liberation dashed in 1944 and 1945, were given one last ray
of hope in 1946, when it was announced that the new United Nations
Organization was to discuss an appropriate international response to
the Francoist regime. On 12 December 1946, the General Assembly
approved Resolution 39 on relations of member states with Spain:

> The peoples of the United Nations, at San Francisco,
> Potsdam and London, condemned the Franco regime in

Spain and decided that, as long as that regime remains, Spain may not be admitted to the United Nations.

The General Assembly, in its resolution of 9 February 1946, recommended that the Members of the United Nations should act in accordance with the letter and the spirit of the declarations of San Francisco and Potsdam. The peoples of the United Nations assure the Spanish people of their enduring sympathy and of the cordial welcome awaiting them when circumstances enable them to be admitted to the United Nations. The General Assembly recalls that, in May and June 1946, the Security Council conducted an investigation of the possible further action to be taken by the United Nations. The Sub-Committee of the Security Council charged with the investigation found unanimously:

"(a) In origin, nature, structure and general conduct, the Franco regime is a fascist regime patterned on, and established largely as a result of aid received from, Hitler's Nazi Germany and Mussolini's Fascist Italy."

"(b) During the long struggle of the United Nations against Hitler and Mussolini, Franco, despite continued Allied protests, gave very substantial aid to the enemy Powers. First, for example, from 1941 to 1945, the Blue Infantry Division, the Spanish Legion of Volunteers and the Salvador Air Squadron fought against Soviet Russia on the Eastern Front. Second, in the summer of 1940, Spain seized Tangier in breach of international statute, and as a result of Spain maintaining a large army in Spanish Morocco large numbers of Allied troops were immobilized in North Africa."

"(c) Incontrovertible documentary evidence establishes that Franco was a guilty party with Hitler and Mussolini in the conspiracy to wage war against those countries which eventually in the course of the world war became banded together as the United Nations. It was part of the conspiracy that Franco's full belligerency should be postponed until a time to be mutually agreed upon."

The General Assembly,
Convinced that the Franco Fascist Government of Spain, which was imposed by force upon the Spanish people with the aid of the Axis Powers and which gave material assistance to the Axis Powers in the war, does not represent the Spanish people, and by its continued control of Spain is making impossible the participation of the Spanish people with the peoples of the United Nations in international affairs; *Recommends* that the Franco Government of Spain be debarred from membership in international agencies established by or brought into relationship with the United Nations, and from participation in conferences or other activities which may be arranged by the United Nations or by these agencies, until a new and acceptable government is formed in Spain.

The General Assembly,
Further, desiring to secure the participation of all peace-loving peoples, including the people of Spain, in the community of nations, *Recommends* that if, within a reasonable time, there is not established a government which derives its authority from the consent of the governed, committed to respect freedom of speech, religion and assembly and to the prompt holding of an election in which the Spanish people, free from force and intimidation and regardless of party, may express their will, the Security Council consider the adequate measures to be taken in order to remedy the situation;

Recommends that all Members of the United Nations immediately recall from Madrid their Ambassadors and Ministers plenipotentiary accredited there.

The General Assembly further recommends that the States Members of the Organization report to the Secretary-General and to the next session of the Assembly what action they have taken in accordance with this recommendation.[18]

The resolution fell far short of proposing any form of intervention designed to force regime change. It was followed by the mass exodus of diplomatic representatives from Madrid, including those of the USA, Britain, the USSR and France. However, once more, the expectations of the fragmented oppositions groups inside Spain were disappointed. To compound Spain's isolation, the government in Paris closed the French border with Spain in response to the execution of Cristino García (21 February 1946). Garcia was a leader of the Maquis within Spain and according to one report, had fought in the Val d'Aran.[19] However, he was also a decorated hero of the French Resistance.

Despite the defeat of his allies, and the hostility from abroad, Franco was able not only to survive but even to consolidate his position. Indeed, the removal of Hitler liberated *franquista* Spain from the status of satellite. Legend has it that one of his acolytes told the general, 'Before you were the third Führer, now that Hitler and Mussolini have been defeated, you are the number one.'[20] The Caudillo persuaded his political class that he was indispensable in the continued struggle against communism and subversion and tapped into a rich vein of nationalism amongst his people. His control of the media and suppression of the opposition allowed him to persuade many Spanish people that the antagonism of the foreign powers was directed against the nation rather than his own person. On 9 December 1946, vast numbers of demonstrators attended a rally in the Plaza de Oriente in Madrid in support of the regime and in protest at the interference from abroad – specifically from the UN. Although it is true that the event was carefully stage-managed by agents of the Falange,[21] it nevertheless reflected a groundswell of 'patriotic' fervour that strengthened the Caudillo's position. The next day, *ABC* led with a headline claiming that the people of Madrid had raised 'the flag of national independence against foreign interference'.

Franco felt secure enough blithely to ignore the demands of Don Juan for the restoration of the Bourbon dynasty and at the same time easily saw off the challenge of the monarchists within his armed forces. He also cynically used international pressure as a pretext to exercise greater control over the troublesome Falange that continued to make demands for radical social change which went against his own ideas of authoritarian conservatism. As an apparent concession to foreign sensibilities, he was able to shift power towards the more amenable Catholic Church and initiated a strategy under which the clergy was entrusted with greater influence in social affairs and censorship, and given sweeping powers in education. Over time, the Falange descended gradually into a secondary role as 'ideological ornament',[22] an indulgence towards the more fanatical supporters of the national crusade.

In the post-war period, the people of Spain endured years of crippling poverty, drought, violent political repression, hunger and disease. In 1950, salaries were no more than 50 per cent of the level of 1936.[23] However, once the Allies opted against military intervention, Franco's right of conquest could not be challenged by a people in dread of renewed civil war. Conditions improved slowly through the 1950s and the appointment of technocrats to the government at the end of the decade led to the reversal of the policy of autarky, and the introduction of a market economy. The 1960s saw rapid economic development and a new prosperity fuelled by the boom in the tourist industry and the income of the million-plus emigrant workers who sought employment throughout Europe.

At the international level, Franco achieved 'redemption' in the way he had predicted in his correspondence with Churchill at the end of the war. In March 1947, before a joint session of Congress and the Senate, the US president formulated a new policy that became known as the 'Truman Doctrine', which committed the USA to a strategy of containment of Soviet expansion. Henry Wallace, thirty-third vice-president (1941–5), complained that Truman's new foreign policy aims meant that: 'There is no regime too reactionary for us provided it stands in Russia's expansionist path.'[24] And thus, the Truman Doctrine proved to be the lifeline that Franco had awaited expectantly. He was now to become the self-proclaimed 'sentinel of the West'.

In the face of Soviet expansion and under pressure from the military, the State Department and business, Truman relaxed his veto on relations with Madrid. Meanwhile, the Labour government in London and the governments of the IV Republic in Paris gradually became aware that treating Spain as a pariah state had not, and would not, achieve the aim of bringing down Franco. France re-opened the border in early 1948. In November 1950, the UN passed Resolution 386, revoking the recommendations to withdraw ambassadors from Madrid and to debar Spain from the specialist international agencies (WHO, FAO, UNESCO).

However, unsurprisingly, it was the Vatican that made the first move actively to rehabilitate the National Catholic dictatorship of Franco and, in the words of Raymond Carr, 'to lift Spain out of international Coventry'.[25] By signing the Concordat of August 1953, the Catholic

Church granted the regime diplomatic recognition, but also established a confessional Catholic state and ensured the inclusion of principles of canon law in the civil code. Article 1 proclaimed:

> The Roman, Apostolic and Catholic Religion shall continue to be the only religion of the Spanish nation and shall enjoy the corresponding rights and prerogatives according to Divine and Canon Law.[26]

More far-reaching were the developments in Washington. General Dwight Eisenhower, elected the thirty-fourth president of the USA in November 1952, had fewer political scruples about the provenance of the Franco regime than his Democrat predecessor. It was impossible to dispute the anti-communist bona fides of Franco, and with the Cold War escalating, the new president ordered immediate détente with the regime in Spain. In September 1953, the USA and Spain signed an agreement (*Pactos de Madrid*) whereby the Americans offered substantial financial and military aid in return for the authorization of four military bases on Spanish territory: Morón, Zaragoza, Torrejón (USAF) and Rota (US Navy).

Spain became a full member of the UN on 14 December 1955, a decade after the defeat of the Axis. In November 1959, Eisenhower made an official visit to Madrid, and was famously photographed embracing Franco before his departure from the Torrejón airbase. Although Spain was not allowed to join NATO or the European Economic Community during Franco's lifetime, the final recognition of his regime came from the millions of foreign tourists who flocked to his beaches from the early 1960s onwards. The dictator died in a hospital bed on 20 November 1975 and was buried in the mausoleum at the Valle de los Caídos – in theory a monument to the fallen of both sides in the Civil War. Of the tens of thousands of Spaniards laid to rest in the basilica, the Caudillo was the only one who had not suffered a violent death. He was mourned by a great swathe of the population who twelve months after his demise would vote in favour of democratic reform and the restoration of civil rights.

In the memoirs he published in 1953, OSS agent Donald Downes, who had worked with Spanish Republicans in North Africa in the period after Operation *Torch*, wrote the following tribute:

No modern story is sadder than the betrayal of the Spanish people. If there is a real hero of the war he is the forgotten Spaniard, abandoned by democracy in 1936 when the Second World War really began, to a choice between Communism and Franco's Fascinazism.

First, we democrats betrayed the Spanish Republic to the Nazis and the Fascists. Then we betrayed the Republican movement to its Communist minority, and then, when rescue would have been so easy, in 1945, we betrayed them by leaving Franco's government in power as the only Axis oasis in Europe.[27]

Notes

Chapter 1: Falling of the Dusk

1. see, for example, Paul Preston: *The Spanish Civil War* (London, 2006) p291, Hugh Thomas: *The Spanish Civil War* (London, 1962) p561, Anthony Beevor: *The Battle for Spain* (London, 2006) p358
2. see, for example, Foreign Minister Julio del Vayo in *The Last Optimist* (London, 1950) pp314–15
3. *The Last Optimist* (London, 1950) p315
4. Quoted in *Public Papers of the Presidents of the United States,* available at https://books.google.es/books?id=nlborifzJnIC&pg=PA1647&lpg=PA1647&dq, p1647
5. in *Arms for Spain* (London, 1998) p250
6. *The Spanish Civil War* (London, 2006) p191
7. 07/09/44, cited in English in *Camus at Combat* (Princeton, 2006) ed. by J. Lévi-Valensi, p30
8. in *My House in Málaga* (London, 2019) p82
9. article republished in *Step by Step* (London, 1949) p37
10. *Step by Step* (London, 1949) p319
11. *Step by Step* (London, 1949) p300
12. in *The Spanish Civil War* (London, 2006) p147
13. *Totalitarian and Authoritarian Regimes* (Colorado, 2000) p155
14. quote is from Hernández de Miguel *Los Campos de Concentración de Franco* (Barcelona, 2019) p68
15. *The Spanish Civil War* (London, 2006) p289
16. *Diario de la guerra española* (Madrid, 1978) p496
17. *The Battle for Spain* (London, 2006) p364
18. in *Memorias* (Barcelona, 1983) p391
19. in Moradiellos, *Textos y Discursos Políticos. Juan Negrín,* (Madrid, 2010) p347
20. *The Battle for Spain* (London, 2006) p372–3

21. *The Spanish Tragedy* (London, 2000) p241
22. *¡Alerta los pueblos!* (Barcelona, 1974) p123
23. Álvaro del Vayo, *Freedom's Battle* (London,1940) p262
24. *¡Alerta los pueblos!* (Barcelona, 1974) p123
25. *Spain 1936–1939* (London, 1963) p128
26. *Guerra y Vicisitudes de los Españoles* Vol. II (Paris, 1968) p204
27. *Freedom's Battle* (London,1940), p265

Chapter 2: *Caminante, no hay camino*

1. *Blood of Spain* (London, 1981) p481
2. *¡Alerta los pueblos!* (Barcelona, 1974) p127
3. *The Spanish Civil War* (London, 1962) p574
4. this is the number quoted by Beevor in *The Battle for Spain* (London, 2006) p378
5. in *Homage to Catalonia* (London,1974) pp8–9
6. *The Spanish Cockpit* (London, 2000) p69
7. *Homage to Catalonia* (London,1974) p9
8. in *Spain: The Vital Years* (London, 1967) p318
9. in *Death's Other Kingdom* (London, 2004) p93
10. according to Martínez Barrio, Speaker of the Cortes in *Memorias* (Barcelona, 1983) p391
11. in the *Yoke and Arrows* by Herbert L. Matthews (New York, 1961) p53
12. from Martínez Barrio, *Memorias* (Barcelona, 1983) p395
13. in *The Life and Death of the Spanish Republic* (London, 2014) p415
14. in *Freedom's Battle* (London,1940) p266
15. *Guerra y Vicisitudes de los Españoles Vol. II* (Paris, 1968) p211
16. *The Life and Death of the Spanish Republic* (London, 2013) p419
17. *Freedom's Battle* (London,1940) p282
18. in *Guerra y Vicisitudes de los Españoles* Vol. II (Paris, 1968) p228
19. in *Hotel in Flight* (New York, 1940) p50
20. in *The Owl of Minerva* (London, 1959) p322
21. *Los Campos de Concentración de Franco* (Barcelona, 2019) p305
22. *Spain 1936–1939* (London, 1963) p134

Chapter 3: Till the Last Gasp

1. *The Spanish Civil War*, (London, 1962) p581
2. *The Diaries of Sir Alexander Cadogan* (London, 1971) p149
3. in *Mi Embajada en Londres durante la Guerra Civil Española* (Barcelona, 1976) p34 and Appendix 19, p308
4. http://hansard.millbanksystems.com/commons/1939/feb/28/spain#S5CV0344P0_19390228_HOC_331
5. http://hansard.millbanksystems.com/commons/1939/feb/28/spain#S5CV0344P0_19390228_HOC_331
6. in *Looking Back on the Spanish Civil War* (London,1974) p235
7. letter in Spanish in *Textos y Discursos Políticos. Juan Negrín,* (Madrid, 2010) pp276–9
8. *Mi Embajada en Londres durante la Guerra Civil Española* (Barcelona, 1976) p 27
9. *Mi Embajada en Londres durante la Guerra Civil Española* (Barcelona, 1976) p351
10. del Vayo *Freedom's Battle* (London, 1940) p282
11. Preston calls him the 'effective leader of the PCE' in *The Last Days of the Spanish Republic* (London, 2017) p35
12. see Preston, *The Last Days of the Spanish Republic* (London, 2017) Chapter 5 'Casado sows the Wind' for an analysis of the relations between Casado, his supporters, the fifth column and Franco's agents
13. for a more detailed account of the bravery of Dickinson and his crew, see Whitehead *Franco: History to the Defeated* (London, 2018) Chapter 5
14. in *The Life and Death of the Spanish Republic* (London, 2014) p423
15. cited in *The Gathering Storm* (London 1948) p191
16. *The Spanish Holocaust* (London, 2012), page xi

Chapter 4: *Allez, allez!*

1. in Spanish: Ian Gibson in *Los últimos caminos de Antomio Machado* (Barcelona, 2019)
2. in *Confieso que he vivido* (Barcelona, 1974) p134
3. cited in *Los movimientos migratorios en el exilio*, Chapter 1 of *El Exilio Republicano Español en Toulouse*, eds. Alted y Domergue, (Madrid, 2003) p31

4. *Los movimientos migratorios en el exilio* in *El Exilio Republicano Español en Toulouse*, Alted y Domergue, (Madrid, 2003) pp30–3
5. see, for example, Scott Soo, *The Routes to Exile* (Manchester, 2017) p33
6. *Los Últimos Españoles de Mauthausen* (Barcelona, 2015) p58
7. *Derrotas y Esperanzas*, (Barcelona, 1994) p190
8. *Images of War* (London: Bookplan, 1966) p52
9. in *Hotel in Flight* (New York, 1940) p359
10. *Hotel in Flight* (New York, 1940) p368
11. *Hotel in Flight* (New York, 1940) p378
12. *En defensa de la Repúblic* (Barcelona, 2010) pp 142–3
13. *El Exodo.* (Barcelona, 1977) pp47–8
14. *Number One Spanish Company* (San Vicente [Alicante] 2001) p50
15. from Frida Stewart *Firing a Shot for Freedom* (London: Clapton Press, 2020) p196
16. *Scum of the Earth* (London, 1941) p91
17. *Scum of the Earth* (London, 1941) p92
18. *The Owl of Minerva* (London, 1959) p334
19. from *En defensa de la República* (Barcelona, 2010) p285
20. Mesquida, *La Nueve* (Barcelona, 2010) pp48–9, and for more details, see Bartolomé Bennassar: *La guerre d'Espagne et ses lendemains*, (Paris, 2006) p378
21. *De Barcelona a la Bretaña Francesa: Memorias* (Sevilla, 2017)
22. *Joys and Sorrow* (London, 1970) p233
23. in *Joys and Sorrow* (London, 1970) p234
24. figures taken from Assumpta Montellà's *La Maternitat d'Elna* (Barcelona, 2017) p23
25. *La Maternitat d'Elna* (Barcelona, 2017) p113
26. for more information on Mary Elmes, see Bailey, *Love and War in the Pyrenees* (London, 2008) pp153–5, and Butler, *The Extraordinary Story of Mary Elmes* (Dublin, 2017)

Chapter 5: Diaspora

1. cited in *En defensa de la Repúblic (*Barcelona, 2010) p 150
2. *Freedom's Battle* (London,1940) p354
3. *Freedom's Battle* (London,1940) p354
4. El único camino (Madrid, 1992) pp613–4

5. see Gregorio Morán, *Miseria, grandeza y agonía del PCE. 1939–1985* (Madrid, 2017) p28

6. *Miseria, grandeza y agonía del PCE. 1939–1985* (Madrid, 2017) p41

7. *Memorias* (Barcelona, 2012) p471

8. *Textos y Discursos Políticos. Juan Negrín* (Madrid, 2010). p382

9. in *Juan Negrín* (Sussex, 2010) p303

10. from *The Cadogan Diaries* (London,1971) p309

11. from *The Cadogan Diaries* (London,1971) p334

12. *As it Happened* (London, 1954) p94

13. in *Ambassador on Special Mission* (London,1946) p173

14. PREM 4/21/1 (National Archives Kew)

15. the inventory is in Rosal, *El oro del Banco de España y la historia del Vita.* (Barcelona,1977) pp114–18. The original title was spelt with an 'x'. In modern Spanish, the title is *Don Quijote*

16. for details of the 'legend' of the treasure, see Rosal, *El oro del Banco de España y la historia del Vita.* (Barcelona,1977)

17. *El oro del banco de España y la historia del Vita* (Mexico, 1976)

18. from *Textos y Discursos Políticos.* (Madrid, 2010). p385

19. https://elpais.com/internacional/2014/06/14/actualidad/14027 52935_649468.html (retrieved 07/01/2018)

20. page 5. The booklet is available on the Warwick Digital Collections website at https://wdc.contentdm.oclc.org/digital/collection/scw/id/3069

21. More information is available at the Association for the UK Basque Children at their website: www.basquechildren.org/

22. *A Chronicle of Small Beer* (Nottingham, 2004) p103

23. in A *Chronicle of Small Beer* (Nottingham, 2004) pp104–9

24. from *Confieso que he vivido* (Barcelona, 1974) pp152–9

25. all figures are taken from Paul Preston, *The Spanish Holocaust* (London, 2012): p135, p447, p191, p321, pp336–7 and p177 respectively

26. see Gabriel Jackson, *Juan Negrín* (Sussex, 2010) p306

27. *Guerra y Vicisitudes de los Españoles Vol. II* (Paris, 1968) p242

28. the diary entry later appeared in Pablo Azcárate's own memoirs edited by Angel Viña: *En defensa de la República* (Barcelona) pp211–13, published in 2010

29. *Derrotas y Esperanzas* (Barcelona,1994) pp211–12

Chapter 6: *Fraternité*

1. *La guerre d'Espagne et sus lendemains*. (Paris, 2017) p424
2. *Los movimientos migratorios en el exilio* in *El Exilio Republicano Español en Toulouse*, Alted y Domergue, (Madrid, 2003) pp36–7
3. from *De Barcelona a la Bretaña* (Sevilla, 2017) pp 217–18
4. *The routes to exile* (Manchester, 2017) p133
5. *The routes to exile* (Manchester, 2017) p133
6. *The routes to exile* (Manchester, 2017) p133
7. *The Origins of the Second World War* (London,1964) p318
8. *Russia at War 1941–45* (New York, 1964) pp47–8
9. *Memorias* (Barcelona, 2012) p383
10. *Memorias* (Barcelona, 2012) p384
11. *The Devil's Alliance* (New York, 2014) p111

Chapter 7: *Fall Rot*

1. *Ian Fleming's Commandos*. (London, 2011) p66. Churchill used the same word 'grapple' in *The Gathering Storm* (London, 1948)
2. *Ian Fleming's Commandos*. (London, 2011) p66
3. *Los movimientos migratorios en el exilio* in *El Exilio Republicano Español en Toulouse*, Alted y Domergue, (Madrid, 2003) p42
4. *The Gathering Storm* (London, 1948) p515
5. *Second World War* (London, 1990) p56
6. according to the account by Pons Prades in *Republicanos españoles en la 2ª Guerra Mundial* (Barcelona,1975) p432
7. see Beevor *The Battle for Spain* (London: 2006) p426
8. *London Gazette* www.thegazette.co.uk/London/issue/38011/ supplement p3180
9. *London Gazette* www.thegazette.co.uk/London/issue/38011/ supplement p3182
10. *London Gazette* www.thegazette.co.uk/London/issue/38011/ supplement p3180–1
11. *London Gazette* www.thegazette.co.uk/London/issue/38011/ supplement p3190
12. in *Republicanos españoles en la 2ª Guerra Mundial* (Barcelona,1975) p446

13. Avi Schlaim: 'Prelude to Downfall: the British offer of Union to France, June 1940' in *Journal of Contemporary History*, July 1974
14. *Mémoirs* (Paris, 1976) pp169–70
15. translation by author, based on manuscript at Fondation de Gaulle: www.charles-de- gaulle.org/espace-pedagogie/dossiers-thematiques/refus-de-larmistice-lappel-18-juin/manuscrit-de-lappel-18-juin/
16. *The Call to Honour (War Memoirs*, Vol. I) (London,1955) p94
17. *Flon-Flon* (Barcelona, 1972) pp233–4
18. *Flon-Flon* (Barcelona, 1972) pp233–4

Chapter 8: *Sauve qui peut*

1. this figure appears in correspondence between Sir Alexander Cadogan and Azcárate, cited in Viñas: *En Defensa de la República* (Barcelona, 2010) p273
2. *The Fall of France* (London, 1954) p225
3. *Their Finest Hour* (London, 1949) p172
4. see, for example, www.lancastria.org.uk/
5. www.nationalarchives.gov.uk/education/worldwar2/theatres-of-war/western-europe/investigation/invasion/sources/docs/1/
6. see, for example: www.lancastria.org.uk/victim-list/
7. from *Number One Spanish Company* (San Vicente, 2001) p52
8. *Number One Spanish Company* (San Vicente, 2001) p61
9. *Escape via Berlin.* (Las Vegas, 1991) p59
10. Carmen Negrín in *Juan Negrín y el exilio* p759 at Biblioteca Virtual … www.cervantesvirtual.com; juan-negrin-y-el-exilio-849673

Chapter 9: The Wall

1. from accounts given by survivors of the Convoy in an RTVE documentary *El Convoy de los 927 Mauthausen* broadcast on 06-02-05.
2. https://bunelik.wixsite.com/bunelik. *Escape from Mauthausen* p23
3. there is some controversy surrounding the story. In *El fotógrafo del horror* (Barcelona, 2018); Spanish historian Benito Bermejo insists that Boix was the mastermind behind the operation.

In *Spaniards in the Holocaust* (London, 2014), American historian David Pike Wingeate, casts doubt on this version and suggests the key role played by Garcia was deliberately belittled by the PCE.

4. the photographs that accompanied Boix's testimony can be found in Benito Bermejo's *El fotógrafo del horror* (Barcelona, 2018) pp185–214

5. taken from the English language transcript of the trial at https://avalon.law.yale.edu/imt/01-28-46.asp#boix

6. in Wingeate's *Spaniards in the Holocaust* (London, 2014), and www.eldiario.es/sociedad/Muere-prisionero-Mathausen-libero-Franco_0_504300323.html

7. see *Los Últimos Españoles de Mauthausen* (Barcelona, 2015) by Carlos Hernández p232

8. *Los Últimos Españoles de Mauthausen* (Barcelona, 2015) p233

9. *Los Últimos Españoles de Mauthausen* (Barcelona, 2015) p142

10. at: www.boe.es/buscar/notificaciones.php?campo[0]=DOC&dato[0]=mauthausen&accion=Buscar&sort_field[0]=FPU&sort_order[0]=desc

11. for further details, see the obituaries that appeared in *El País* (04/10/20) and *The Guardian* (05/10/20)

12. all subsequent spellings and figures are taken from the *Historical Dictionary of the Spanish Empire* (New York, 1992)

13. from the Fundación Nacional Francisco Franco: www.fnff.es/Las_relaciones_entre_Franco_y_Petain_2769_c.htm

14. from the *New York Times* (10/09/25), cited by Charles William (London, 2005) p238

15. see, for example, *Pétain* by Charles Williams (London, 2005) p303

16. *Pétain* by Charles Williams (London, 2005) p305

17. see *Pétain and de Gaulle*, J-R Tournoux (London: Heinemann, 1966) p91

18. figure quoted by Dreyfus-Armand in *El exilio republicano español en Toulouse.* (Madrid, 2003) p36

19. *By Safe Hand* (London, 1983) p21

20. *Pétain* by Charles Williams (London, 2005) p529

21. *Los movimientos migratorios en el exilio* in *El Exilio Republicano Español en Toulouse*, Alted y Domergue, (Madrid, 2003) p40

22. see, for example, Preston, *The Spanish Holocaust* (London, 2013) p491

23. Preston, *The Spanish Holocaust* (London, 2013) p495
24. see Mesquida, *La Nueve* (Barcelona, 2010) p150
25. Loreto Urraca in *Entre Hienas* (Madrid, 2018) p217
26. see *Le Monde* 06/02/2015, and *El País* 28/09/2008
27. in *Eisenhower's Guerrillas* by Benjamin F. Jones (Oxford 2016) p68
28. details of Aguirre's adventure are from his own version: *Escape via Berlin* (Las Vegas, 1991)
29. *The Rise and Fall of the Third Reich* (London, 1971) p1041
30. *Half of Spain Died* (New York, 1973) pp234
31. *Half of Spain Died* (New York, 1973) pp233
32. https://grupos.es.amnesty.org/es/castillaleon/grupos/salamanca/paginas/noticia/articulo/desaparecidos-del-franquismo-cuarenta-anos-sin-justicia/

Chapter 10: Forests of the Night

1. *The Call to Honour* (London,1955) p89
2. for more details, see *Saturday at M.I.9* by Airey Neave, *The Escape Room* (New York, 1970) pp49–60
3. see Airey Neave, *The Escape Room* (New York, 1970) p63
4. the names of the five evaders are taken from *Saint-Nazaire* by James Dorrian: (Barnsley: Pen & Sword, 2006) pp180–1
5. Airey Neave, *The Escape Room* (New York, 1970) p127
6. The Escape Lines Memorial Society website at www.ww2escapelines.co.uk/
7. see *The Basque History of the World* by Kurlansky (London, 1999) pp 217–20
8. *The Escape Room* (New York, 1970) p138
9. see Airey Neave, *Little Cyclone* (London, 2013) pp176–9
10. *The Basque History of the World* (London, 1999) p220
11. for an excellent and concise account of the Resistance in Marseille, see the website of the Alliance Française in London: www.alliancefrancaise.london/Marseille-First-Capital-of-the-Resistance.php
12. for more detail, see Airey Neave, *The Escape Room* (New York, 1970) pp64–7
13. *The Way Back. The Story of Pat O'Leary* (London,1957) pp173–83
14. see his sister's account in Montseny *El Exodo* (Barcelona, 1977) p137

15. *Cruel Crossing* (London, 2013) p213
16. *The Escape Room* (New York, 1970) pp 30–7
17. Pons Prades, *Republicanos españoles en la 2ª Guerra Mundial* (Barcelona,1975) p303
18. for a detailed account of Ponzán's operations, see *Republicanos españoles en la 2ª Guerra Mundial* (Barcelona,1975) pp296–309
19. Airey Neave, *The Escape Room* (New York, 1970) pxiii
20. in *Fight Another Day* (Barnsley, 2013) p251
21. according to OSS agent Donald Downes in *The Scarlet Thread* (Maryland, 2018) p107
22. for more information, see the two documentaries *El rey de Canfranc* (Manuel Priede and José Antonio Blanco, 2013) and *Juego de espías* (Ramón J. Campo, Germán Roda, 2013)
23. *MI9* (London, 1979) p19
24. in *Los Campos de Concentración de Franco* (Barcelona, 2019) p417
25. *I Walked Alone* (London, 1950) pp179–81
26. see Hernández de Miguel in *Los Campos de Concentración de Franco* (Barcelona, 2019) p 420
27. *Ambassador on Special Mission* (London,1946) p226
28. in *Fight another Day* (Barnsley, 2013) p117
29. from Foot and Langley's *MI9* (London, 1979) p77
30. *Sunday at Large* (London, 1977) p140
31. details from the Encyclopaedia of New Zealand at: https://teara. govt.nz/en/biographies/5m46/miles-reginald; also: Sir Samuel Hoare, *Complacent Dictator* (New York, 1947) p229
32. *Ambassador on Special Mission* (London,1946) p238

Chapter 11: Violins of Autumn

1. *Fighters in the Shadows* (London, 2015) p17
2. for more detail see the Musée de L'Homme website: www. museedelhomme.fr/en/museum/history-musee-homme/1941-musee-homme-resistance-network
3. see, for example, *Carboneros, leñadores y maquis* by Fernando Hernández Sánchez.at: https://laestaciondefinlandia.wordpress. com/2014/01/15/carboneros-lenadores-y-maquis-los-guerrilleros-espanoles-en-francia-1939-1950/

4. in *Maquis* by Serrano, Secundino (Madrid, 2004) p126
5. in *Call to Honour* (London, 1955) p266
6. *Call to Honour* (London, 1955) p271
7. from a memo. to Halifax (03/07/40), cited in *Behind the Lines* by Miller (London, 2002) pp1-2
8. *Unity 1942–1944* (London, 1959) p258
9. SOE Archives File (D/R)D:1 (a) quoted in The Secret History of the SOE (W. Mackenzie) p602
10. from CIA Library: www.cia.gov/library/center-for-the-study-of-intelligence/csi-publications/csi-studies/studies/vol-60-no-2/eisenhowers-guerrillas.html
11. *Crusade in Europe* (London,1948) pp323–5
12. in *Fighters in the Shadows* (London, 2015) p16
13. *The Spanish Civil War* (Oxford, 2005) pp117–19
14. in *Das Reich* (London, 1983) p78
15. there are suggestions that there may have been as many as 30,000 Republican conscripts working on the Atlantic Wall. See, for example, *D-Day in Numbers: The Facts behind Operation Overlord* by Jacob F. Field (London; O'Mara Books, 2014)
16. Imperial War Museum. Oral History. Available at: www.iwm.org.uk/collections/item/object/80009851
17. for more information, see *Esclavos de Hitler. Republicanos en los campos nazis del Canal de la Mancha* by Martí Crespo (Barcelona: Voc, 2014); more details based on the personal experience of Juan Taule are available at the website: www.theislandwiki.org/index.php/Spanish_Republican_Juan_Taule; and in George Forty's *Atlantic Wall: Channel Islands* (Pen & Sword; Barnsley, 2011)
18. for more details, see Caroline Sturdy Colls's documentary *Adolf Island* on her research into the Alderney camps, available on the Smithsonian Channel
19. *El Exodo* (Barcelona 1977) pp122–3
20. in *Maquis* (Madrid, 2004) p129
21. Braddon in *Nancy Wake* (London, 1956) p181.
22. *Nancy Wake* (London, 1956) pp200–1
23. taken from the French edition, translation by author, *La Gestapo m'appelait la Souris Blanche* (Paris, 2001) p147
24. in *Moondrop to Gascony* (London, 1946) p172
25. *Moondrop to Gascony* (London, 1946) p173 and 174

26. in *L'Esprit de Résistance* (Paris, 1995) p269
27. *L'Esprit de Résistance* (Paris, 1995) p269
28. *The Call to Honour* (London, 1955) p115
29. this version of events is from *Three Marshalls of France* by A. Clayton (London, 1992) p45
30. the Fighting Basques Project suggests the Republicans represented 25–30% of the total brigade; see *Combatientes Vascos en la Segunda Guerra Mundial* (Madrid, 2018) p25. Of these twenty were Basques or from Navarre)
31. *Republicanos españoles en la 2ª Guerra Mundial* (Barcelona,1975) p460
32. *Republicanos españoles en la 2ª Guerra Mundial* (Barcelona,1975) p477
33. *Memoirs* (London, 1960) p144
34. see his memoirs *Carnets de Route* (Paris, 1984) p265
35. this figure appears in *Republicanos españoles en la 2ª Guerra Mundial* (Barcelona,1975) p362

Chapter 12: The Devil, the Deep Blue Sea and the Rock

1. PREM/4/21/1 (National Archives Kew)
2. see Eccles: *By Safe Hand* (London, 1983) p101. According to Hoare, it was the Foreign Office that took this emergency precaution: Ambassador on Special Mission (London,1946) p24
3. *Ambassador on Special Mission* (London,1946) p22
4. *By Safe Hand* (London, 1983) p104
5. *Ambassador on Special Mission* (London,1946) p40
6. *Ambassador on Special Mission* (London,1946) p109
7. quoted in *The Cadogan Diaries* (London, 1971) p326
8. *Wartime Mission in Spain* (New York, 1945) pp77–8
9. in *Hitler's Interpreter* (Stroud, [Gloucestershire], 2016) p190 and Serrano Suñer in *Memorias* (Barcelona, 1977) p290
10. *Hitler's Interpreter* (Stroud, [Gloucestershire], 2016) p191
11. *Memorias* (Barcelona, 1977) p294
12. quoted by Serrano Suñer in *Memorias* (Barcelona, 1977) p294
13. in *Memorias* (Barcelona, 1977) p298
14. *Hitler's Interpreter* (Stroud, [Gloucestershire], 2016) p193

15. cited in *Franco's Friends* by Peter Day (London, 2011) p186
16. ABC 30 June 1940, p5
17. *Ambassador on Special Mission* (London,1946) p42
18. in *The Grass and the Asphalt* (Cádiz, 1997) pp186–8
19. *Defending the Rock* (London, 2017) pp250–1
20. *Thorns of Memory* (London, 1961)
21. *The Grass and the Asphalt* (Cádiz, 1997) p190
22. *Ambassador on Special Mission* (London,1946) p53
23. memo to Churchill. CAB 84/26/29. 12/01/41 (National Archives Kew)
24. *Ambassador on Special Mission* (London,1946) p53
25. CAB 66/12/12. 21/08/40 (National Archives Kew)

Chapter 13: Golden Eyes

1. *Number One Spanish Company* (San Vicente [Alicante] 2001) p62
2. CAB 84/26/29 pp126-129 (National Archives Kew)
3. CAB 84/26/29. 12/01/41 (National Archives Kew)
4. *Number One Spanish Company* (San Vicente [Alicante], 2001) pp65–7
5. in *En defensa de la República* (Barcelona, 2010) p387
6. this account is from his autobiography, *Adventures of a Doctor* (London, 1962) pp137–9
7. *Adventures of a Doctor* (London, 1962) p138
8. *Secret History of SOE*, Mackenzie, William (London, 2000) p730
9. this account is taken from his autobiography, *Thorns of Memory*: (London, 1961) pp147–9
10. *Thorns of Memory* (London, 1961) p145
11. from Cunningham, *Beaulieu.* (Barnsley, 2011). p82
12. both quotes are taken from *My Silent War* by Kim Philby (London,1983) p57. Kemp's comment was made in his own memoirs, *No Colours or Crest*.
13. Cunningham, *Beaulieu.* (Barnsley, 2011). First published in 1998. pp82–3
14. Rankin, *Defending the Rock* (London, 2017) p439
15. *Thorns of Memory* (London, 1961) p149
16. as told to Marcel Jullian in *HMS Fidelity* (London, 1957) Chapter 8 'Waters of Anger'
17. Appendix VI / *H.M.S. Fidelity* by Marcel Jullian (London 1957)
18. *Number One Spanish Company* (San Vicente [Alicante], 2001) p67

19. see *Franco and Hitler*, Stanley Payne (Yale, 2008) p94
20. *A Game of Moles,* Bristow (London, 1993) p49
21. taken from E. Butler's *Mason-Mac: The Life of Lieutenant-General Sir Noel Mason-Macfarlane* (London, 1972) p124
22. quoted by Serrano Suñer in *Memorias* (Barcelona, 1977) p306
23. see, for example, Rudolph von Ribbentrop's biography of his father: *My Father Joachim von Ribbentrop* (Barnsley: Pen and Sword, 2019) pp249–51
24. in *Present at the Creation* (New York, 1969) p53.
25. for example, see Nicholas Rankin, *Defending the Rock* (London, 2017) p345
26. PREM 3/438B. 14–15 Nov 1942 (National Archives Kew)
27. quoted by Donald Downes in *The Scarlet Thread* (Maryland, 2018) p108
28. in *The Scarlet Thread* (Maryland, 2018) p110
29. this account is based mainly on Donald Downes's own version in *The Scarlet Thread* (Maryland, 2018) pp103–29 (Rowman & Littlefield, 2005*),* supported by Richard Harris Smith's account *OSS: The Secret History of America's First Central Intelligence Agency* (University of California, 1972) pp76–83

Chapter 14: *Con la camisa nueva*

1. in *Homage to Catalonia* (London,1974*)* p48
2. published in *News Chronicle*, 24 October 1936
3. *Ambassador on Special Mission* (London,1946) p112
4. *Ambassador on Special Mission* (London,1946) pp114–15
5. *Memorias* (Barcelona, 1977) p206
6. figures from Kleinfield and Tambs *Hitler's Spanish Legion* (Pennsylvania, 1979) p335
7. for footage and individual testimonies, see: www.rtve.es/alacarta/ videos/documaster/documaster-espanoles-2-guerra-mundial-frente-del-este-rojos-azules/5380259/
8. Caballero: *Hitler's Spanish Legion* (Pennsylvania, 1979) p26
9. the translation is from the text prepared for Churchill: PREM 4/21/1 (National Archives Kew)
10. from Caballero *Españoles contra Stalin* (Madrid, ND) p60

11. see Caballero *Españoles contra Stalin* (Madrid, ND) p63 and Kleinfield and Tambs' *Hitler's Spanish Legion* pp4344
12. for detailed accounts, see Salisbury: *The 900 Days: The Siege of Leningrad* (London: Pan, 2000) and Werth: *Russia at War 1941–45* (New York: Dutton, 1964) Part III
13. *Hitler's Table Talk*, (New York 2000) p71
14. for a more detailed account, see Caballero: *Españoles contra Stalin* pp149–52 or Kleinfield and Tambs: *Hitler's Spanish Legion* (Pennsylvania, 1979) pp148–54
15. Kleinfeld and Tamb *Hitler's Spanish Legion* (Pennsylvania, 1979) p186
16. Kleinfeld and Tamb *Hitler's Spanish Legion* (Pennsylvania, 1979) p220
17. figures are taken from Kleinfeld and Tamb *Hitler's Spanish Legion* (Pennsylvania, 1979) p299
18. figures from *Oxford Companion to World War II*, (Oxford 2005) p110
19. *Oxford Companion to World War II*, (Oxford 2005) p110
20. Werth *Russia at War 1941–45* (New York,1964) p324
21. from *The 900 Days: The Siege of Leningrad* (London, 2000) pvii
22. in an article published by *El País* on 10/05/1985 at https://elpais.com/diario/1985/05/10/internacional/484524015_850215.html
23. in *The Battle for Spain* (London, 2006) p419
24. according to Beevor, the figure was 50%: *The Battle for Spain* (London, 2006) p419
25. these figures are given by Serna in: *Heroísmo español en Rusia* (Madrid, 1981) p55
26. the anecdote is from Pons: *Republicanos Españoles en la Segunda Guerra Mundial* (Barcelona, 1975) p566
27. *ABC* 09/03/2015 at: www.abc.es/espana/20150308/abci-dia-internacional-de-La-Mujer-201503072004.html
28. Preston *Doves of War* (London, 2002) p386
29. See www.warheroes.ru/hero/hero.asp?Hero_id=281
30. This is the figure given by Serna Martínez in the article that appeared in *El País* 10/05/85. Other sources suggest the number is between 200 and 300 (see, for example, www.publico.es/opinion/espanoles-defendieron-urss.html)
31. for more information on the role of the exiles in the service of the USSR, see Serna Martínez: *Heroísmo en la URSS* (Madrid, 1981), Pons Prades: *Republicanos españoles en la 2ª Guerra Mundial* (Barcelona, 1975) and Arasa: *Los españoles de Stalin* (Barcelona: Belacqua, 2005)

Chapter 15: Back Entrances, Side Doors, Secret Elevators

1. Pujol, (with Nigel West) *Garbo* (London, 1986) p56
2. Pujol, *Garbo* (London, 1986) p64
3. Public Record Office – Garbo. *The Spy who Saved D-Day* p43
4. in Pujol, *Garbo* (London, 1986) pp64–5
5. Public Record Office – Garbo. *The Spy who Saved D-Day* pp 58–9. www.mi5.gov.uk/agent-garbo. In his autobiography Garbo claims he was referring to Liverpool dockers – [Pujol, Garbo (London, 1986) p119].
6. see *Sunday at Large* (London,1977) Chapter 11 'The Spare Room'
7. Desmond Bristow, *A Game of Moles* (London, 1993) p40
8. Beevor, *D-Day* (London, 2009) p523
9. Christopher Andrew, *The Defence of the Realm* (London, 2009) p297
10. Public Record Office – Garbo. The Spy who saved D-Day p205
11. Pujol, *Garbo* (London, 1986) p199
12. quoted in *The Defence of the Realm* (London, 2009) p256

Chapter 16: *Ubique*

1. Second Lieutenant José Cortés in Pons Prades *Republicanos españoles en la 2ª Guerra Mundial* (Barcelona, 1975) p360
2. Dronne, *Carnets de Route d'un Croisé de la France Libre* (Paris, 1984) p242 and 249–50
3. Dronne, *Carnets de Route d'un Croisé de la France Libre* (Paris, 1984) ibid pp 262–3
4. in *La Nueve* (Barcelona, 2010) p107
5. for more information about Lucio Sauquillo: *Combatientes Vascos en la Segunda Guerra Mundial* (Madrid, 2018) by Tabernilla; also *Commonwealth War Graves Commission* at: www.cwgc.org
6. from *Combatientes Vascos en la Segunda Guerra Mundial* (Madrid, 2018) p75 and the BBC Archive at www.bbc.co.uk/history/ww2peopleswar/stories/38/a4460438.shtml. There is footage of the king's visit to Normandy at: www.youtube.com/watch?v=02O6TD-EG8c
7. in *A Game of Moles* (London, 1993) p24

8. in *Number One Spanish Company* (San Vicente [Alicante] 2001) pp77–8

9. *Number One Spanish Company* (San Vicente [Alicante] 2001) pp82–5

10. this account is based on the information available in his records at www.paradata.org.uk/people/jose-m-irala, also *Commonwealth War Graves Commission* at: www.cwgc.org

11. for more information on Kirkpatrick, see *The Scotsman* 29/09/2016 at: www.scotsman.com/whats-on/arts-and-entertainment/ww2-mad-scots-piper-who-remains-hero-italy-1466065; also *Operation Tombola* (London: Arms and Armour, 1986) by Roy Farran, p73 and p110

12. this is the account given by Major Roy Farran in *Operation Tombola* (London: Arms and Armour, 1986) pp113–14

13. in *Operation Tombola* (London: Arms and Armour, 1986) p192. There is a second version on pages 231–2, but the details are essentially the same.

14. for more details on Balerdi and his two friends, see *Combatientes Vascos en la Segunda Guerra Mundial* (Madrid, 2018) and on the role of Ramos, see *SAS in Tuscany, 1943–1945* by Brian Lett (Barnsley: Pen and Sword, 2011) chapters 19–21

15. Dronne, *Carnets de Route d'un Croisé de la France Libre* (Paris, 1984) p264

16. in *Unity* (London 1959) p297

17. *Unity* (London 1959) p297

18. Beevor, *D-Day* (London, 2009) p498

19. de Gaulle, *Unity* (London 1959) bid p301

20. Pons Prades *Republicanos españoles en la 2ª Guerra Mundial* (Barcelona,1975) p389

21. passenger list in *Una presó amb vistes al mar* (University of Alicante, 2008)

22. *El País*, 20/04/2017. Almudena Grandes is the author of *Inés y la alegría* (Barcelona: Tusquets, 2010), a compelling novel that maps the story of the Republicans in Toulouse and describes the invasion of the Val d'Aran. The novel is part of her series. *Episodios de una guerra interminable.*

23. in *La Nueve* (Barcelona, 2010) p214

24. from his obituary in *La Vanguardia* 24/04/2020 and Mesquida's *La Nueve* (Barcelona, 2010) pp181–7
25. Pons Prades *Republicanos españoles en la 2ª Guerra Mundial* (Barcelona,1975) p19

Chapter 17: But Sometimes You Might Make the Wrong Decisions, Comrades

1. estimates from a range of sources put the figure between 40,000 and 59,000. The numbers for Britain/Ireland are taken from the *International Brigade Memorial Trust* website at: www.international-brigades.org.uk/
2. for details and figures see Gerald Howson: *Arms for Spain* (London, 1998) and Michael Alpert: *A New International History of the Spanish Civil War* (London,1994)
3. *Tres Años de Lucha* (Paris, 1970) p270
4. *Memoirs of a Revolutionary* (London, 1963) p336
5. for a full description of their quarrel, see S. Koch's *The Breaking Point. Hemingway, Dos Passos, and the Murder of José Robles* (New York: Counterpoint, 2005)
6. *Memoirs of a Revolutionary* (London, 1963) p337
7. quoted by Richard Davenport-Hines: *Auden* (New York: Pantheon, 1995) p164
8. the details of these events are from Preston's *The Last Stalinist* (London, 2015) pp114–17 and Moran's *Miseria, grandeza y agonia del PCE* (Madrid, 2017) pp70–92. They are contrasted with Carrillo's version in *Memorias* (Barcelona, 2012) pp496–500
9. *Memorias* (Barcelona, 2012) p496
10. the narrative is from *Miseria, grandeza y agonía del PCE* by Morán (Madrid, 2017) pp86–7
11. *Derrotas y Esperanzas* (Barcelona, 1994), p206
12. *Derrotas y Esperanzas* (Barcelona, 1994), p218
13. for example see *Jesús Monzón* by Manuel Martorell (Pamplona, 2000) p99
14. *Jesús Monzón* by Manuel Martorell (Pamplona, 2000) p101
15. cited by Azcárate, in *En defensa de la República* (Barcelona, 2010) p187

16. from *Reconquista de España*, October–November 1943
17. see *La verdad de mis relaciones con Franco* (Barcelona, 1981) p283
18. *La verdad de mis relaciones con Franco* (Barcelona, 1981) p317
19. in *Jesús Monzón* by Manuel Martorell (Pamplona, 2000) p142
20. Daniel Arasa, *Años 40* (Barcelona: 1984) p90
21. Zaragoza Fernández in *Radio Toulouse y la invasión del Valle de Arán*, p132
22. in Secundino Serrano's *Maquis* (Madrid, 2004) p131
23. see *Jesús Monzón* by Manuel Martorell, p129
24. from a letter to Franco, in Shirer, *The Rise and Fall of the Third Reich* (London, 1971) p980

Chapter 18: *Une certaine idée de la France*

1. from Ricardo Sicre's novel *The Tap on the Left Shoulder* (London: Cassell, 1950) p229
2. in *Das Reich* (London, 1983) p185.
3. details of this account from Serge Vernal, *L'Esprit de Résistance*, (Paris, 1995) pp 304–14
4. *L'Esprit de Résistance* (Paris, 1995) p269
5. *Fighters in the Shadows* (London, 2015) p386
6. *Moondrop to Gascony* (London, 1946) p178
7. from *Moondrop to Gascony* (London, 1946) p191
8. There are many versions of this battle. The numbers in this account are based mainly on the version offered by Mesquida in *Y ahora volved a vuestras casas* (Barcelona, 2020) pp181–93. She also includes a list with the names of the 36 men in the original unit.
9. *Ambassador on Special Mission* (London, 1946) p278
10. in Mackenzie, *Secret History of the SOE* (London, 2000) p584
11. *L'Esprit de Résistance*, (Paris, 1995) p271
12. in *Maquis y Pirineos* (Pirineos, 2001) p35
13. *Salvation* (London, 1960) p18
14. *Salvation* (London, 1960) p20
15. *Love and War in the Pyrenees* (London, 2008) p104
16. from Daniel Arasa, *Años 40* (Barcelona: 1984) p50

17. for a detailed account of the battle and the role of the Basques, see Guillermo Tabernilla's *Combatientes Vascos en la Segunda Guerra Mundial* (Madrid: 2018) pp40–54
18. the *Basque History of the World* (London, 1999) pp22–3
19. https://ianasagasti.blogs.com/mi_blog/2018/09/entrevista-a-kepa-ordoki-en-1977.html. there are suggestions that it was not de Gaulle who made this promise but General Larminat (see for example *Combatientes Vascos en la Segunda Guerra Mundial* [Madrid: 2018] p54)

Chapter 19: *¿qué gigantes? – dijo Sancho Panza*

1. for a detailed account, see Antonio Maestre's *Franquismo S.A.* (Madrid: Akal, 2019)
2. in *Spain, 1833–2002* (OUP, 2013) p161. Vincent paraphrases Serrano's phrase in Spanish in *Maquis* (Madrid, 2004) p374
3. *Complacent Dictator* (New York, 1947) p245
4. in *The Scarlet Thread* (Maryland, 2018) p122
5. Churchill in *Triumph and Tragedy*, (London, 1954), p520
6. See, for example, Ferran Sánchez Agustí in *Maquis y Pirineos* (Pirineos, 2001) p34
7. https://hansard.parliament.uk/commons/1944-05-24/.../ForeignAffairs
8. see, for example, Richard Wigg, *Churchill and Spain* (Sussex, 2008) p154
9. in *Closing the Ring*, (London, 1954), pp487–8
10. in Richard Wigg, *Churchill and Spain* (Sussex, 2008) p115–16
11. *My Silent War* (London, 1983) p116
12. from Hoare's memoirs, *Complacent Dictator* (New York, 1947) p96
13. https://hansard.parliament.uk/commons/1944-05-24/.../ForeignAffairs
14. See *Wartime Mission in Spain* (New York, 1945) p303
15. *Wartime Mission in Spain* (New York, 1945) p96
16. *Wartime Mission in Spain* (New York, 1945) pp307–8
17. in Viñas *En defensa de la República* (Barcelona, 2010) pp283–6
18. in *The Scarlet Thread* (Maryland, 2018) pp 121–2

19. he later wrote a novel, *The Tap on the Left Shoulder*, based on his experiences, where his name is spelt Sicré
20. the details of his experiences are taken from the website of the *Ministro de Trabajo, Migraciones y Seguridad Social* at: www. mitramiss.gob.es/cartaespana/es/noticias/Noticia_0333.htm
21. in *Maquis* (Madrid, 2004) p137
22. from *Salvation* (London, 1960) p20

Chapter 20: Republic Across the Mountains

1. in *Derrotas y Esperanzas* (Barcelona, 1994) p286
2. *Derrotas y Esperanzas* (Barcelona, 1994) p280
3. see *Memorias* (Barcelona, 2012) and *Miseria, grandeza y agonía del PCE* (Madrid, 2017) respectively
4. *Miseria, Grandeza y Agonía del PCE* (Madrid, 2017) p268
5. Azcárate in *Derrotas y Esperanzas* (Barcelona, 1994) p266 and Carrillo in Archivos Históricos del PCE. Dirigentes/Santiago Carrillo/Informes Caja 30. Carpeta 1.2
6. *Miseria, Grandeza y Agonía del PCE* (Madrid, 2017) p156
7. in *Años 40* (Barcelona: 1984), p78
8. see, for example, *Radio Toulouse y la invasión del Valle de Arán* by Luis Zaragoza p133
9. Arasa in *Años 40* (Barcelona: 1984), p78
10. quoted in Riera Socasau, *Juán Blazuez y Lola Clavero* (Lleida, 2013) p73
11. compare: *Años 40* (Barcelona: 1984), p78 and *Derrotas y Esperanzas* (Barcelona, 1994) p286
12. *Derrotas y Esperanzas* (Barcelona, 1994) p287
13. *Años 40* (Barcelona: 1984), p78
14. Archivos Históricos del PCE. Dirigentes/Santiago Carrillo/ Informes Caja 30. Carpeta 1.2
15. *Memorias* (Barcelona, 2006) pp476
16. from War Memoirs III – *Salvation* (Weidenfeld and Nicolson) p20
17. *La invasión de los maquis* (Barcelona, 2004), p142
18. interview in *Les guérilléros du Val d'Aran 1944* www.youtube. com/watch?v=MJdrh9A8ANQ

19. Archivos Históricos del PCE. Dirigentes/Dolores Ibárruri/ Escritos/16.2
20. in *La invasión de los maquis* (Barcelona, 2004) p320
21. in Arasa, *Años 40* (Barcelona: 1984), p117
22. quoted by Mesquida in *Y ahora volved a casa* (Barcelona, 2020) p111
23. see the interview in Las Ilusiones Perdidas. Episode 6. La Invasion del Valle de Arán, directed by Eugenio Monesma. Pyrene P.V., Spain 2004 www.youtube.com/watch?v=wAezYe9gcgM
24. in Arasa, *Años 40* (Barcelona: 1984), p88
25. in Arasa, *La invasión de los maquis* (Barcelona, 2004), p166

Chapter 21: For Courage Mixed with Prudence is not Foolish

1. details from a singularly unenthusiastic pamphlet produced by the Ministry of Foreign Affairs: *Ángel Sanz Briz. El ángel de Budapest*. at: www.exteriores.gob.es/Embajadas/BUDAPEST/es/ Embajada/Paginas/Historia-Sanz-Briz.aspx
2. from *La invasión de los maquis* (Barcelona, 2004) p158
3. these and all figures in this chapter as well as descriptions of conditions and events are based on the work of cited authors in: *La invasión de los maquis* (Barcelona, 2004) and *Años 40* (Barcelona: 1984); *Maquis y Pirineos* (Pirineos, 2001); *Maquis* (Madrid, 2004); and *Radio Toulouse y la invasión del Valle de Arán,* respectively.
4. cited by Daniel Aras in *Años 40. Los maquis y el PCE* (Barcelona: 1984), p90
5. *Aqueth dia i auie ua nòça.* (2014) by Mireira Boya and Natàlia Lloreta (Production: ARIUAN)
6. *Maquis y Pirineos* (Pirineos, 2001) p80
7. this account of the battle for Salardú is provided by the local authorities of the village and is reproduced on a tourist information board in the public car park.
8. the quotation is from Sánchez Agustí's *Maquis y Pirineos* (Pirineos, 2001) p85
9. for example: Serrano, in *Maquis* (Madrid, 2004) p134
10. in Aras's *Años 40. Los maquis y el PCE* (Barcelona: 1984), p168. The figure was repeated by Pinocho's son in an interview with

Mesquida, published in her book *Y ahora, volved a vuestras casas* (Barcelona, 2020) p247

11. in Arasa, *La invasión de los maquis* (Barcelona, 2004), p216–17
12. in *Nosotros los Franco* (Barcelona, 1980), p132
13. *Años 40* (Barcelona: 1984), pp134–5
14. in Arasa, *La invasión de los maquis* (Barcelona, 2004), p219
15. quoted in Riera Socasau, *Juán Blazuez y Lola Clavero* (Lleida, 2013) p73
16. see Riera Socasau, *Juán Blazuez y Lola Clavero* (Lleida, 2013) p72
17. according to Riera Socasau, *Juán Blazuez y Lola Clavero* (Lleida, 2013) p30
18. for example, Arasa, *La invasión de los maquis* (Barcelona, 2004), p222
19. from *Memorias* (Barcelona, 2006) pp465–7
20. *Memorias* (Barcelona, 2012) p466
21. *Memorias* (Barcelona, 2012) p468
22. *Memorias* (Barcelona, 2012) p471
23. recording and transcript available at: https://millercenter.org/the-presidency/presidential-speeches/july-28-1943-fireside-chat-25-fall-mussolini

Chapter 22: *Broma baisha*

1. from *Memorias* (Barcelona, 2012) p472, *Derrotas y Esperanzas* (Barcelona, 1994) p288 and *La invasión de los maquis* (Barcelona, 2004), p244
2. *Memorias* (Barcelona, 2012) p472, and interviews in *Les guérilléros du Val d'Aran 1944* by Jorge Amat and *Las Ilusiones Perdidas*. Episode 6. *La Invasion del Valle de Arán*, directed by Eugenio Monesma. Also: Archivos Históricos PCE Dirigentes/ Santiago Carrillo/Informes Caja 30. Carpeta 1.2
3. *La invasión de los maquis* (Barcelona, 2004), p257
4. *Derrotas y Esperanzas* (Barcelona, 1994) p288
5. *Les guérilléros du Val d'Aran 1944* by Jorge Amat and *Las Ilusiones Perdidas*. Episode 6. *La Invasion del Valle de Arán*, directed by Eugenio Monesma. *La invasión de los maquis* (Barcelona, 2004), p244
6. *La invasión de los maquis* (Barcelona, 2004), p244–5

7. Archivos Históricos del PCE. Dirigentes/Santiago Carrillo/ Informes Caja 30. Carpeta 1.2
8. *La invasión de los maquis* (Barcelona, 2004), p227
9. *Maquis y Pirineos* (Pirineos, 2001) p93
10. *Maquis y Pirineos* (Pirineos, 2001) p94–116
11. *Maquis y Pirineos* (Pirineos, 2001) p226
12. retrieved from http://prensahistorica.mcu.es/clandestina/es
13. in *Wartime Mission in Spain* (New York, 1945)
14. in *Nosotros los Franco* (Barcelona,1980), p134
15. *The Undefeated* Collier's 03/03/1945
16. for more details, see Molanes Pérez, Pablo *El Hospital Varsovia de Toulouse, un proyecto del exilio español.* Cultura de los Cuidados. Año XVII, n. 35 (1. cuatrimestre 2013) at http://rua.ua.es/dspace/handle/10045/28068

Chapter 23: Veil of Oblivion

1. in *The Last Stalinist* (London: 2014) p147
2. *Años 40* (Barcelona: 1984), pp 308
3. Archivos Históricos del PCE. Dirigentes/Santiago Carrillo/ Informes Caja 30. Carpeta 1.2 pp19–20.
4. *Derrotas y Esperanzas* (Barcelona, 1994) p290
5. *Memorias* (Barcelona, 2012) p508
6. in *Maquis y Pirineos* (Pirineos, 2001) p278
7. cited by Serrano in *Maquis* (Madrid, 2004) p312
8. *Santiago Carrillo* (Barcelona, 1983) p81
9. *Así destruyó Carrillo el PCE* (Barcelona, 1983), p79
10. *Así destruyó Carrillo el PCE* (Barcelona, 1983), p83
11. *Jesús Monzón* by Manuel Martorell (Pamplona, 2000) p75
12. *Así destruyó Carrillo el PCE* (Barcelona, 1983), pp74–5
13. in *The Last Stalinist* (London: 2014) p162
14. quoted in English by David Wingeate in *Spaniards in the Holocaust* (London, 2000) p165
15. *Así destruyó Carrillo el PCE* (Barcelona, 1983), pp86–7
16. Archivos Históricos del PCE. Report 11.07.1951. Caja 35. Carpeta 16
17. in *The Last Stalinist* (London: 2014) p156
18. in *Maquis* (Madrid, 2004) p315

19. *Así destruyó Carrillo el PCE* (Barcelona, 1983), pp87–8
20. comments from his great-niece to *Público*: at www.publico.es/sociedad/figura-oculta-comunista-luis-montero.html
21. in *Joys and Sorrows* (London, 1970) p230

Chapter 24: *Die Welt des freien Menschen*

1. Appendix A of Hoare: *Ambassador on Special Mission* (London,1946) p300
2. the reply is also in Appendix A of *Ambassador on Special Mission* (London,1946) pp304–6
3. published in *Complacent Dictator* (New York, 1947) p244
4. for a detailed account of the relations between Churchill, Hoare and the FO, see Wigg, *Churchill and Spain* (Sussex, 2008) pp 177–95
5. *Ambassador on Special Mission* (London,1946) p284
6. quote from Secretary of State Dean Acheson in *Present at the Creation* (New York, 1969) p169
7. from Foreign Relations of the United States: Diplomatic Papers, The Conference of Berlin (The Potsdam Conference), 1945 at: https://history.state.gov/historicaldocuments/frus1945Berlinv02/d710a-29
8. telegrams from *Archivo General de la Administración* (10)026.002 SIGNAGA 54/12434
9. in Wayne H. Bowen: *Truman, Franco's Spain and the Cold War* (Missouri, 2017)
10. Department of State Bulletin Volume 25, p402 and Bowan: *Truman, Franco's Spain, and the Cold War* (Missouri, 2017) p67
11. Viñas: *En defensa de la República* (Barcelona, 2010) p233,
12. in *Triumph and Tragedy*, (London,1954), p520
13. *As it Happened* (London, 1954) p95
14. *As it Happened* (London, 1954) p147
15. at: https://api.parliament.uk/historic-hansard/commons/1945/aug/20/debate-on-the-address#S5CV0413P0_19450820_HOC_31
16. 07/09/44, cited in English in *Camus at Combat* (Princeton, 2006) ed. by J. Lévi-Valensi, p30
17. see, for example, *Pétain and de Gaulle* by J-R Tournoux (London, Heinemann, 1966) p148

18. www.un.org/documents/ga/res/1/ares1.htm. The italics in the text are as appears in original document.
19. www.un.org/documents/ga/res/1/ares1.htm. The italics in the text are as appears in original document. UNED, 2003) p157
20. from Hermanos*: El fin de la esperanza* (Buenos Aires, 1956) p50
21. for more details, see, for instance: Hermanos*: El fin de la esperanza* (Buenos Aires, 1956) pp80–3
22. Mary Vincent, *Spain 1833–2002* (OUP, 2013) p162
23. figure taken from A. Garzón, *¿Quién vota a la derecha?* (Barcelona: Península, 2019) p141
24. text of radio address in the Congressional Record, 80th Congress, First Session, Appendix, Volume 93, Part 10, (January 3, 1947– April 1, 1947), A1329
25. in *Spain 1808–1975* (Oxford, 1982) p721
26. www.vatican.va/roman_curia/secretariat_state/archivio/documents/ rc_seg-st_1530827_concordato-spagna_sp.html
27. *The Scarlet Thread* (Maryland, 2018) p103

Glossary

Abwehr: German Military Intelligence

Afrikakorps (DAK): German expeditionary force in North Africa (1941–3), under the command of General Rommel

AGE: Agrupación de Guerrilleros Españoles, autonomous Spanish Maquis group in French Resistance

BOE: *Boletín Oficial del Estado/Official State Gazette*

Carlistas: traditionalist (anti-liberal), ultra-Catholic followers of the dynastic line of Prince Carlos, pretender who claimed his right to the throne under Salic Law when his niece was proclaimed Queen Isabel in 1833

Caudillo: title bestowed on Franco, similar to 'Führer' or 'Duce'

CC.OO.: Comisiones Obreras, trade union aligned with Communist Party

checas: headquarters of self-appointed autonomous militia police forces whose aim was to expose and eliminate pro-Franco elements in Republican territory (especially Madrid)

Comintern: Third Communist International (1919–43), organization promoting the world Communist movement

Condor Legion: autonomous military legion/unit deployed by Hitler in support of Franco in Spanish Civil War

CNT: Confederación Nacional del Trabajo, confederation of anarcho-syndicalist labour unions

CNT-FAI: Confederación Nacional de Trabajo/Federación Anarquista Ibérica, anarchist group

Cortes: the historical name for the Spanish Parliament

CTE: Compagnies de travailleurs étrangers/foreign workers companies, set up by decree law on 12 April 1939. The companies (250 men in each unit) were attached to the French Army; the enlisted men carried out public and military works.

Deuxième Division Blindée: Second Armoured Division of the Free French, under General Leclerc

División Azul (Blue Division): Spanish volunteer force that fought alongside Wehrmacht on the Eastern Front against the USSR

EFE: Spanish news agency, set up in 1939

Euskadi: the Basque Country

Falange: Fascist 'Party' founded by José Antonio Primo de Rivera

Fall Gelb (Case Yellow): first stage of German offensive in western Europe (May 1940)

Fall Rot (Case Red): second stage of German offensive in France (June 1940)

FET de las JONS: Falange Española Tradicionalista y de las Juntas de Ofensiva Nacional Sindicalista, Franco's single party, the result of an enforced union between the Falange and the Carlists

FFI: Forces Françaises de l'Intérieur, the unified Resistance movement in France

Frente Popular: Popular Front, alliance of left-wing and Republican parties that won the 1936 general election

Fuero de los Españoles: one of Franco's 'Fundamental Laws' that established the rights, liberties and duties of the Spanish people (1945)

Gallego: native of Galicia in north-west Spain

Generalísimo: Franco's military title as 'supreme commander'

Generalitat: autonomous government of Catalonia

Gestapo (Geheime Staatspolizei): Nazi secret police

GTE: Groupes de travailleurs étrangers

Guardia Civil: paramilitary police force

gudari: the Basque word for warrior often used by Spanish speakers; the plural in Basque is Gudariak

huidos: Republican partisans who 'took to the hills' rather than surrender to Franco's forces and who organized the guerrilla resistance to the new regime

International Brigades: volunteers who fought for the Republic during the Spanish Civil War

JARE: Junta de Auxilo a los Republicanos Españoles, board set up by the Prieto faction to administer Republican funds

JSU: Juventudes Socialistas Unificadas, united left-wing organization, the result of the merger between the youth movements of the Socialists and Communists

Kapo (*Kameradschaftspolizei*): trusted prisoner/functionary in German concentration camps with responsibility for supervising forced labour and some administrative tasks

Lehendakari: President of the Basque government

Luftwaffe: German Air Force

MEW: Ministry of Economic Warfare

MI5: British military intelligence service, also known as the Secret Service; responsible for domestic security and counter-espionage

MI6: British military intelligence services, also known as the Secret Intelligence Service (SIS); responsible for overseas intelligence operations

MI9: British intelligence section (1939–45) with responsibility for escapers and evaders in occupied Europe

Milice: paramilitary police force set up in Vichy France to suppress the French Resistance

Movimiento Nacional: commonly used name for Franco's single party (FET y de las JONS), later shortened to Movimiento

Nationalists: the forces that supported the military uprising of July 1936 and fought for the cause of General Franco

NKVD: People's Commissariat for Internal Affairs, secret police of the Soviet Union

OKW: Oberkommando der Wehtmacht/German High Command

Operation *Ariel*: extraction of Allied troops from western French seaports (June 1940)

Operation *Backbone*: Allied plans for intervention in Spain and Spanish Morocco after *Torch* (1942)

Operation *Banana*: Infiltration of OSS operatives in Spain and Spanish Morocco after *Torch* (1942)

Operation *Barbarossa*: German invasion of USSR (June 1941)

Operation *Bolero-Paprika*: French police campaign against PCE (1950)

Operation *Catapult*: Royal Navy attack on French fleet at Mers-el-Kébir after French surrender (July 1940)

Operation *Cobra*: Allied breakout from Normandy (1944)

Operation *Cycle*: extraction of Allied troops from Le Havre (June 1940)

Operation *Dragoon*: (initially Operation *Anvil*) Allied invasion of southern France (August 1944)

Operation *Dynamo*: Dunkirk evacuation (June 1940)

Operation *Exporter*: the Australian/British-led invasion of Lebanon and Syria (June/July 1941)

Operation *Felix*: plans for a German invasion of Spain and an offensive against British positions in Gibraltar (1941)

Operation *Fortitude*: deception plan to persuade Germans that main thrust of Allied invasion of France would be through Pas de Calais

Operation *Galia*: SAS mission to support partisans in northern Italy (1945)

Operation *Goldeneye*: plans for British intervention in Spain and the defence of Gibraltar in the case of a German occupation

Operation *Market Garden*: the Arnhem offensive (September 1944)

Operation *Overlord*: Allied landings in Normandy (June 1944)

Operation *Pilgrim*: British plans to invade the Canary Islands, should Gibraltar fall to the Axis

Operation *Polar Star* (*Polyarnaya Zvezda*): Soviet counter-attack on Leningrad front

Operation *Relator*: plans for behind-the-lines commando organization in preparation for a German occupation of Spain

Operation *Rupert*: SOE sabotage mission behind German lines in eastern France

Operation *Sconce*: SOE plans for operations in Spain if Franco granted Germans land access to Gibraltar

Operation *Sealion* (*Unternehmen Seelöwe*): Nazi plan for the invasion of Britain

Operation *Sprinkler*: SOE plans in case of a hostile German invasion of Spain

Operation *Sunflower* (*Unternehmen Sonnenblume*): the deployment of German troops in North Africa (February 1941).

Operation *Tombola*: SAS mission behind German lines in northern Italy (1945)

Operation *Torch*: Allied landings in North Africa (November 1942)

Operation *Tracer*: plans to leave a covert observation post in Gibraltar in the case of a German occupation of the British colony

OSS: Office of Strategic Services, US intelligence service, predecessor of CIA; the American equivalent of Britain's SOE

parachutage: parachute drop (of weapons and other supplies)

passeur (French)/*pasador* (Spanish): men and women who guided escapers/evaders across the border into Spain

PCE: Partido Comunista Español/Spanish Communist Party

PNV: Partido Nacionalista Vasco/Basque Nationalist Party

POUM: Partido Obrero de Unificación Marxista, left-wing party identified with ideology of Trotsky

PSOE: Partido Socialista Obrero Español/Socialist Party

PSUC: Partit Socialista Unificat de Catalunya/Catalan Communist Party

Q-ship: armed merchant ship, operating as non-military vessel and carrying concealed weapons

Regia Marina: Italian Navy (until 1946)

Regulares: 'indigenous' colonial troops recruited in Morocco that fought in Franco's army

RMVE: Régiments de Marche de Voluntaires Étrangers/March Battalions of Foreign Volunteers, temporary units consisting of last-minute recruits, reserves and support personnel sent to join French troops at the front

Rojos: Reds, term used pejoratively by Franco's supporters to refer not only to Socialists and Communists, but also to all those loyal to the Republic

Rotspanier: German label for Spanish Republican prisoners in Mauthausen

SAS: Special Air Service, British special forces

SCAEF: Supreme Commander Allied Expeditionary Force

Second Republic (1931–9): proclaimed when an increasingly unpopular King Alfonso XIII abandoned Spain

SERE: Servicio de Evacuación de Refugiados Españoles, commission set up by Negrín's government to coordinate and finance aid to refugees

SIM: Servicio de Inteligencia Militar/Republican Military Intelligence Service

SOE: Special Operations Executive, set up on Churchill's orders to provide support to resistance movements in occupied Europe.

Spahis: French colonial army troops recruited mainly from North Africa

SS: Schutzstaffel: elite Nazi 'defence' force, lit. protection squads

STO: *Service du travail obligatoire* (compulsory work service)

UGT: Unión General de Trabajo/General Workers' Union, Socialist trade union

UNE: Unión Nacional Española, organization sponsored by the PCE to create a unified opposition to the Franco regime

Wehrmacht: German armed forces

Sources

Bibliography

Aguirre, José Antonio: *Escape via Berlin: Eluding Franco in Hitler's Europe* (Las Vegas: University of Nevada, 1991)

Alted, Alicia and Lucienne Domergue (editors): *El exilio republicano español en Toulouse (1939–1999)* (Madrid: UNED, 2003)

Álvarez del Vayo, Julio: *Freedom's Battle* (London: Heineman, 1940)

Álvarez del Vayo, Julio: *The Last Optimist* (London: Putnam, 1950)

Arasa, Daniel: *Años 40: Los Maquis y el PCE* (Barcelona: Argos Vergara, 1984)

Arasa, Daniel: *La invasión de los Maquis* (Barcelona: Belacqua, 2004)

Attlee, Clement: *As it Happened* (London: Heinemann, 1954)

Azaña, Manuel: *La velada en Benicarló* (Barcelona: Edhasa, 2017)

Azcárate, Manuel: *Derrotas y Esperanzas: La República, la Guerra Civil y la Resistencia* (Barcelona: Tusquest,1994)

Azcárate, Pablo: *Mi Embajada en Londres durante la Guerra Civil Española* (Barcelona: Ariel, 1976)

Bailey, Rosemary: *Love and War in the Pyrenees* (London: Wiedenfeld & Nicholson, 2008)

Beevor, Anthony: *The Battle for Spain: The Spanish Civil War 1936–1939* (London: Wiedenfeld & Nicholson, 2006)

Bennassar, Bartolomé: *La guerre d'Espagne et sus lendemains.* (Paris: Perrin, 2017)

Bermejo, Benito: *El fotógrafo del horror. La historia de Francisco Boid y la fotos robadas a los SS de Mauthhausen.* (Barcelona: RBA, 2018)

Borkenau, Franz: *The Spanish Cockpit* (London: Phoenix, 2000)

Borman, Martin: *Hitler's Table Talk* (Ostara Publications, ND)

Bowen, Wayne H.: *Truman, Franco's Spain and the Cold War* (Missouri: University of Missouri, 2017)

Braddon, Russell: *Nancy Wake* (London: Cassell, 1956)

Bristow, Desmond (with Bill Bristow): *A Game of Moles* (London: Little, Brown & Co., 1993)

Brome, Vincent: *The Way Back: The Story of Pat O'Leary* (London: Cassell & Co.,1957)

Brudenell-Bruce, Cedric (Earl of Cardigan): *I Walked Alone* (London: Routledge, 1950)

Buckley, Henry: *The Life and Death of the Spanish Republic* (London: I.B. Tauris, 2013)

Butler, Ewan: *Mason-Mac: The Life of Lieutenant-General Sir Noel Mason-Macfarlane* (London: Macmillan,1972)

Caballero Jurado, Carlos: *Españoles contra Stalin* (Madrid: Susaeta, ND)

Carnés, Luisa: *De Barcelona a la Bretaña* (Sevilla: Renacimiento, 2017)

Carr, Raymond: *Spain 1808–1975* (Oxford: Clarendon Press, 1982)

Carr, Raymond: *The Spanish Tragedy: The Civil War in Perspective* (London: Phoenix Press, 2000)

Carrillo, Santiago; *Memorias* (Barcelona: Planeta, 2012)

Casals, Pablo: *Joys and Sorrow* (London: Macdonald & Co., 1970)

Chalmers Mitchell, Sir Peter: *My House in Málaga* (London: Clapton Press, 1938)

Churchill, Winston: *The Gathering Storm* (London: Cassell & Co., 1948)

Churchill, Winston: *Their Finest Hour* (London: Cassell & Co., 1949)

Churchill, Winston: *Step by Step* (London: Odhams, 1949)

Claudín, Fernando: *Santiago Carrillo: Crónica de un secretario general* (Barcelona: Planeta, 1983)

Clayton, Anthony: *Three Marshals of France* (London: Brassey's, 1992)

Cunningham, Cyril: *Beaulieu: The Finishing School for Secret Agents* (Barnsley [South Yorkshire]: Pen & Sword, 2011)

Darling, Donald: *Sunday at Large* (London: William Kimber, 1977)

Day, Peter: *Franco's Friends* (London: Biteback, 2011)

Dear, I.C.B. (editor): *Oxford Companion to World War II* (Oxford: OUP, 2005)

Diaz, José: *Tres años de lucha* (Paris: Ebro, 1970)

Dilks, David (ed): *The Diaries of Sir Alexander Cadogan 1938–1945* (London: Cassell, 1971)

Downes, Donald: *The Scarlet Thread Adventures in Wartime Espionage* (Maryland: Wildside Press, 2018)

Dronne, Raymond: *Carnets de Route d'un Croisé de la France Libre* (Paris: France Empire, 1984)

Eccles, David: *By Safe Hand* (London: Bodley Head, 1983)
  Eisenhower, Dwight: *Crusade in Europe* (London: Heineman,1948)
Foot, M.R.D and J.M. Langley: *MI9* (London: Bodley Head, 1979)
Fox, Rosalinda: *The Grass and the Asphalt* (Cádiz: J.S. Harter, undated)
Franco, Pilar: *Nosotros los Franco* (Barcelona: Planeta, 1980)
Fraser, Ronald: *Blood of Spain* (London: Penguin, 1981)
de Gaulle, Charles: *The Call to Honour* (*War Memoirs*, Vol. I) (London: Collins, 1955)
de Gaulle, Charles: *Unity 1942-1944* (*War Memoirs*, Vol. II) (London: Wiedenfeld & Nicholson, 1959)
de Gaulle, Charles: *Salvation 1944-1946* (*War Memoirs*, Vol. III) (London: Wiedenfeld & Nicholson, 1960)
Gilbert, Martin: *Second World War* (London: Fontana,1990)
Gildea, Robert: *Fighters in the Shadows* (London: Faber & Faber, 2015)
Graham, Helen: *The Spanish Civil War* (Oxford: OUP, 2005)
Grande Catalán, Antonio: *Number One Spanish Company* (San Vicente [Alicante]: ECU Narrativa, 2001)
Green, Nan: *A Chronicle of Small Beer. The Memoirs of Nan Green* (Nottingham: Trent, 2004)
Hart-Davis, Duff: *Man of War: The Secret Life of Captain Alan Hillgarth* (London: Random House, 2012)
Hastings, Max: *Das Reich* (London: Pan, 1983)
Hastings, Max: *The Secret War: Spies, Codes and Guerrillas 1939– 1945.* (London: William Collins, 2015)
Hayes, Carlton H. J.: *Wartime Mission in Spain* (New York: Macmillan, 1945)
Hernández de Miguel, Carlos: *Los Últimos Españoles de Mauthausen* (Barcelona: Grupo Zeta, 2015)
Hernández de Miguel, Carlos: *Los Campos de Concentración de Franco* (Barcelona: Penguin Random, 2019)
Hoare, Samuel: *Ambassador on Special Mission* (London: Collins,1946)
Hoare, Samuel: *Complacent Dictator* (New York: Knopf,1947)
Ibárruri, Dolores: *El único camino* (Madrid: Castalia, 1992)
Iniesta, Serapio: *Flon-Flon* (Barcelona: Brugera, 1972)
Jackson, Gabriel: *Juan Negrín: Spanish Republican War Leader* (Sussex: Cañada Blanch, 2010)
Johnstone, Nancy J.: *Hotel in Flight* (New York: Longmans, Green & Co., 1940)

Jones, Benjamin F.: *Eisenhower's Guerrillas* (Oxford: OUP, 2016)

Jullian, Marcel: *H.M.S. Fidelity* (London: Souvenir, 1957)

Kemp, Peter: *The Thorns of Memory* (London: Sinclair-Stevenson,1990)

Kindelán, Alfredo: *La verdad de mis relaciones con Franco* (Barcelona: Planeta 1981)

Kleinfield, Gerald and Lewis Tambs: *Hitler's Spanish Legion* (Pennsylvania: Stackpole, 1979)

Koestler, Arthur: *Scum of the Earth* (London: Jonathan Cape, 1941)

Koltsov, Mikhail: *Diario de la guerra española* (Madrid: Akal, 1978)

Kurlansky, Mark: *Basque History of the World* (London: Jonathan Cape, 1999)

Lévi-Valensi, Jacqueline (editor): *Camus at Combat. Writing 1944–1947* (Princeton University, 2006)

Lister, Enrique: *Así destruyó Carrillo el PCE* (Barcelona: Planeta, 1983)

Mackenzie, William: *The Secret History of the Secret Operations Executive 1940–1945* (London: St. Ermin's Press 2000)

Martínez Alonso, E.: *Adventures of a Doctor* (London: Robert Hale, 1962)

Martínez Barrio, Diego: *Memorias* (Barcelona: Planeta, 1983)

Matthews, Herbert L.: *The Yoke and the Arrows: A Report on Spain* (New York: George Braziller, 1961)

Matthews, Herbert L.: *Half of Spain Died: A Reappraisal of the Spanish Civil War* (New York: Scribners, 1973)

Mesquida, Evelyn: *La Nueve* (Barcelona: Zeta, 2010)

Mesquida, Evelyn: *Y ahora volved a vuestras casas* (Barcelona: Penguin-Random, 2020)

Miller, Russell: *Behind the Lines* (London: Secker & Warburg, 2002)

Montellà, Assumpta: *La Maternitat d'Elna* (Barcelona: Ara Mini/SOM, 2017)

Montseny, Federica: *El Exodo. Pasión y muerte de españoles en el exilio* (Barcelona: Galba, 1977)

Moradiellos, Enrique: *Textos y discursos políticos* (Madrid: Centro de Estudios Políticos y Constitucionales, 2010)

Morán, Gregorio: *Miseria, grandeza y agonía del PCE. 1939-1985* (Madrid: Akal, 2017)

Neave, Airey: *Escape Room* (New York: Doubleday & Co. Inc,1970)

Neave, Airey: *Little Cyclone* (London: Biteback, 2013)

Neruda, Pablo: *Confieso que he vivido* (Barcelona: Circulo de Lectores, 1974)

Olson, James S. (Editor-in-Chief): *Historical Dictionary of the Spanish Empire, 1402–1975* (New York: Greenwood, 1992)

Orwell, George: 'Looking Back on the Spanish Civil War' in *Homage to Catalonia* (London: Penguin, 1974*)*

Payne, Stanley G.: *Franco and Hitler: Spain, Germany and World War II* (Yale University, 2008)

Payne, Stanley: *Fascism in Spain 1923–1977* (University of Wisconsin, 1987)

Philby, Kim: *My Silent War* (London: Granada 1983)

Pollitt, Harry: *How to Win the War* (London: CPGB, 1939)

Pons Prades, Eduardo: *Republicanos españoles en la 2ª Guerra Mundial* (Barcelona: Planeta, 1975)

Preston, Paul: *Doves of War: Four Women of Spain* (London: Harper, 2003)

Preston, Paul: *The Spanish Civil War: Reaction, Revolution and Revenge* (London: Harper, 2006)

Preston, Paul: *The Spanish Holocaust: Inquisition and Extermination in Twentieth-Century Spain* (London: Harper, 2013)

Preston, Paul: *The Last Stalinist: The Life of Santiago Carrillo* (London: William Collins, 2015)

Preston, Paul: *The Last Days of the Spanish Republic* (London: William Collins, 2017)

Pujol, Juan (with Nigel West) *Garbo* (London: Grafton, 1986)

Rankin, Nicholas: *Ian Fleming's Commandos: The Story of 30 Assault Unit in WWII* (London: Faber and Faber, 2011)

Rankin, Nicholas: *Defending the Rock* (London: Faber and Faber, 2017)

Ravanel, Serge (with Jean-Claude Raspiengeas): *L'Esprit de Résistance* (Paris: Seuil, 1995)

Riera Socasau, Juan Carlos: *Juan Blázquez "General César" y Lola Clavero* (Lleida: Milenio, 2013)

Rojo, Vicente (General): *¡Alerta los pueblos!* (Barcelona: Ariel, 1974)

Rosal, Amaro del: *El oro del banco de España y la historia del Vita* (Mexico: Grijalbo, 1976)

Salisbury, Harrison E.: *The 900 Days: The Siege of Leningrad* (London: Pan, 2000)

Sánchez Agustí, Ferran: *Maquis y Pirineos: La gran invasión* (Lleida: Milenio, 2001)

Sandoval, José and Manuel Azcárate: *Spain 1936–1939* (London: Lawrence & Wishart, 1963)

Serna Martínez: *Heroísmo en la URSS* (Madrid: Roque Serna, 1981)

Serrano, Secundino: *Maquis* (Madrid: Temas de Hoy, 2004)

Serrano Suñer, Ramón: *Memorias* (Barcelona: Planeta, 1977)

Serge, Victor: *Memoirs of a Revolutionary, 1901–1941* (London: OUP, 1963)

Schmidt, Paul: *Hitler's Interpreter* (Stroud, [Gloucestershire]: History Press, 2016)

Smith, Richard Harris: *OSS: The Secret History of America's First Central Intelligence Agency* (University of California 1972)

Soo, Scott: *The Routes to Exile: France and the Spanish Civil War Refugees, 1939–2009* (Manchester University, 2017)

Spears, (Sir) Edward: *The Fall of France* (London: Heinemann, 1954)

Stourton, Edward: *Cruel Crossing. Escaping Hitler across the Pyrenees* (London: Random House, 2013)

Sweets, John F.: *Choices in Vichy France* (New York: OUP, 1986)

Thomas, Hugh: *The Spanish Civil War* (London: Readers Union, 1962)

Tabernilla, Guillermo and Ander González: *Combatientes vascos en la Segunda Guerra Mundial* (Madrid: Desperta Ferro, 2018)

Trevor-Roper, H.R.: *Hitler's Table Talk: His Private Conversations.* Translated by N. Cameron & R.H. Stevens (New York: New York: Enigma 2000)

Urraca Luque, Loreto: *Entre Hienas* (Madrid: Funambulista, 2018)

Vincent, Mary: *Spain, 1833–2002: People and State* (Oxford University, 2017)

Viñas, Angel: *En Defensa de la República* (Barcelona: Crítica, 2010)

Wake, Nancy: *La Gestapo m'appelait la Souris Blanche* (Paris: Editions du Félin, 2001)

Walters, Anne-Marie: *Moondrop to Gascony* (London: MacMillan, 1946)

Werth, Alexander: *Russia at War, 1941–45* (New York: Dutton, 1964)

Wigg, Richard: *Churchill and Spain: The Survival of the Franco Regime, 1940–1945* (Sussex: Cañada Blanch/Sussex Academic Press 2008)

Williams, Charles: *Pétain* (London: Little Brown, 2005)

Wingeate Pike, David: *Spaniards in the Holocaust: Mauthausen, the Horror on the Danube* (London: Routledge, 2000)

Woolsey, Gamel: *Death's Other Kingdom* (London: Eland, 2004)

Zugazagoitia, Julián: *Guerra y Vicisitudes de los Españoles* Vol. II (Paris: Librería Española, 1968)

Archives

Archivos de la Democracia (University of Alicante)
Archivo General de la Administración (Alcalá de Henares – Madrid)
Archivos Históricos del Partido Comunista de España (Madrid)
Archivos Municipales (Alicante)
Archivos Provinciales (Alicante)
Boletín Oficial del Estado (www.boe.es)
Imperial War Museum Collections (www.iwm.org.uk)
National Archives (Kew)
Portal de Archivos Españoles (Ministerio de Educación, Cultura y
   Deporte) (http://pares.mcu.es/)

Press

ABC
Collier's
Diario Información (Alicante)
El País
Hansard
La Vanguardia
Mundo Obrero
Picture Post
Reconquista de España
The Guardian
The Times

Online Articles

Santos, Felix: *Españoles en la liberación de Francia: 1939-1945*:
   www.cervantesvirtual.com/obra-visor/espanoles-en-la-liberacion-de-
   francia-19391945--0/html/ffdeef08-82b1-11df-acc7-002185ce6064_7.
   html
Negrín, Carmen: www.cervantesvirtual.com/descargaPdf/juan-negrin-
   y-el-exilio-849673/
Carboneros, leñadores y maquis: Los guerrilleros españoles en
   Francia (1939-1959): https://laestaciondefinlandia.wordpress.

com/2014/01/15/carboneros-lenadores-y-maquis-los-guerrilleros-espanoles-en-francia-1939-1950/ by Fernando Hernández Sánchez.

Radio Toulouse y la invasión del Valle de Arán (Article) by Luis Zaragoza: Dialnet-RadioTeWolhandViedVallDeAran-3673698%20

Collier's 03/03/1945. 'The Undefeated', an article by Martha Gellhorn

Schlaim, Avi: 'Prelude to Downfall: The British offer of Union to France in June 1940' in *Journal of Contemporary History*, July 1974

Velázquez Hernández, Aurelio: *LA OTRA CARA DEL EXILIO Los organismos de ayuda a los republicanos españoles en México (1939-1949)*. Doctoral Thesis: https://gredos.usal.es/jspui/bitstream/10366/115618/1/DHMMC_*Velazquez_Hernandez_A._La_otra_cara.pdf*

National Joint Committee for Spanish Relief (booklet) at: The Warwick Digital Collections: https://wdc.contentdm.oclc.org/digital/collection/scw/id/3072/

Websites

Reconquista de España (Órgano de la UNE): https://argonnaute.parisnanterre.fr/ark:/14707/a011403267989ilw1Jl/5baef7fad5

Diario Público: www.publico.es/

El Diario: www.eldiario.es

www.exteriores.gob.es/Embajadas

www.vatican.va/roman_curia/secretariat_state/archivio/index_sp.htm

The Association of the UK Basque Children: www.basquechildren.org

Fondation de Gaulle: www.charles-de-gaulle.org/

Fundación Nacional Francisco Franco: www.fnff.es/

Robert Capa: The forgotten army: www.slightly-out-offocus.com/robert_capa_forgotten_army.html

United Nations: www.un.org/en/

WW2 Escape Lines Memorial Society: www.ww2escapelines.co.uk/

Musée de l'Homme: www.museedelhomme.fr/en/museum/history-musee-homme/1941-musee-homme-resistance-network

www.alliancefrancaise.london/Marseille-First-Capital-of-the-Resistance.php

www.cia.gov/library/center-for-the-study-of-intelligence/csi-publications/csi-studies/studies/vol-60-no-2

https://ianasagasti.blogs.com/

Supplement to the London Gazette: www.thegazette.co.uk/London/
  issue/38011/supplement/3179
https://avalon.law.yale.edu/imt/01-28-46.asp#boix
http://saintnazairesociety.org

Audiovisual

Les guérilléros du Val d'Aran 1944 by Jorge Amat. France 3: www.
  youtube.com/watch?v=MJdrh9A8ANQ
Jesús Monzón, el líder olvidado por la historia. RTVE: www.youtube.
  com/watch?v=Oj16mzrzA1s
La Clave. *El marxismo*. 10/11/1979 RTVE: www.youtube.com/
  watch?v=cfeY8FUPjlI
La Nueve. Los olvidados de la victoria RTVE: www.youtube.com/
  watch?v=sCTzkiBmMFU
www.rtve.es/alacarta/videos/documaster/documaster-espanoles-2-
  guerra-mundial-frente-del-este-rojos-azules/5380259/
El Convoy de los 927 Mauthausen. RTVE documentary broadcast on
  06-02-05
Las Ilusiones Perdidas. Episode 6. *La Invasion del Valle de Arán*,
  directed by Eugenio Monesma. Pyrene P.V., Spain 2004: www.
  youtube.com/watch?v=wAezYe9gcgM
Aqueth dia i auie ua nòça. (2014) by Mireira Boya and Natàlia Lloreta
  (Production: ARIUAN) www.youtube.com/watch?v=y8weozX7Afw
  (and review in L*a Vanguardia* 08/12/2015)
Interview with SOE agent Jacques Poirier Imperial War Collections:
  www.iwm.org.uk/collections/item/object/80010224

Notes on Chapter Titles

The quotation at the beginning of the book is taken from *La Complainte du Partisan* by Resistance leader Emmanuel D'Astier de la Vigerie, written in London in 1943 and set to music by Anna Marly. This original song inspired Leonard Cohen's version *The Partisan*.

Chapter 1. The title of is taken from Hegel's aphorism, 'The owl of Minerva spreads its wings only with the falling of the dusk.'

Chapter 2. The title of is taken from Antonio Machado's most famous poem *Proverbios y cantares (XXIX)*. '*Caminante, no hay camino, se hace camino al andar*' can be translated as 'there is no path, the path is made by those who walk it'.

Chapter 3. 'Till the last gasp' (is taken from Shakespeare's *Henry IV*, Part 1 (1:2): 'Fight till the last gasp.'

Chapter 6. *Fraternité* is the third pillar of the revolutionary motto of the French Republic: *Liberté, Égalité, Fraternité*.

Chapter 7. *Fall Rot* (Case Red) was the German strategic plan for the second stage of the invasion of France in June 1940, following the campaign against the Benelux countries

Chapter 8. '*Sauve qui peut*' is a popular French expression that can be translated as 'every man/woman for himself/herself' or 'run for it'.

Chapter 9. Apart from the obvious connotation, *The Wall* (*Le Mur*) is also the title of a short story by Jean-Paul Sartre, based on an incident during the Civil War.

Chapter 10. William Blakes's *Forests of the Night* is the title of the novel by French writer Jean-Louis Curtis, describing life in a small town in south-west France under the Vichy regime.

Chapter 11. 'Violins of autumn' is part of the opening lines of Verlaine's poem *Chanson d'Automne* chosen by the SOE to warn the Resistance of an imminent Allied landing in northern France.

Chapter 13. 'Golden Eyes' is a reference to Ian Fleming's home in Jamaica (Goldeneye) where he wrote his James Bond books.

Chapter 14. '*Con la camisa nueva*' ('in my new shirt') is the second line of the hymn of the Falange – '*Cara al sol*' ('Face to the Sun')

Chapter 15. 'Back entrances, side doors, secret elevators' is taken from a description of her own life by Greta Garbo. The complete quote is 'The story of my life is about back entrances, side doors, secret elevators and other ways of getting in and out of places so that people won't bother me.'

Chapter 16. *Ubique* (Everywhere) is the motto of the Royal Engineers.

Chapter 17. 'But sometimes you might make the wrong decisions, comrades' are the words spoken by Squealer in George Orwell's *Animal Farm*, in defence of Napoleon's particular approach to democratic centralism

Chapter 18. *Une certaine idée de la France*: General de Gaulle's vision of France

Chapter 19. '*¿Qué gigantes – dijo Sancho Panza?*' ('What giants? said Sancho Panza') from *Don Quijote*.

Chapter 20. '... *de sabios es guardarse hoy para mañana*' is a proverb used by Sancho Panza to his master: 'wise men save themselves for tomorrow and do not risk everything in a single day'.

Chapter 21. 'for courage mixed with prudence is not foolish' is from *The Song of Roland*; as the Christian army fights to the death at Roncesvalles

Chapter 22. *Broma biasha* is the typical mist of the Val d'Aran (in aranés)

Chapter 23. 'Veil of oblivion' is taken from Sir Samuel's Hoare's memoirs of his time as ambassador in Madrid.

Chapter 24. *Die Welt des freien Menschen* is part of the oath taken by Mauthausen survivors in May 1945, in the name of the victims of fascism, to struggle for an international community of peace and fraternity: 'the World of free people'.

Index